I0284449

There has been no greater controversy in our contemporary Churches than that of the binding nature of God's Moral Law upon men and nations. In his book, *The Necessity of Absolutes*, Dr. Stodghill has demonstrated once again the historic theological view as set forth in the *Westminster Confession of Faith* (1647). The view that both men and nations are bound to the Moral Law of God is the Reformed and Puritan position maintained in the historic Christian Church. With careful precision Dr. Justin B. Stodghill works his way through the Theonomist and Antinomian controversies, demonstrating and defending the historic position of the Church. This is a must for pastors, college and seminary students, and Christian laymen alike.

Rev. Dr. Kenneth G. Talbot, President
Whitefield Theological Seminary
Lakeland, Florida

A Study of the Westminsterian view of the Law of God is helpful to all Christians, but especially to those of us who have taken vows stating that the *Westminster Standards* are what we believe and what we will teach. Dr. Justin B. Stodghill shows us the Reformed historical understanding of the Law's threefold division and the Law's uses in our salvation by examining the teaching of the *Westminster Standards* on the Law of God. Furthermore, this study helps us deal with issues related to the Law of God both within and outside of Reformed theological circles.

Rev. Dr. Kyle E. Sims, Pastor
First Associate Reformed Presbyterian Church (ARP)
Lancaster, South Carolina

Much of modern Reformed thinking and teaching on Biblical Law has been shaped by Theonomy or Reconstructionism, particularly as taught by the late R. J. Rushdoony. Many of Rushdoony's disciples, including Greg Bahnsen, Gary DeMar, Gary North, and David Chilton have taken the baton and advocated his neo-Westminsterian view of the Law. Theonomy denies the three-fold distinction of the Law taught by the Westminster divines. Some such as Rushdoony would reject the covenant of works, which in my opinion opens the floodgate for the Federal Vision error. Dr. Justin B. Stodghill has provided the Reformed world with a clear, precise, and articulate defense of Biblical Law as it is outlined in the Westminster Standards. *The Necessity of Absolutes* is a refreshing work on the classical Reformed view of the Law that is certainly necessary for the Reformed world in our day. I highly recommend this book as a study of our Reformed standards on this important doctrine. Dr. Stodghill writes with clarity and has done an outstanding work on this topic.

Rev. Stephen Welch, Pastor
Reformation Presbyterian Church (RPCGA)
Sheboygan, Wisconsin

The Necessity of Absolutes

The Westminsterian Doctrine of Biblical
Law Defined, Defended, and Applied

Justin Benjamin Stodghill

Presbyterian Reformation Books

Royse City, Texas

MMXX

The Necessity of Absolutes: The Westminsterian Doctrine of Biblical Law Defined, Defended, and Applied

© 2020 by Justin Benjamin Stodghill

Published by Presbyterian Reformation Books
Royse City, TX 75189

All rights reserved. No part of this book may be reproduced, stored in a retrieval system, or transmitted in any form or by any means—electronic, mechanical, photocopy, recording, or otherwise—except for brief quotations for the purpose of review or comment, without the prior permission of the author.

Cover Design: Rachael Ritchey

Images reproduced by courtesy of Westminster Abbey. The picture of the Jerusalem Chamber is © The Dean and Chapter of Westminster.

First Printing 2020

Printed in the United States of America

Unless otherwise indicated, Scripture quotations are from the *Authorised (King James) Version* of the Bible.

All emphases in Scripture quotations have been added by the author.

Hardcover ISBN: 978-1-7357605-0-6
ePub ISBN: 978-1-7357605-1-3

Library of Congress Control Number: 2020917951

Soli Deo Gloria

For my wife,

Tonya,

and for my parents,

John and Jane,

with my humble gratitude for your love,

support, and patience

Contents

Acknowledgments vi
Preface vii
Foreword viii
Introduction 1

I. The Nature of Biblical Law 29
1. Westminster's Definition of the Law 34
2. The Tripartite Division of the Law 62
3. Love as the Fulfilling of the Law and Christ as the End of the Law 71

II. The Moral Law: Perpetuity, Nature, and Uses 87
1. The Nature, Perspicuity, and Perpetuity of the Moral Law 89
2. *Natural Law* and Man Left Without Excuse 109
3. The Three *Uses* of the Moral Law 121

III. The Moral Law: Presented in Two Tables   145
1. Rules for the Right Understanding of the Ten Commandments   147
2. The Preface to the Ten Commandments   163
3. The First Table of the Decalogue   171
4. The Second Table of the Decalogue   217
5. Indwelling Sin and the Christian's Inability to Keep the Law Perfectly   233

IV. The Ceremonial Law Abrogated and Judicial Law Expired   245
1. The Ceremonial Law and Its Abrogation in Christ   248
2. The Judicial Law and Its Expiration with the New Testament Church   269
3. The Principle of *General Equity*   275
4. *Theonomy* Considered in Light of Westminster   286

V. The Law for Today: Defense and Practice   311
1. Antinomianism and New Covenant Theology   315
2. The Biblical Practice of the Law: Good Works   336
3. The Biblical Practice of the Law: Biblical Ethics   342

Conclusion   361
Bibliography   367
Scripture Index   383

Acknowledgments

I wish to express my humble gratitude to the faculty and staff of Whitefield Theological Seminary and to the members of the examination committee: Rev. Dr. Kenneth Talbot, Rev. Dr. Bill Higgins, Rev. Dr. Dewey Roberts, and Rev. Todd Ruddell. I am very grateful to my thesis advisor, Dr. Talbot, for his encouragement and patience throughout the duration of this project. I am particularly thankful to my pastor, friend, and mentor, Rev. Todd Ruddell, for his many suggestions, advice, unwavering support, and for his kind Foreword to this work. I also wish to thank the Presbyters of New Geneva Presbytery (RPCGA) for their prayers and Godly counsel. My sister, Joy E. Rancatore, deserves special notice and my deepest appreciation for utilizing her editorial skills in reviewing and correcting the format and content of this work.

Preface

The work before you is the culmination of several years of research and prayerful meditation. It is the result of preparation for two series of sermons on the Decalogue and the Sermon on the Mount, as well as academic research in pursuit of my doctorate. Our gracious Lord has not left us to wonder about our chief end or how we are to live. In a culture of ever-changing social mores, the moral principles of Scripture remain unaltered because the Triune God is immutable. As such, and in the face of relativistic presuppositions even in the modern Church, the ethical absolutes of Scripture are most necessary.

It is my humble prayer that this simple treatise will advance the manifest glory of God before men and be used by Him to encourage the faithful ministers of Christ, equip His saints in their spiritual pursuits, and convict the lost of their eternal condition apart from the merits of the Lord Jesus. **Sola Deo Gloria**

Foreword

There are, I suppose, theological treatises that ought to push the boundaries, advance the usefulness of the novel, and incorporate the latest perspectives, illuminating the readers to a more perfect pondering of what is "out there" in theological debate current to every age. Some of these treatises will be polemical, critiquing the latest trend or promoting it, in the trenches of theological work. Others will interact in the rarified air of the academy, where academic freedom reigns and no perspective is taboo. However, the work you have before you is like none of these. Rather, it calls for a return to what many of us would call a more orthodox age, an age more in keeping with the Scriptures in its theological work — an age of not only confessionalism but of the writing of the great Confessional Standards of the Protestant Reformation. If this work is novel in the art of theological treatise in our age, it is so in that it calls for a *return* to our Confession of Faith, written over three centuries ago. I am pleased to call the author, Rev. Dr. Justin B. Stodghill, my friend and fellow-laborer in the Ministry of the Word. In the work before you he reminds us all of our roots and, in so doing, he reminds us of the fruits we ought to be bearing as those coming from that noble stock. There we have the rarified air of a true theological academy. But far more, there is the meeting of the Church of Jesus Christ in the British Isles, the literary issue of which is one of the most beloved, enduring, technically brief, yet full statements of Reformed Theology proper—the *Westminster Confession of Faith*, *Larger* and *Shorter Catechisms*, and *Directories of Worship* and *Church Government*.

In the following pages you will find a broad outline covering a very narrow topic, the Law of God, as it was discussed and brought to confessional expression in the formal literary output of the Westminster Assembly. This is a treatise for further study in the facets of the Law it covers, since truly as there is no end to the writing and reading of books as the wise King once told us (Ecclesiastes 12:12), so each chapter itself might be expanded to a book-length handling of its subject. What you have before you is a good introduction, with some polemics and discussion, chapter by chapter. It also includes a good and very workable bibliography for further research into the thrust of each chapter as it pertains to the Assembly's confessional output, teaching and "standardizing" the Church's view of the Law of God. Largely a work of historical theology (although with more than simple reporting), the author seeks to bring to light what he calls the "Westminsterian position" in various doctrinal and practical positions and applications of the Law of God. Any student of Scripture or Reformed Theology would do well to place this work on his reading list, make use of the bibliography, and work through the issues that seemed so clear to the Westminster Divines but have become so unclear in later ages.

The title of the work is indicative of the importance of the topic being "The Necessity of Absolutes," and herein lies the value of considering the Law of God as an absolute moral standard, for we live in an age which has lost its ethical moorings. Our author calls us to this consideration in the work before you, and this is *always* a worthy endeavor. The Scriptures command us to meditate upon the Law of God (Joshua 1:8), to memorize the Law of God (Proverbs 3:1), to keep the Law of God (Proverbs 7:2), to talk of the Law of God making it part of our daily conversation (Deuteronomy 6:4-9). Further, space would fail if we brought the Scripture passages to bear that show the commitment of the godly to the Law of God, and the numerous examples of obedience and attendant blessing upon that obedience in the Word. The Lord gives encouragement to obeying Him; and, truly as new creatures in Christ, the Law of God is given to us not as a covenant of works, but as a rule of godly and blessed living before our Savior. So simply considered in that light this is an important work, even if all it ever does for us is to set our eyes and attention toward the Law of God for our meditation and edification.

But it does more than that. In five sections the author walks us through what today's Christian ought to understand—yea, *needs* to understand—regarding ethics and Scripture and walking humbly before His God. In section one we learn that not all "law" is law, but that the wise Lord has given His law in both historical and supra-historical settings. Drawing wisdom from the Assembly at Westminster, we learn what the Law of God is, why there are three divisions in the Law, and what these mean and how the law relates to Christ and His Gospel. We hear of the Bible's own understanding of what love truly is, and what a refreshing change is this Biblical love to the bondage and perversion that passes for love in our age. This is the foundational section upon which the rest is built, and without which the superstructure of the Bible's ethic falls upon the rocks of relativism and popular vote. This section includes various quotations from theologians of the Westminster era and before, speaking to this perpetuity and use of the Law of God.

In section two we are reminded of the perpetuity of the Moral Law of God and in what way it continues for all men, in the preaching of the Gospel, and for the Christian himself. We learn what it means to be created in the image of God and have that natural, moral underpinning that resides in all men, although marred and even hated by the "natural man" yet in his sins but because of which he is "without excuse" (Romans 1:18-20). Drawing heavily upon the work of Ernest Kevan, our author shows that Law and Grace are not necessarily opposed to one another, but do comport in the life of the Christian without violating the principles of the Gospel or of obedience. Further in this section we see the abiding use of the Moral Law for all kinds of men, as our *Westminster Larger Catechism* puts it—for all men considered as a race of men, for those who are yet in their sins, and for those who have been redeemed by Christ. This is a very valuable line of reasoning in a day when in many Churches the Law is all but forgotten and believed *passé* for the New Testament professor.

In section three we are taken to the *Larger Catechism*, which by all accounts presents a *tour de force* interpretation of the Law of God for our instruction and keeping. Our author carefully presents this material which is withering in its Biblical scope and force to the interested Christian who seeks to love God and obey His commandments (Deuteronomy 30:20; Ecclesiastes 12:13; John 14:15). Wisely he follows this section with a statement on obedience and the Covenant of Grace, indwelling sin in the believer, and the part that the law plays in these spiritual verities.

Section four speaks to the abiding validity of the Moral Law as compared to the Ceremonial Law (abrogated according to the Westminster Divines) and the Judicial Law (said by the Divines to "expire" along with the estate of the Jewish nation) and the relationship between all of these and the general or moral equity which obtains in all ages and all societies of men. This is perhaps the most controversial section of the book, and our author ably maintains the "Westminsterian" position against some others, namely the theonomic position of Dr. Greg Bahnsen. And while books and libraries might be written on this topic, certainly we have an overview here with some detail that can be the springboard for further study in this area of debate among reformed theologians.

Section five enters into a discussion of the other pole from "Theonomy" and speaks about a species of antinomianism, namely "New Covenant Theology," which (although new in name and manifestation) presents errors that are not all that new, as our author points out. Relying on historical sources, our author presents those orthodox divines of the past who opposed the same errors that rise up today, especially antinomianism, and applies these arguments from the past to today's errors, updating and exposing the want of Biblical support for those doctrines and practices. This fifth section presents a consistently Biblical ethic against those who would replace the Law of God with some other teaching. It draws us back to the Westminster Subordinate Standards and presents Biblical truth regarding ethics for the New Testament Christian, revealing what truly the "Law of Christ" is.

Following this fifth section is an able conclusion. In it, we are called to the only conclusion that we can possibly draw from an examination of the relevant portions of history, theology, and confessional standard. Let us return to our secondary standards, and in so doing, in the area of ethics and morality, we will be returning to the Bible as God's own ethic which He has declared to us. We are reminded of our confessional heritage and urged not to abandon it, for it is a right presentation of the Biblical data. The inspired authors wrote those Spirit-indicted norms of morality—this is God's own publication and the index of His own moral excellence.

As a pastor in the Church of Jesus Christ, I commend this work to those who will take up and read. Meditation upon the Law of God is a great exercise, commendable, useful, convicting, stretching, and even at times withering. But when taken up according to the comprehensive teaching of Scripture, it is also encouraging. In its study we capture the life of Jesus Christ and His righteousness for sinners in our thoughts. We are reminded that He is the one who is holy, harmless, separate from sinners, made higher than the heavens, who is able to save to the uttermost those who come to God by Him, seeing He ever lives to make intercession for them. And He gives His Law back to His own as the means of love-expression from Him to them, and from them to Him. Dear Christian, do not neglect one of His commandments.

Rev. Todd Ruddell, Pastor
Christ Covenant Reformed Presbyterian Church (RPCGA)
Wylie, Texas
October 2020

Introduction

> For I say unto you, That except *your righteousness* shall exceed the righteousness of the scribes and Pharisees, ye shall in no case enter into the kingdom of heaven.
> (Matt. 5:20)

The Christian Church reached the pinnacle of her beauty during the Second Reformation period, particularly in England and Scotland. Manifesting her maturity and perspicuity in doctrine, worship, discipline, and government, her priceless jewels having been rescued from the dark cesspool of the Medieval papacy during the sixteenth century Reformation, she openly displayed her brightly polished gems before the whole world when the Church "... reached its high-water mark at the

THE NECESSITY OF ABSOLUTES

Westminster Assembly."[1] William Hetherington goes so far as to say that "... the Westminster Assembly's Confession of Faith ... may be safely termed the most perfect statement of Systematic Theology ever framed by the Christian Church."[2] It would be in error, however, to presume that the divines assembled at Westminster formulated something never before seen in the Christian religion.[3] On the contrary, they presented no new doctrine, no novelty in worship, no unprecedented practice of discipline, and no previously unseen system of ecclesiastical government. Instead, by stripping away the filthy rags of human superstition, minutely examining the whole of the

---

[1] Anthony T. Selvaggio, ed., *The Faith Once Delivered: Essays in Honor of Dr. Wayne R. Spear* (Phillipsburg, NJ: P&R, 2007), xiii.

[2] William Maxwell Hetherington, *History of the Westminster Assembly of Divines*, 5th ed., ed. Robert Williamson (New York: Anson D. F. Randolph, 1890), 353.

[3] "By the time of the Confession, the divines do not create doctrinal categories but merely codify doctrines that have already been in the theological air for quite some time." J. V. Fesko, *The Theology of the Westminster Standards: Historical Context and Theological Insights* (Wheaton, IL: Crossway, 2014), 137.

Introduction

Scriptures, and concisely presenting the Biblical prescription for the Church as preserved by her careful Husband and matchless King, the Westminster divines presented arguably the best human summary of what the Scriptures principally teach. In the *Confession of Faith*, *Larger* and *Shorter Catechisms*, and *Directories*, are found the most faithful and complete collection of Biblical faith and practice ever produced since the days of the apostles and the closing of the inspired Canon of Scripture. In fact, the true genius and importance of the Westminster Assembly lies in the fact that, rather than a novel enterprise, the divines faithfully incorporated the tenets of legitimate Church councils, convocations, and assemblies from the previous sixteen centuries, while decidedly rejecting and removing the errors that had crept in through the indefatigable efforts of popery and pagan superstition.

The successful enterprise of the divines assembled at Westminster Abbey has, however, been largely overlooked, or even openly rejected, by their very spiritual descendants. The English Church never adopted or exercised the tenets of the Assembly's efforts. Scotland was the only national

THE NECESSITY OF ABSOLUTES

Church to adopt the Standards; but an unwavering subscription to them began to crumble by the end of the seventeenth century, and, today, the Church of Scotland bears a marked dissimilarity to the historic national Kirk. Perhaps the greatest tragedy is the Presbyterian Church in America.[4] From the very foundation of the United States, the Presbyterians in this country immediately set out to abandon the fullness of their heritage, to cast off the Biblical precedent for an established national Church, and to alter the Westminster Standards better to fit the scheme of eighteenth century Enlightenment thought. Once the subordinate standards of the Church have been pronounced editable, they can no longer serve as a genuine standard but lose their original authoritative character, and ancient landmarks are easily moved. The bitter fruit of these deformations in England, Scotland, and the United States has ripened to the extent that the Confessionally consistent Reformed and Presbyterian Churches have decreased to a

---

[4] Note, this is a reference to the various mainstream bodies of the Presbyterian Church in the United States, not a reference to a particular denomination (i.e., the Presbyterian Church in America, PCA).

Introduction

number of scattered "micro-Presbyterian" bodies, while the "mainstream" thieves who have stolen the names of the National Churches have not only joined in the corruptions of the early twenty-first century culture but, in many cases, they have led the way in the pursuit of unspeakable abominations against the very Majesty of the God they still pretend to worship.[5]

To recover from the moral morass into which the present-day Church has descended, there must be a return to that system of doctrine and practice embodied in the Westminsterian System. By Westminsterian System is meant those doctrines set forth in the Westminster *Confession of Faith* and *Larger* and *Shorter Catechisms*, along with the approved *Directories* of the Church of Scotland, as adopted and implemented during the Second Reformation period of the mid-seventeenth

---

[5] A Church is a *continuing Church* only insofar as it embodies and perpetuates the foundational principles of that historic institution from which it claims to originate. While many of the mainstream Presbyterian bodies demonstrate an organizational continuation, in practice they have deviated from the actual confessional practice of the historic Scottish Presbyterian Church of the seventeenth century.

THE NECESSITY OF ABSOLUTES

century, primarily within the national Kirk of Scotland. Because these Standards preserve the greatest level of maturity ever presented by Christ's Church, no lesser system of doctrine, worship, discipline, or government will withstand the powerful onslaught of the humanistic system of thought that has enslaved many modern civil and ecclesiastical bodies.

Clearly, a study of this nature can focus only on a single part of the Westminsterian System. For that reason, the focus of this study will be upon the Westminsterian view of Biblical Law. This is a pertinent topic for the type of Reformation that is needed because the Lord God has presented and preserved His appointed remedy for every evil in His own "breathed-out"[6] ethic. Any discussion of the Second Reformation view of Biblical Law, therefore, must take into account the Westminster divines' fundamental presupposition of the primacy of Scripture. The orthodox divines of the Second Reformation era—whether English Puritan, Scottish Covenanter, or Dutch *Nadere Reformatie* divine—unanimously and tenaciously

---

[6] See 2 Tim. 3:16.

Introduction

systematized, adhered to, and promulgated an entire world and life view founded upon, and driven by, an unwavering commitment to the Holy Scriptures as the *very* Word of God inscripturate, which was understood to be the exclusive Standard for belief and practice. If, therefore, as the Westminster divines maintained, "Man's chief and highest end is to glorify God, and fully to enjoy him for ever,"[7] then only God Himself can dictate the manner in which man is to glorify Him. This led to a mature system of thought that went far beyond any merely academic theology to a level of Christian practice—both collectively and individually—in which God condescended to address every aspect of life.

By way of example, one of the most controversial aspects of the Westminsterian System is the regulative principle of worship, which contends that "… the acceptable way of worshipping the true God is instituted by himself, and so limited by his

---

[7] "The Larger Catechism," [hereafter, WLC] in *The Westminster Confession: The Confession of Faith, The Larger and Shorter Catechisms, The Directory for the Public Worship of God: With Associated Historical Documents* (Edinburgh: Banner of Truth Trust, 2018/1646), Q.1, 179.

own revealed will, that he may not be worshipped according to the imaginations and devices of men, or the suggestions of Satan, under any visible representation, or any other way not prescribed in the holy scripture."[8] That God and his Word, rather than man and his superstitions, would be the sole authority defining and delineating the mode, method, and means of worship was somewhat novel in a century so recently freed from the tyranny of the Roman antichrist. Building upon the solid foundation of *Sola Scriptura* laid by the previous generation of Reformers in Britain and the Continent, it was precisely because the Word of God *alone* was the standard for faith and practice (rather than traditions, councils, or popes) that the Westminsterian System could produce successive generations of Godly, learned, and articulate ecclesiastical leaders in the pulpits and mature Christians in civil and social life. As the legitimate heirs of the sixteenth century Reformers, the

---

[8] "The Confession of Faith," [hereafter, *WCF*] in *The Westminster Confession: The Confession of Faith, The Larger and Shorter Catechisms, The Directory for the Public Worship of God: With Associated Historical Documents* (Edinburgh: Banner of Truth Trust, 2018/1646), XXI.i, 110-111.

Introduction

Westminster divines inculcated a consistent, experiential religion in keeping with the Reformation mindset of their predecessors. Arguing that he was the legitimate father of Puritanism, D. Martyn Lloyd-Jones referred to John Knox as a man who was driven by the guiding principles of the centrality and absolute authority of Scripture and the application of the Scriptures to the whole of life. Emphatically, he concludes, Knox "… applied his principles. There is no such thing, it seems to me, as a theoretical or academic Puritan."[9] So it was that the Westminsterian System of thought produced not only a regulative principle of worship but it also developed a Biblical system that regulated ecclesiastical doctrine, discipline, and government. The aim was to take the whole of the Bible and apply the precepts and principles found within it to society by application of the light of nature, Christian prudence, and the general rules of Scripture. Rightly understood, there is nothing adiaphorous in the Christian's life. Rather, the whole of life—public and private, civil and

---

[9] D. Martyn Lloyd-Jones, *John Knox and the Reformation* (Edinburgh: Banner of Truth Trust, 2011), 56.

THE NECESSITY OF ABSOLUTES

ecclesiastical, whether at labor or at rest—must be governed by the Word of God and focused upon God's glory and service.

God alone, not only as the Creator, but as the Lawgiver and King, has the sovereign right to legislate the conduct of humankind. He has not left ethics to be debated by philosophers, sociologists, or politicians. He has already given His good Law to men, for "… what doth the LORD require of thee, but to do justly, and to love mercy, and to walk humbly with thy God?" (Mic. 6:8). What is the standard of justice, mercy, and a humble walking with God? Is it left to each successive generation to define such terms for themselves? Absolutely not. Indeed, "He hath shewed thee, O man, what *is* good" (Mic. 6:8). The one, true, and living God, Who has been pleased to reveal Himself in the direct propositions of Scripture, is the eternal and unchanging I AM. As He is unchanging and unchangeable, so is His standard for morality. In an age when many confessional Churches are rejecting Biblical standards of morality to appeal to the prevailing immorality of the culture, it is imperative for the Church of the Lord Jesus Christ to stand up and return to the fundamental

Introduction

presupposition of the infallibility, inerrancy, and all-sufficiency of the God-Breathed Word as the alone Standard for faith and practice. If the Church truly has a love for the lost and a desire for the salvation of sinners, then there must be the unashamed presentation of the fact of sin and the standard of morality from Scripture. There is simply no Gospel message without addressing man as a sinful, fallen creature separated from God because of that sin. The Good News of the Savior Jesus Christ can be nothing more than a fable unless the purpose of His incarnation is fully published; namely, "Behold the Lamb of God, which taketh away the sin of the world" (Jn. 1:29). Without *this* Savior, man is an eternally condemned creature, lost and without hope in the world. The solution to reaching the lost for Christ is not to appease their lawlessness by perverting the clear Biblical teaching about sin. Rather, it is the vital return to the preaching of the *whole* counsel of God, beginning with the fact that the thrice Holy God abhors sin and will not tolerate it in His sight. Society must be made cognizant of the fact that "Sin is any want of conformity unto, or transgression of,

THE NECESSITY OF ABSOLUTES

the law of God."[10] They must further be made aware of the fact that there is nothing in the ability of fallen man to earn a place in the good graces of God. Sin must be expiated, and the sinner must be reconciled to God; and this can only be done through the vicarious atonement of the spotless Lamb of God, Jesus Christ.

For this reason, there *must* be a return to Biblical teaching of the Law of God. To be certain, there are many ecclesiastical lawyers in the Church today. Sadly, they seem more intent on novelty (i.e., the revival of old heresies) than they are about the clear teaching of the Scriptures. A popular error prevalent in American evangelical Churches is antinomianism—the faulty idea that Biblical Law was something given by the God of the Old Testament and has no binding effect upon modern man. On the opposite extreme, many in the Reformed circles have overcompensated by espousing the notion that every part of the Law of

---

[10] "The Shorter Catechism," [hereafter, *WSC*] in *The Westminster Confession: The Confession of Faith, The Larger and Shorter Catechisms, The Directory for the Public Worship of God: With Associated Historical Documents* (Edinburgh: Banner of Truth Trust, 2018/1646), Q.14, 426.

Introduction

the Mosaic economy, except for most of the Ceremonial Law, is still binding, in every particular, for every nation. While there is much to be said for the high view of Biblical Law espoused by the theonomic/reconstructionist position, its view of the binding nature of the Judicial Law is exegetically untenable, beyond the general equity of it. True continuing reformation requires the rejection of all forms of antinomianism, no matter how appealing they may, on the surface, appear.

Instead, the Church must return to the Biblical presentation of the Law. There must be a determined purging of every facet of un-Biblical novelty and an unwavering return to the clear teaching of Scripture as rightly understood and promulgated by the historic Reformed Church. Nowhere is that view more succinctly and accurately presented than in the documents produced by the Westminster Assembly of Divines. The Westminster divines rightly understood that God, as the Creator and Sovereign, is also the only absolute Legislator. Rules of conduct and principles of ethics are necessarily determined by God the Creator as He has revealed them in the propositions of Scripture. Just as God is the One

THE NECESSITY OF ABSOLUTES

Who is the Object of worship and thereby has absolute authority over the manner in which He will be worshiped, so also as the sovereign Legislator, God alone can dictate those basic legal principles which must govern and direct the whole of human affairs. Hearts and lives transformed by Christ's salvific cross work and justified by His vicarious, propitiatory, and atoning Sacrifice, and which are (thereby) the subjects of the regenerative and sanctifying work of the Holy Spirit, look to the Triune God as Father and Covenant LORD. With the heart of stone excised, the new heart of flesh desires to be obedient to its heavenly Father. Relieved from the curse of the Law of God as a covenant of works, the regenerate soul is made free to pursue obedience out of love and gratitude, with a deep desire to be conformed to the Image of Jesus Christ. The Moral Law remains the same as before in its content but is wholly desirable to the believer as a rule of life. To justify the rejection of this good Law—itself the reflection of God's own Holiness—is rebellion against the very One Who has redeemed His people to Himself. God's Law is absolute and remains the sole standard by which all men shall be judged. As a rule of life, it is a tool in

Introduction

the Hand of the Holy Spirit in fitting His saints for heaven. *God's absolutes are, therefore, most necessary for the believer.* Christ has shown His people that His Law is a joy and not an oppressive burden: "Take my yoke upon you, and learn of me; for I am meek and lowly in heart: and ye shall find rest unto your souls. For my yoke *is* easy, and my burden is light," (Matt. 11:29-30). Should the modern Church desire further reformation, she must abandon the myriad schemes designed to marginalize God's perfect Law and return, without hesitation, to that most necessary of moral principles, the absolute Moral Law of God.

Biblical instruction regarding this necessity is given by the Lord Jesus Christ in His Sermon on the Mount. In the second major division of the Sermon, the Lord Jesus states: "Ask, and it shall be given you; seek, and ye shall find; knock, and it shall be opened unto you: for every one that asketh receiveth; and he that seeketh findeth; and to him that knocketh it shall be opened" (Matt. 7:7-8). Even though this passage has been grossly misapplied by errorists as a reference to sinners "getting saved," this passage applies (as the entirety of the Sermon on the Mount does) to Christians (i.e., those already

THE NECESSITY OF ABSOLUTES

in Christ). Even though the Lord's sermon was given in the hearing of the multitudes, His intended audience was comprised of His immediate disciples and, by inference, the whole of His Church.[11] These verses address the manner in which the people of God are to live. They must first *ask* (αἰτεῖτε) of Him all things necessary for this life. They must diligently *seek* (ζητεῖτε) His Word for their sole direction. They must unwaveringly *knock* (κρούετε) at the Throne of Grace in prayer, looking to the Author and Finisher of their faith every step of the way. If the sole purpose of the Gospel is to get people "saved," then why would Christ insist that they must live a life of asking, seeking, and knocking? Simply, it is that the Christian is to be conformed more and more to the Image of Christ; for, as Christ makes evident in this sermon, "…

---

[11] Matt. 5:1-2, "And seeing the multitudes, He went up into a mountain: and when He was set, His disciples came unto Him: and He opened His Mouth, and taught them." The Greek original reads: προσῆλθον αὐτῷ οἱ μαθηταὶ αὐτοῦ· καὶ ἀνοίξας τὸ στόμα αὐτοῦ, ἐδίδασκεν αὐτούς. The near and necessary antecedent of αὐτούς is μαθηταὶ; therefore, the Lord's address was primarily to His disciples and only secondarily to the gathered Jews as the members of the visible Church in that day.

Introduction

except your righteousness shall exceed *the righteousness* of the scribes and Pharisees, ye shall in no case enter into the kingdom of heaven" (Matt. 5:20).[12] Such righteousness is entirely impossible for men, unless the Lord Himself intervenes and imputes this righteousness to them.

Christ's principle of a preceptive Biblical ethic is then very clearly set forth as He continues, "Therefore all things whatsoever ye would that men should do to you, do ye even so to them: for this is the law and the prophets" (Matt. 7:12). Although the statement may at first appear to bear a striking resemblance to pagan philosophers,[13] this statement is completely different than anything

---

[12] See John Calvin, *Commentary on a Harmony of the Evangelists Matthew, Mark, and Luke*, vol. 1, trans. William Pringle (Bellingham, WA: Logos Bible Software, 2010), 351–354.

[13] One is immediately reminded of the *Analects* of Confucius (551-479 B.C.), for example. "Zigong asked, 'Is there a single saying that one may put into practice all one's life?' The Master said, 'That would be 'reciprocity': That which you do not desire, do not do to others.'" Robert Eno, trans., *The Analects of Confucius: An Online Teaching Translation*, xx, accessed May 21, 2018, http://www.indiana.edu/~p374/Analects_of_Confucius_%28 Eno-2012%29.pdf.

previously propounded. Rather than a pagan ethic of reciprocity, the Lord Jesus Christ insists upon the fulfillment of the Moral Law, with which Christ—in fulfillment of its negative commandments—summarizes the whole Second Table positively with this statement that inculcates a loving treatment of all human beings—regardless of their treatment of Christians—simply because they are image-bearers of God. The emphasis, when understood in this light, eclipses the focus on human beings altogether for a clearer focus upon the Creator Who made them. The principle of Biblical love toward fellow men becomes an important pursuit of those who have been "born from above" (John 3:16). Christ's "Golden Rule," then, is the *response* of those who have been regenerated, for whom the summary of the whole Moral Law is *love* in action—first toward God and, consequently, toward man. Indeed, the first word in the statement, "therefore," places a direct connection with the preceding "ask ... seek ... knock" principle. It may be stated thus: *Since* God in His infinite grace and mercy has condescended to redeem a people to Himself through Christ, supplying them with true blessedness in Himself, a

Introduction

transformed nature, and life everlasting, they *therefore* respond from that new nature with an ethic and determination to do good to others. It is not a response to the good done by other men (an ethic of reciprocity) but, rather, the response of the infinite and everlasting good done to them by God (an ethic of just equity founded upon the precepts of the Moral Law). Hereby the Christian life can be said to be entirely *responsive,* so that every demand of the Moral Law becomes a desirable pursuit in the life of Christ's people. It is never a slavish obedience in order to gain salvation or favor; it is, instead, a response of thankfulness for the salvation freely given to undeserving sinners.

The Lord Jesus does not leave His people without a standard of righteousness nor does He leave them to "feel" for the standard by which they are to live. That Standard of righteousness is the Moral Law. Christ continues His instruction in this Sermon by saying, "Enter in at the strait gate: for wide is the gate, and broad is the way, that leadeth to destruction, and many there be which go in thereat: because strait is the gate, and narrow is the way, which leadeth unto life, and few there be that find it" (Matt. 7:13-14). The autonomous man

THE NECESSITY OF ABSOLUTES

theory falls apart in the light of the perspicuity of Christ's teaching. Relativism proves itself to be a counterfeit morality, and reciprocity reveals itself as a destructive ethic. There are two (and only two) ways in this life: Christ as the Door vs. autonomous man as the counterfeit door; the Way of Truth in Christ vs. the counterfeit way of deceit; genuine heart-religion as the gift of God's free grace vs. a works-righteousness that is futile. The end of the first way is everlasting life, and the way is traveled by comparatively few. The end of the second way is everlasting damnation, and that way is flooded with the masses of the unregenerate with their relativistic ethic.

When understood in this light, it becomes apparent that the giving of the Moral Law is a great gift of God to His people. While all men will be judged by the Moral Law as the Standard, it can only condemn all those outside of Christ. To those in Christ, however, it is no longer a curse or a burden. Instead, it is a joy and delight as the reflection of the Majesty and Holiness of God Who is absolute Righteousness. Two tenets of Biblical salvation resonate this principle; namely, Adoption and Sanctification. Notice, true Biblical religion is

Introduction

not only about "getting saved." It is always a fitting for heaven, a preparation for the eternal Sabbath in the Presence of the Triune God. Hence, observe the Westminster divines, "Adoption is an act of the free grace of God, in and for his only Son Jesus Christ, whereby all those that are justified are received into the number of his children, have his name put upon them, the Spirit of his Son given to them, are under his fatherly care and dispensations, admitted to all the liberties and privileges of the sons of God, and made heirs of all the promises, and fellow-heirs with Christ in glory."[14] It is impossible to imagine a more glorious truth than this Biblical doctrine, especially in the light of its implications and ramifications. But, further, it is impossible to think that God the LORD, Who is Holiness and Righteousness, would adopt into His own family and place His Name upon those that He, at the same time, excuses from a conformity to the Image of Jesus Christ. Note the impossibility of this notion: "A son honoureth *his* father, and a servant his master: if then I *be* a Father, where *is* Mine

---

[14] *WLC*, Q.74, 237.

THE NECESSITY OF ABSOLUTES

honour? And if I *be* a Master, where *is* My fear?" (Mal. 1:6a). Since all who are in Christ have been adopted into the very family of God Himself, therefore "… put ye on the Lord Jesus Christ, and make not provision for the flesh, to *fulfil* the lusts *thereof*" (Rom. 13:14).

The infinite grace of God extends even so far as to do the actual work of this transformation of sanctification in His people by the work of His Holy Spirit. The Westminster divines observe:

> Sanctification is a work of God's grace, whereby they whom God hath, from the foundation of the world, chosen to be holy, are in time, through the powerful operation of His Spirit applying the death and resurrection of Christ unto them, renewed in their whole man after the image of God; having the seeds of repentance unto life, and all other saving graces, put into their hearts, and those graces so stirred up, increased, and strengthened, as that they more and more die unto sin, and rise unto newness of life.[15]

This great work of the Holy Spirit graphically demonstrates Christ's "strait gate … narrow way" principle as intended for believers alone, due to the

---

[15] *WLC*, Q.75, 238.

Introduction

fact that this is not something that proceeds from man but from God Himself. Man simply cannot will or work himself into the state of sanctification. It is entirely the gift of God imparted to His Covenant people in Christ through the sanctifying work of the Holy Spirit.

The purpose of this treatise is to present the doctrine of Biblical Law as unfolded in the Westminsterian System. Examining these Second Reformation documents and the way in which seventeenth and eighteenth century pastors and theologians applied them in the world of their own day will establish the basis for the application of God's unchanging truth for this modern world. The first chapter presents the definition of Biblical Law and its Tripartite division, defending the foundational principles of the Westminsterian view of Biblical Law. The second chapter focuses on the Westminsterian position on the perpetuity and universality of the Moral Law, the concept of Natural Law from a Biblical perspective, and the Three Uses of the Moral Law. The third chapter is a summary of the treatment of the Decalogue by the Westminster divines, including their explanation of each of the Ten Commandments and the Biblical requirement of Christians to obey the Moral Law, despite their inability to do so perfectly. In the fourth chapter, the Westminsterian treatment of the Ceremonial and Judicial Law is presented, along with a consideration and rejection of *theonomy*. The final chapter is dedicated to a defense of the Westminsterian doctrine of Biblical Law against Antinomianism, including New Covenant Theology, along with insights into applying the Moral Law in Good Works and in Ethics.

The formal thesis of this work is that the Westminsterian System presents the consistent, Biblical hermeneutic on Biblical Law and that the further reformation of the Church today and its relevance for lawless modern society is the reaffirmation of said System of doctrine and its application to the individual, family, Church, and society. It is the author's genuine desire that the following study will reinvigorate a deep respect and love for God's Law within Christ's Church. But such an aim can never be realized unless, first, the Church seeks to restore a deep awareness of, and zeal for, the eternal majesty and holiness of God Himself. This author is firmly convinced from Scripture that the right view of Biblical Law can

Introduction

only arise from a heart enraptured with the beauty and glory of the majesty of God. This was the fundamental view of the Westminster divines who labored to formulate their statements on the Law. Ernest Kevan's observation is well worth noting:

> The Puritans began their thinking on this subject, not with an abstract concept of "law," but with the experimental awareness of the exalted Lawgiver: behind the *lex* stood the Legislator. This thoroughly Biblical approach was characteristic of the whole of their preaching and writing. To them, the Law must always be the Law of God, and all their doctrinal formulations were dominated by the recognition of God's overwhelming greatness.[16]

Unless there is a restoration of genuine Biblical *theology* proper, it is futile to pursue the development of any form of Christian *ethic*.

Any study of this sort, therefore, cannot be done merely as an academic exercise. The very honor of the living God is the real subject and must be the first principle for the right understanding of His

---

[16] Ernest F. Kevan, *The Grace of Law: A Study in Puritan Theology* (Grand Rapids: Soli Deo Gloria Publications, 2015/1964), 47.

THE NECESSITY OF ABSOLUTES

Law. Without the right heart-view of the Legislator through the mediation of Christ and the regenerating work of the Holy Spirit, the Law of Scripture can do nothing more than leave mankind guilty and without excuse before the eternal Judge. For Christ's people, however, the Law of God is no longer that letter that kills,[17] but is "… a perfect rule of life for us … [and you must] continually hold this law before you as being the will of God; approve of it, love it, obediently subject yourself to it, and in your entire conduct behave yourself according to this rule, and keep it in view as a carpenter does his blueprint."[18] May the Lord be pleased to make the prayer of the Psalmist the perpetual prayer of His saints today.

> Teach me, O LORD, the way of thy statutes; and I shall keep it *unto* the end. Give me understanding, and I shall keep thy law; yea,

---

[17] See 2 Cor. 3:6.

[18] Wilhelmus à Brakel, *The Christian's Reasonable Service in which Divine Truths concerning the Covenant of Grace are Expounded, Defended against Opposing Parties, and their Practice Advocated as well as The Administration of this Covenant in the Old and New Testaments*, vols. 1-4, ed. Joel R. Beeke, trans. Bartel Elshout (Grand Rapids: Reformation Heritage Books, 1994/1700), 3:81.

Introduction

I shall observe it with *my* whole heart. Make me to go in the path of thy commandments; for therein do I delight. Incline my heart unto thy testimonies, and not to covetousness. Turn away mine eyes from beholding vanity; *and* quicken thou me in thy way. Stablish thy word unto thy servant, who *is devoted* to thy fear. Turn away my reproach which I fear: for thy judgments *are* good. Behold, I have longed after thy precepts: quicken me in thy righteousness.
        (Ps. 119:33-40)

Chapter One

The Nature of Biblical Law

> *It is* time for thee, LORD, to work: *for* they have made void thy law. Therefore I love thy commandments above gold; yea, above fine gold. Therefore I esteem all *thy* precepts *concerning* all *things to be* right; *and* I hate every false way.
>
> (Ps. 119:126-128)

The confessional standards produced by the divines at the Westminster Assembly in the middle of the seventeenth century display a particular presuppositional foundation. From the very outset of the *Confession*, they freely admit that humankind is capable of "thinking God" simply because of the created order and the very nature of man himself, having been created in the image of God. God is at

THE NECESSITY OF ABSOLUTES

the very center of man's makeup and God Himself is essential to the being and right expression of man. Despite this reality—that man "thinks God"—there is a catastrophic and universal flaw in humanity that prevents human beings from *rightly* perceiving God. Hence, "although the light of nature and the works of creation and providence do so far manifest the goodness, wisdom, and power of God, as to leave men unexcusable; yet they are not sufficient to give that knowledge of God and of His will, which is necessary unto salvation."[1] The presuppositional foundation upon which the entire Westminsterian System is based follows immediately:

> Therefore it pleased the Lord, at sundry times, and in divers manners, to reveal Himself, and to declare that His will unto His Church; and afterwards, for the better preserving and propagating of the truth, and for the more sure establishment and comfort of the Church against the corruption of the flesh, and the malice of Satan and of the world, to commit the same wholly unto writing: which maketh the Holy Scripture to be most necessary; those

---

[1] *WCF*, I.i, 3.

The Nature of Biblical Law

former ways of God's revealing His will unto His people being now ceased.[2]

The divines did not begin their system with a statement about God, man, Christ, or salvation. Instead, they began with the presuppositional statement that "The holy scriptures of the Old and New Testament are the word of God, the only rule of faith and obedience."[3] As such, Scripture, and Scripture alone, is the only possible Standard for any discussion of the Person and Nature of God and the nature, needs, and hopes of human beings.

Man is designed to "think God" but, left to his own flawed and finite nature, he is incapable of *rightly* perceiving anything about God, himself, other human beings, or the created universe around him. Man is, without question, still capable of rational thought. But he simply cannot muster the correct view of himself or his surroundings because he is a creature who is morally corrupted, in all of his faculties, by his depraved nature. Incapable of *right* knowledge but driven by the

---

[2] Ibid.
[3] *WLC*, Q.3, 180.

THE NECESSITY OF ABSOLUTES

innate need for meaning and purpose, human beings exhibit an uninterrupted history of building systems of thought and even entire civilizations based upon faulty perceptions. Yet, even in the midst of this corruption, small sparks of the *imago Dei* remain and these sparks are reflected by the fact that even in the most barbarous of civilizations one will find *laws*. "For when the Gentiles, which have not the law, do by nature the things contained in the law, these, having not the law, are a law unto themselves: which shew the work of the law written in their hearts, their conscience also bearing witness, and *their* thoughts the mean while accusing or else excusing one another" (Rom. 2:14-15). These human laws are substitutions for that pure Law of God, which is programmed into the very nature of man since, on account of sin's damaging effects, man is incapable of any upright view of the Law. Even though the Bible is widely distributed, when the Law of God is read by unbelievers, it is not received uprightly by them. There remains a rejection of this Revelation because "… the natural man receiveth not the things of the Spirit of God: for they are foolishness unto him: neither can he know *them*, because they are

The Nature of Biblical Law

spiritually discerned" (1 Cor. 2:14). Because of this natural blindness, the discussion of ethics and morality must, therefore, originate with the authoritative Source; namely, the Word of God. Founded upon the presupposition that the Bible is the very Word of God inscripturate, the Westminsterian System looks to Scripture alone as the Guidebook for its discussion of the Law.

THE NECESSITY OF ABSOLUTES

1. Westminster's Definition of the Law

Chapter Nineteen of the *Westminster Confession of Faith*, "Of the Law of God," presents a broad summary of Biblical Law. It begins with the statement that "God gave to Adam a law, as a covenant of works, by which He bound him and all his posterity to personal, entire, exact, and perpetual obedience."[4] This is a very important beginning to the discussion of Biblical Law since, in the Westminsterian System, only God can reveal His will to mankind. The LORD God revealed His Law to Adam in some special way and he passed on this Law to his posterity after the fall. Since the time of Moses, God has revealed this same Law through the direct propositions of Scripture. Any correct knowledge that man can have regarding God and His will must be given by God Himself. The divines began their discussion of the Law by echoing what they had previously stated with respect to the doctrine of the covenants; namely, "The distance between God and the creature is so

---

[4] *WCF*, XIX.i, 95.

The Nature of Biblical Law

great, that although reasonable creatures do owe obedience unto Him as their Creator, yet they could never have any fruition of Him as their blessedness and reward, but by some voluntary condescension on God's part, which He hath been pleased to express by way of covenant."[5] In his commentary on the *Confession*, Robert Shaw explains, "Man is naturally and necessarily under a law to God. This results from the necessary and unalterable relation subsisting between God and man, as the one is the Creator, and the other his creature."[6] The rejection of this fact is the source of the unspeakable evils in this fallen world. God gave His good Law to Adam, the head and fountain of mankind, as a public person.[7] Two points need to be elucidated from this statement. First, in revealing His good Law to Adam, God revealed the *moral law* as the rule of life for Adam and his posterity. Further, He gave to Adam a *positive law* as a test of obedience. Second,

---

[5] *WCF*, VII.i, 38.

[6] Robert Shaw, *An Exposition of the Westminster Confession of Faith* (Ross-shire, Scotland: Christian Focus Publications, 1992), 84.

[7] Rom. 5:12.

THE NECESSITY OF ABSOLUTES

God established a *covenant of works* with Adam and made him the *federal head* of all his posterity.

As to the first point, not only did God reveal His *Moral Law* to Adam, He further gave to Adam a *positive law*, as a test of faithfulness. There is an important distinction between these two types of law. The *Moral Law*, founded in the very Nature of God Himself, is a revelation of His own righteousness and holiness and cannot be annulled or altered. According to John Owen (1616-83), on the other hand,

> *Positive laws* are taken to be such as have no reason for them in themselves ... but do depend merely and solely on the sovereign will and pleasure of God. Such were the laws and institutions of the sacrifices of old. ...Being fixed by mere will and prerogative ... God had in his purpose fixed a determinate time and season wherein they should expire or be altered by his authority.[8]

---

[8] John Owen, *An Exposition of the Epistle to the Hebrews*, in *Works of John Owen*, vol. 19, ed. W. H. Goold (Edinburgh: T&T Clark, 1862), 328–329.

The Nature of Biblical Law

James Durham (1622-58) makes a slightly different distinction, arguing that all laws given by God are, properly speaking, *moral* laws; yet there are laws that are *naturally moral* (i.e., the *moral law* of God as explained above) and laws that are *positively moral* (i.e., the positive commands of God as expressed above). Durham's distinction is not, however, substantially different than Owen's, for he states the difference:

> ... we are to distinguish between things *naturally moral*, that is, such (as love to God and our neighbor, and such like) which have an innate rectitude and holiness in them, which cannot be separate from them; and things *positively moral*, that have their obligation by a special, positive, super-added sanction; so that their rectitude flows not from the nature of the things themselves, as in the former.[9]

To distinguish between *moral* and *positive* laws, Durham uses the same example as Owen by referring to the Fourth Commandment. Arguing that human beings know by nature that God is to

---

[9] James Durham, *A Practical Exposition of the Ten Commandments*, ed. Christopher Coldwell (Dallas: Naphtali Press, 2002/1675), 56.

THE NECESSITY OF ABSOLUTES

be worshiped (the *moral* law), yet that he is to be worshiped on a specific day of the week as appointed by God in a *positive* command. While the first, being *naturally moral,* cannot be altered, the second, being *positively moral,* can be changed at God's discretion. The Fourth Commandment remains morally binding on all mankind in every age as requiring one day in seven to be set apart for the worship of God and a holy resting the whole day. But the specific day upon which the Sabbath is kept was changed from the seventh day of the week from the beginning of the world to the resurrection of Christ at God's discretion to the first day of the week since Christ's resurrection thus to continue to the consummation of the ages.[10]

Such also was the *positive* commandment that God gave to Adam in the Garden of Eden: "And the LORD God commanded the man, saying, 'Of every tree of the garden thou mayest freely eat: but of the tree of the knowledge of good and evil, thou shalt not eat of it: for in the day that thou eatest thereof thou shalt surely die'" (Gen. 2:16-17). The Westminster divines maintained that, upon his

---

[10] Ibid.

The Nature of Biblical Law

creation, God entered "... into a covenant of life with [Adam], upon condition of personal, perfect, and perpetual obedience, of which the tree of life was a pledge; and forbidding to eat of the tree of the knowledge of good and evil, upon the pain of death;"[11] "which while they kept, they were happy in their communion with God, and had dominion over the creatures."[12] This was a *positive* commandment by God to Adam because, in the thing itself—that is, in the fruit of that specific tree in the Garden—there was nothing inherently good or evil. Instead, it was set apart from the other fruit trees purely at God's own discretion as a test of Adam's fidelity. David Dickson (c.1583-1663) clarified this point:

> ... a positive law was superadded to [the law of nature], that Adam should not eat of the tree of knowledge of good and evil: that by obeying the same, he might give a specimen or proof of his obedience to the law of nature, in the perfect obedience whereof, so long as he should continue, he should live for ever. For the Lord

---

[11] *WLC*, Q.20, 193.
[12] *WCF*, IV.ii, 23-24.

THE NECESSITY OF ABSOLUTES

> threatened death to him only if he should sin: and death is the wages of sin, which by sin entered into the world.[13]

Had Adam kept the *positive* law by abstaining from eating the forbidden fruit as evidence of his keeping the *moral* law of God, Adam would not have fallen from the original righteousness in which he had been created, would not have had the fellowship and communion with God interrupted by his expulsion from the Garden, and would not have become subject to spiritual and physical death. As Gordon Clark affirms, "… had Adam refused to eat the forbidden fruit, sheer obedience to the divine command could have been the only motive. God set a test of obedience uncomplicated by extraneous considerations."[14] The distinction between the *moral* law and *positive* law is an important one to distinguish between those laws

---

[13] David Dickson, *Truth's Victory Over Error: A Commentary on the Westminster Confession of Faith*, ed. and trans. John R. de Witt (Edinburgh: Banner of Truth Trust, 2007/1684), 118.

[14] Gordon H. Clark, *What do Presbyterians Believe? The Westminster Confession Yesterday and Today* (Unicoi, TN: Trinity Foundation, 2001/1965), 69.

that are moral in and of themselves because they are reflective of the very Nature of God, and those which were given by God for specific purposes and at appointed times. The first are universally and perpetually binding, but the latter can be altered, abrogated, or can expire at God's direction, although during their tenure they are binding, alongside that which is *naturally moral*.

The second point, that God established a *covenant of works* with Adam upon his creation and made Adam the *federal head* of all his posterity which proceeded from him by natural generation, is of equal importance when establishing the view of Biblical Law in the Westminsterian System. It is not the purpose of this study to enter into a thorough discussion of the Federal, or Covenant, Theology of the Westminster divines. Several comments, however, are important for any valid discussion of the Westminsterian view of Biblical Law. One central point is that, at his creation, Adam received from God His law (both the *moral* law and the *positive* law) "... as a covenant of works, by which He bound him and all his posterity to personal, entire, exact, and perpetual obedience; promised life upon the fulfilling, and threatened death upon the breach of it: and endued him with power and ability to keep it."[15] It is already established that Adam fell from his original righteousness upon his disobedience of the *positive* command not to eat of the forbidden fruit. But the explanation continues that this rebellion, on Adam's part, infected and affected every member of the human race proceeding from Adam by ordinary generation. "[Our first parents] being the root of all mankind, the guilt of this sin was imputed, and the same death in sin and corrupted nature conveyed, to all their posterity descending from them by ordinary generation."[16]

At this point, it is vital to recognize that the Westminster Standards comprise a unit. Although divided into the *Confession*, *Catechisms*, and *Directories* and while further divided into chapters/paragraphs, questions, and answers, the collection forms a unit that presents a complete body of divinity and practical instruction for Christian living. Because these documents present,

---

[15] *WCF*, XIX.i, 95.
[16] *WCF*, VI.3, 34.

The Nature of Biblical Law

in summary form, what the Scriptures principally teach, the entire collection is to be viewed as a single body of work. What is spoken of in the nineteenth chapter of the *Confession* regarding Biblical Law is incomplete unless viewed in light of statements, within the same *Confession* and the *Catechisms*, respecting the eternal decrees, creation, the fall of man, good works, Christian liberty, and the doctrine of the Covenants. The Westminster divines realized that Scripture itself forms a unit and must be taken as a whole. They rightly concluded that

> The whole counsel of God concerning all things necessary for His own glory, man's salvation, faith, and life, is either expressly set down in Scripture, or by good and necessary consequence may be deduced from Scripture. ... [and, that while] All things in Scripture are not alike plain in themselves, nor alike clear unto all: yet those things which are necessary to be known, believed, and observed for salvation, are so clearly propounded and opened in some place of Scripture or other, that not only the learned, but the unlearned, in due use of the ordinary means, may attain unto a sufficient understanding of them.[17]

---

[17] *WCF*, I.vi-vii, 8-9.

THE NECESSITY OF ABSOLUTES

Furthermore, "The infallible rule of interpretation of Scripture is the Scripture itself: and therefore, when there is a question about the true and full sense of any Scripture (which is not manifold, but one) it must be searched and known by other places that speak more clearly."[18] In speaking of Biblical Law, the divines could not rightly discuss the subject apart from the overall context of Scripture which presents God as the Covenant God. It is not for man to speculate as to the reason why God has chosen to relate to the creature by means of the covenant; it is merely for man to see, in Scripture, that such is God's good pleasure and accept that this is His way of relating to the creature He made in His own Image. Baseless speculation about other means God *might* have used are irrelevant. So too are doctrines that attempt to present the unfolding of redemptive history as a series of various means of communicating salvation to man in successive and disparate "dispensations."

Quite to the contrary, God reveals Himself as the Covenant God of His people Who saves His

---

[18] *WCF*, I.ii, 10.

The Nature of Biblical Law

people—elected and foreordained from eternity—in time through the salvific cross work of His only-begotten Son Incarnate, the Lord Jesus Christ.[19] The fundamental evil of the autonomous man theory that pervades every sub-Christian system of thought and infects so many of the professing Christian systems of doctrine openly rejects the

---

[19] Although not explicit in the *WCF*, *WLC*, or *WSC*, the Scottish divines David Dickson and James Durham composed the treatise, "The Sum of Saving Knowledge," which is often bound with printed editions of the Westminster Standards. Under Head II of this document, they observe: "II. The sum of the covenant of redemption is this: God having freely chosen unto life a certain number of lost mankind, for the glory of his rich grace, did give them, before the world began, unto God the Son, appointed Redeemer, that, upon condition he would humble himself so far as to assume the human nature, of a soul and a body, unto personal union with his divine nature, and submit himself to the law, as surety for them, and satisfy justice for them, by giving obedience in their name, even unto the suffering of the cursed death of the cross, he should ransom and redeem them all from sin and death, and purchase unto them righteousness and eternal life, with all saving graces leading thereunto, to be effectually, by means of his own appointment, applied in due time to every one of them. This condition the Son of God (who is Jesus Christ our Lord) did accept before the world began...." ["The Sum of Saving Knowledge," in *The Westminster Confession*, 476-77.]

THE NECESSITY OF ABSOLUTES

Biblical position, tenaciously accepted and carefully presented by the Westminster divines, that

> The distance between God and the creature is so great that although reasonable creatures do owe obedience unto Him as their Creator, yet they could never have any fruition of Him as their blessedness and reward, but by some voluntary condescension on God's part, which He hath been pleased to express by way of covenant.[20]

All fellowship with God was broken when Adam rebelled against his Creator and, so absolute was this breach, that man can never reach up to God or, by his own volition or by his own means, ever find any reconciliation with God. God is absolute perfection and cannot, and will not, allow any hint or stain of sin to enter His Presence.

Adam did not sin for himself alone. Instead, Scripture makes very evident that Adam was not acting only as a private individual but also as the federal head of all his posterity. Adam's rebellion was not merely a breaking of God's positive law, it

---

[20] *WCF*, VII.i, 38.

The Nature of Biblical Law

was the breach of the covenant originally made between God the Creator and Adam His own creation. The Westminster divines refer to this original covenant as the *covenant of works*[21] or *covenant of life*.[22] The requirement for the maintenance of that first estate in which he was created was that Adam had to keep God's Law in its entirety—both the *moral* precepts and the *positive* command not to eat of the forbidden fruit. Life was promised to Adam, *and to his posterity*, if he kept God's good Law; while death was threatened upon Adam, *and upon his posterity*, if he violated God's good Law. This federal headship of Adam is no mere seventeenth century scholastic formulation but is clearly articulated in Scripture. In defense of this position, Gordon Clark clearly states: "[Adam] was the representative of his natural posterity. In this connection a careful study of Romans 5:12-21 should be made. Note that men are sinners because

---

[21] WCF, VII.ii, 39.

[22] *WLC*, Q.20, 193; *WSC*, Q.12, 425. [This is not to be confused with Samuel Rutherford's *The Covenant of Life Opened*, which was a treatment of the Covenant of Redemption.]

of the one act of the one man."[23] Adam, with respect to the *positive* law of God whereby he was forbidden to eat of the fruit of the tree of the knowledge of good and evil, was standing before God as a *public* person and representative *head* in the place of every single man, woman, and child that would proceed from him by natural generation. The guilt he acquired by his rebellion against God was *imputed* to the account of all who proceeded from him. "The grounds of this imputation are, that Adam was both the *natural root* and the *federal head* or representative of all his posterity."[24] From this poisoned root of original sin present throughout all of Adam's posterity, springs the actual transgressions of human beings. From the very time of Adam and his transgression, it can truly be said of all humankind that "The imaginations of man's heart is evil from his youth" (Gen. 8:21) and "The carnal mind is enmity against God: for it is not subject to the law of God, neither indeed can be" (Rom. 8:7).

---

[23] Clark, *What do Presbyterians Believe?*, 74.
[24] Shaw, 79; Shaw's emphasis.

The Nature of Biblical Law

Despite man's rebellion (which was no unforeseen occurrence[25]), in order that God's purpose of the redemption of His elect would certainly come to fruition in time, the Lord immediately established the Covenant of Grace at the very moment that Adam violated the Covenant of Works. The *protevangelium*, pronounced immediately following the fall of Adam, states: "And I will put enmity between thee and the woman, and between thy seed and her seed; it shall bruise thy head, and thou shalt bruise his heel" (Gen. 3:15). As the divines so clearly state,

> God doth not leave all men to perish in the estate of sin and misery, into which they fell by the breach of the first covenant, commonly called the Covenant of Works; but of His mere love and mercy delivereth His elect out of it,

---

[25] This section maintains that God's providence extends to the first fall of man and all other sins of angels and men "... and that not by a bare permission, but such as hath joined with it a most wise and powerful bounding, and otherwise ordering and governing of them, in a manifold dispensation, to His own holy ends; yet so, as the sinfulness thereof proceedeth only from the creature, and not from God, Who, being most holy and righteous, neither is, nor can be, the Author or Approver of sin." See *WCF*, V.iv, 28.

THE NECESSITY OF ABSOLUTES

and bringeth them into an estate of salvation by the second covenant, commonly called the Covenant of Grace.[26]

This second Covenant is the very heart of the Gospel of Jesus Christ toward sinners, apart from which there is no possibility of salvation—neither by the works of the law, nor by any other means imagined by men. While the Covenant of Works was made by God with Adam as the federal head of all humanity, "The covenant of grace was made with Christ as the second Adam, and in Him with all the elect as His seed."[27] It is apparent that God had entered into covenant directly with Adam in the prelapsarian estate in which he was created because God made man "... with reasonable and immortal souls, endued with knowledge, righteousness, and true holiness, after His own image; having the law of God written in their hearts, and power to fulfill it."[28] Though it was truly a condescension on God's part to covenant with Adam, even as a righteous and rational creature,

---

[26] *WLC*, Q.30, 199.
[27] *WLC*, Q.31, 200.
[28] *WCF*, IV.ii, 23-24.

The Nature of Biblical Law

yet it is contrary to the very nature of the thrice holy God that He would ever condescend to covenant with a sinful creature, which man, by Adam's transgression, has become, being "... utterly indisposed, disabled, and made opposite to all good, and wholly inclined to all evil."[29] The salvation of fallen man, therefore, is made possible only by way of reconciliation between the holy God (the *offended* Party) and sinful man (the *offending* party) through the means of a Mediator. The *Confession of Faith* eloquently presents this Mediator:

> It pleased God, in His eternal purpose, to choose and ordain the Lord Jesus, His only begotten Son, to be the Mediator between God and man; the Prophet, Priest, and King, the Head and Savior of His Church, the Heir of all things, and Judge of the world: unto Whom He did from all eternity give a people, to be His seed, and to be by Him in time redeemed, called, justified, sanctified, and glorified.[30]

As with everything else produced in the Westminsterian System, this statement is designed

---

[29] *WCF*, VI.iv, 35.
[30] *WCF*, VIII.i, 44.

THE NECESSITY OF ABSOLUTES

for practical application to the Church. The salvation of sinners by God, and the distribution of His free grace to them through the Person and Work of the Mediator Jesus Christ, is the scope of the whole of Scripture.

Though this introductory material may seem labored and long, it is the necessary foundation to the divines' view of Biblical Law, especially as it pertains to the redeemed in Christ. Before Adam's sin, the law of God, written on Adam's heart, was a delight and a joy. But, upon his transgression of the *positive* law, the *moral* law became a curse to him and to all his posterity proceeding from him by natural generation. The evidence of this change in the relationship between man and the law was immediate as Adam hid himself from the Voice of God walking in the Garden. Adam was keenly aware of the absolute holiness of God and his own guilt and shame as a law-breaker. The Covenant of Works had been broken by man and he justly received the sentence of death from his righteous and holy Judge. Upon his violation of the Covenant, Adam brought upon himself and all his posterity a perpetual curse from which there could be no escape at man's own fallen hands. There remains no possibility of justification by the works of the law, as Paul makes eminently clear when he concludes that "… by the deeds of the law there shall no flesh be justified in his sight: for by the law is the knowledge of sin" (Rom. 3:20). To those outside of Christ, the curse of the Covenant of Works remains a perpetual condemnation. But God, in His infinite grace and mercy toward His elect, for His own glory according to His own will, established the Covenant of Grace in Christ Jesus so that through His vicarious, propitiatory atonement on the cross at Calvary, all those ordained to life had not only the *possibility* but the *certainty* of everlasting salvation in Him,

> … being justified freely by his grace through the redemption that is in Christ Jesus: Whom God set forth *to be* a propitiation through faith in his blood, to declare his righteousness for the remission of sins that are past, through the forbearance of God; to declare, *I say*, at this time his righteousness: that he might be just, and the justifier of him which believeth in Jesus (Rom. 3:24-26).

Just as Adam at his creation, being the federal head of the whole of his posterity, procured

THE NECESSITY OF ABSOLUTES

everlasting damnation and death by his disobedience, so Christ Jesus, as the Divinely-appointed federal Head of all the elect, procured everlasting life to all of those ordained to life from eternity. As by Adam's sin death was *imputed* to every human being proceeding from him by ordinary generation, so all those who are in Christ by faith have His perfect righteousness *imputed* to their accounts.[31] This last point is very important, because the Biblical doctrine of *imputation*, like that of *justification*, is a legal pronouncement by God the supreme Judge of all men and angels. Shaw summarizes this point:

> By the *imputation* of Adam's first sin, it is not intended that his personal transgression becomes the personal transgression of his posterity; but that the *guilt* of his transgression is reckoned to their account. And it is only the guilt of his *first* sin, which was committed by him as a public representative, that is imputed to his posterity, and not the guilt of his future sins, after he had ceased to act in that character.[32]

---

[31] Paul fully spells out this doctrine especially in Rom. 5:12-19.

[32] Shaw, 79; Shaw's emphasis.

The Nature of Biblical Law

With the Covenant of Works established, the Westminster divines proceed to state that the selfsame *Moral Law* given to Adam in his original state of innocence, "… after his fall, continued to be a perfect rule of righteousness, and, as such, was delivered by God upon Mount Sinai, in ten commandments, and written in two tables."[33] And further, they contend that "The rule of obedience revealed to Adam in the estate of innocence, and to all mankind in him … was the moral law."[34] Although written with the Finger of God on the tables of stone for the first time at Sinai, the Scriptures reveal that the *same* moral law was inscribed on the being of Adam at his creation and, though marred by the depravity resulting from man's fall,[35] remains an indelible part of human

---

[33] *WCF*, XIX.ii, 96.

[34] *WLC*, Q.92, 255. (See also *WSC*, Q.40, 440.)

[35] See *WLC*, Q.25, 196; which states, "The sinfulness of that estate whereinto man fell, consisteth in the guilt of Adam's first sin, the want of that righteousness wherein he was created, and the corruption of his nature, whereby he is utterly indisposed, disabled, and made opposite unto all that is spiritually good, and wholly inclined to all evil, and that continually; which is commonly called Original Sin, and from which do proceed all actual transgressions."

THE NECESSITY OF ABSOLUTES

nature. This *natural law* is the God-given standard that leaves all men inexcusable before Him. This Biblical view of natural law is made very clear in the Book of Romans. All of mankind, by Adam's rebellion, have forfeited the ability and the will to keep the moral law in thought, word, or deed; yet all men are subject to judgment, and that selfsame moral law is the standard of their judgment before the righteous Judge. As Paul states, "For the wrath of God is revealed from heaven against all ungodliness and unrighteousness of men, who hold the truth in unrighteousness; because that which may be known of God is manifest in them; for God hath shewed *it* unto them" (Rom. 1:18-19).

There can be no plausible definition of the terms "ungodliness" and "unrighteousness" apart from an objective standard that defines what is "Godly" and "righteous." This the Lord God has been pleased to do in His moral law. Nor is the moral law *only* recorded in the Ten Words of Exodus 20. Instead, as has been stated, it is a part of the actual nature of man created in the *imago Dei* (hence, a *natural law*). Paul continues,

The Nature of Biblical Law

> For when the Gentiles, which have not the law [that is, the written Ten Commandments], do by nature the things contained in the law [that is, the selfsame *moral* law], these, having not the [written] law, are a law unto themselves: which shew the work of the [*moral*] law written in their hearts, their conscience also bearing witness, and *their* thoughts, the mean while accusing or else excusing one another (Rom. 2:14-15).

This *moral law*, as the remnant of that marred *imago Dei* wherein man was first created, remains the standard by which all men shall be judged. It must be remembered that, for the largest part of human history (from the fall of Adam to the propagation of the Church after Christ's ascension and the outpouring of the Holy Spirit), the true religion was kept by a small portion of humanity. The rest of the world remained in superstition and darkness. Even with the spread of the Gospel, true Biblical religion has remained the minority in a world of paganism. Yet, all men are culpable before God and stand eternally condemned before Him even though they do not acknowledge the Holy Scripture as the written Word of God. As Gordon Clark states, "The heathen, who have never heard the Gospel of salvation, are nonetheless responsible

THE NECESSITY OF ABSOLUTES

for their sins because of this original endowment of knowledge which is part of the divine image in which man was created."[36] Hence, even though the majority of humanity rejects the Word of God, all men do have the *natural law* within them. This *natural law* can never lead any man to happiness in God; instead it leaves all men without excuse. Thomas Manton (1620-77) maintained that "It is God's prerogative to give a law to the conscience and the renewed motions of the heart."[37] He also stated, "God's right is valid whether you will consent or not."[38] Man, as a creature, is culpable for his thoughts and actions before His Creator, whether or not in his sinful pride he recognizes the absolute authority of God Who is the Creator and Lawgiver. And, it is imperative to note, God's *Moral Law* has not changed since His creation of man in the beginning [although some positive commands have changed]. As G. I. Williamson explains, "[The moral law] was 'written in the

---

[36] Clark, *What Do Presbyterians Believe?*, 182.

[37] Thomas Manton, *The Complete Works of Thomas Manton* (Birmingham: Solid Ground Christian Books, 2008), VI:10.

[38] Ibid., 333.

hearts' of men. ... What was right for Adam and wrong for Adam is precisely the same as that which is commanded and forbidden us by the Ten Commandments."[39] There is no other account of good or evil apart from this *Moral* or *natural law*.

Humanity can be divided into but one of two categories: either, first, all those in Christ under the Covenant of Grace, being assured of everlasting life in Him and His perfect obedience, for whom the Moral Law as a Covenant of Works has been abolished, but for whom the Moral Law remains the perpetual rule of obedience; or, second, all those still in fallen Adam under the broken Covenant of Works, remaining in their depravity and assured of everlasting damnation, for whom the Moral Law remains the standard by which they are held guilty, but by which they can have no salvation or restoration of fellowship with God. There is no universal salvation of men, nor is there any salvation by the works of the Law.

---

[39] G. I. Williamson, *The Westminster Confession of Faith for Study Classes*, 2nd ed. (Phillipsburg, NJ: P&R, 2004), 179.

THE NECESSITY OF ABSOLUTES

To summarize, God created man with a rational and upright mind in His own image, having deposited His Law within him and given him power to fulfill it. But Adam, in his rebellion against God's *positive law*, also violated the *Moral Law* and, as the federal head of the whole human race, plunged his entire posterity into a state of guilt and condemnation before God. Further, due to his inherited corruption, every faculty of fallen man is tainted by sin even though the innate Moral Law was never totally eradicated. This *natural law* remains within man's being, and it is because of their rejection of this innate law that all men outside of Christ stand guilty before the judgment seat of God. There is no excuse for fallen man, nor can any plead ignorance since the law remains a central part of man's constitution. God, in His infinite mercy, according to His own perfect and eternal will, by His own free grace, ordained to redeem an elect portion from among fallen men through the establishment of the Covenant of Grace in time through the Person and work of God the Son Incarnate, the Lord Jesus Christ. All those in Christ are freed from the curse of the Moral Law. The Law remains "… holy, and just, and good" (Rom. 7:12), not as the means of salvation but as a rule of life and obedience for the redeemed; and the same law continues as the perpetual standard by which everyone, including those outside of Christ, will be judged and by which they stand condemned before Him.

THE NECESSITY OF ABSOLUTES

2. The Tripartite Division of the Law

Jewish tradition, dating back to the early days of the Talmud, holds that there are 613 Mitzvot (commandments) in the Torah. The list was codified in the twelfth century A.D. by Maimonides and presents a listing with 365 negative laws (corresponding to the number of days in the solar year) and 248 positive laws (corresponding to the number of bones in the human body).[40] *"There are two basic categories of the commandments in the Torah: those that were enjoined for all generations, and those that were not."*[41] Even within modern Judaism, there is a clear distinction between Biblical laws that remain binding and those which have expired because they were specific to Old Testament Israel in the land of Canaan during the period of the Tabernacle/Temple economy.

---

[40] David D. Mahoney and James J. Mahoney, *The Torah Concordance: A Reference Guide for Biblical Law* (Hebrew Heritage Learning Center, 2012/2009), 17; Mahoney's emphasis. [Please note: Use of this reference is not an endorsement of its contents.]

[41] Ibid.

The Nature of Biblical Law

The right understanding of the distinction in the Old Testament laws, therefore, can come only from the sound exegesis of Scripture. There is common reference to a distinction of the Law in the history of Biblical doctrine, stretching back to the time of Moses. Philip S. Ross in his thesis, *From the Finger of God*,[42] traces the history of the tripartite division from the Pentateuch itself, through the whole of Scripture, and traces its development from the early Church fathers through the Reformation. Since the present work focuses upon the Westminsterian position, it is to this latter period that the following observations will be confined. The development of the articulation of this Biblical division of the Law is ably traced out by Ross; and sufficient evidence exists from patristic Church literature and the presentation of this subject by Aquinas confidently to assert the fact that, by the time of John Calvin (1509-64), he could exhort his readers that "We must bear in mind the *common* [emphasis added] division of the whole law of God

---

[42] Philip S. Ross, *From the Finger of God: The Biblical and Theological Basis for the Threefold Division of the Law*, (Ross-shire, Scotland: Christian Focus Publications, 2010, xx.

THE NECESSITY OF ABSOLUTES

published by Moses into moral, ceremonial, and judicial laws."[43] He was confident in making this statement through his knowledge of the doctrines of his orthodox predecessors and those of his contemporaries within the Reformed Churches. Calvin summarizes each of these divisions, stating that the Moral Law "... is the true and eternal rule of righteousness, prescribed for men of all nations and times,"[44] the Ceremonial Law was the rule of worship for the Church under age, and the Judicial Law was established within the Israelite nation as a body politic. Theodore Beza (1519-1605), Calvin's successor in Geneva, concurs when he states that "The law of the Lord our God that was handed down to His people through Moses is partly ethical, partly sacrificial, and partly political."[45] Heinrich

---

[43] John Calvin, *Institutes of the Christian Religion*, ed. John T. McNeill, trans. Ford Lewis Battles (Philadelphia: The Westminster Press, 1960), IV.xx.14, 1502.

[44] Ibid., IV.xx.15, 1503.

[45] Theodore Beza, Appendix B: "The Moral, Ceremonial, and Political Law of God as Derived from the Books of Moses and Distributed into Particular Classes," in *A Clear and Simple Treatise on the Lord's Supper: In Which the Published Slanders of Joachim Westphal Are Finally*

The Nature of Biblical Law

Bullinger (1504-75), successor to Zwingli the Reformer in Zurich, presents the identical view when he states:

> [The law of God] is divided into the moral, ceremonial, and judicial laws. ... The moral law is that which teacheth men manners, and layeth down before us the shape of virtue. ... The ceremonial laws are they which are given concerning the order of holy and ecclesiastical rites and ceremonies. ... The judicial laws give rules concerning matters to be judged between man and man, for the preservation of public peace, equity, and civil honesty.[46]

Of the three divisions, Bullinger maintains that the moral law is perpetually binding upon all of humankind declaring, "... the ten commandments are the very absolute and everlasting rule of

---

Refuted, trans. David C. Noe (Grand Rapids: Reformation Heritage Books, 2016), 171.

[46] Henrich Bullinger, "Of God's Law, and of the Two First Commandments of the First Table," in *The Decades of Henry Bullinger, Minister of the Church of Zurich*, vols. 1-2, 2nd decade, 2nd sermon, ed. for the Parker Society by Rev. Thomas Harding, trans. H. I. (Cambridge: Cambridge University Press, 1849), 209-10.

righteousness and all virtues, set down for all places, men, and ages, to frame themselves by."[47]

The clarity of the tripartite division of Biblical Law is summarized by the Westminster divines as they confess that

> God gave to Adam a law, as a covenant of works, by which He bound him and all his posterity to personal, entire, exact, and perpetual obedience. ... [Which] law, after his fall, continued to be a perfect rule of righteousness, and, as such, was delivered by God upon Mount Sinai, in ten commandments, and written in two tables. ... Beside this law, commonly called moral, God was pleased to give to the people of Israel, as a church under age, ceremonial laws. ... To them also, as a body politic, He gave sundry judicial laws.[48]

Anthony Burgess (d. 1664), English Puritan divine and member of the Westminster Assembly, was very diligent to establish this accepted division not upon tradition, but upon a solid exegetical basis. If a doctrine cannot be established upon the authority of the Scriptures, it is nothing more than

---

[47] Ibid., 211.
[48] *WCF*, XIX.i-iv, 95-98.

The Nature of Biblical Law

the commandment or doctrine of men. If, however, a doctrine is directly commanded in Scripture or, by good and necessary consequence may be deduced from Scripture, it is authoritative because it originates from God and is preserved in the absolute Standard of truth, the revealed Word of God. As Stephen J. Casselli observes in his excellent discussion of Burgess' view:

> The threefold division of the law is employed as a way to organize large tracts of biblical literature in a coherent fashion and to begin to sort out the continuities and discontinuities in the progress of redemptive history in relation to the law of God. There is a basic continuity in regard to the moral dimension of the law from Adam to the present. However, there is a major discontinuity with reference to the ceremonial and civil law, particularly with the epochal change at the coming of Christ ...[49]

To establish the primacy and abiding nature of the Moral Law, Burgess argued from Scripture that

---

[49] Stephen J. Casselli, *Divine Rule Maintained: Anthony Burgess, Covenant Theology, and the Place of the Law in Reformed Scholasticism* (Grand Rapids: Reformation Heritage Books, 2016), 85-86.

THE NECESSITY OF ABSOLUTES

there is a marked distinction between the giving of the Moral Law to Israel and the promulgation of the ceremonial and judicial laws. Only the "Ten Words" were verbally given by God to the whole congregation of Israel. Only the "Ten Words" were twice written with the Finger of God upon two tables of stone. Only the "Ten Words" were placed in the Ark of the Covenant as a testimony to succeeding generations. Even though the Ceremonial Law was an expression of the First Table of the Moral Law to the Church under age as the Church of the Living God at that time, and the Judicial Law was an expression of the Second Table of the Moral Law to Israel as the theocratic Kingdom of God, these bodies of Law were applications of the Moral Law, which lay at the foundation of them. Hence, the abiding nature of the Moral Law to all mankind, and especially to the Church, is clearly indicated in the very nature of the mutability of the Ceremonial and Judicial Laws vis-à-vis the inherent immutability of the Moral Law.[50]

Later in the seventeenth century, the Church continued to maintain this doctrine. James Durham

---

[50] Ibid., 83.

The Nature of Biblical Law

concurred that there is a Biblical distinction between the moral, ceremonial, and judicial Law. The Moral Law, he states, "... concerns manners, and the right ordering of a godly conversation: and, because these things are of perpetual equity and rectitude, the obligation of this law, as to that, is perpetual."[51] The judicial law was given to the nation of Israel as a body politic; and, therefore, its binding authority as to every specification ended with the dissolution of Israel as a unique state. The ceremonial law, regulating the outward worship of God in Israel as the Church of the Old Testament period and pointing to the Messiah to come in its outward forms and shadows, is fully abrogated since those Old Testament types have all been fulfilled in Christ. As such, Durham provides an important caution to be observed concerning the judicial and ceremonial laws. He posits: "... the judicial law is but *mortua*, dead; and may, where it is thought fit ... be used under the New Testament. But the ceremonial law is *mortifera*, deadly, and cannot be revived without falling from grace (Gal.

---

[51] Durham, 55.

THE NECESSITY OF ABSOLUTES

5:2, 4)."[52] This point is axiomatic and essential to a right understanding and application of Biblical Law for the Church and modern society. Concurring with his contemporary in his early commentary on the *Westminster Confession of Faith*, David Dickson confirms that Biblical Law is presented in a three-fold division, and maintains that the Moral Law is perpetually binding, the ceremonial law abrogated in Christ, and the judicial law has no binding authority upon Gentile nations.[53] Francis Turretin (1623-87), the Genevan professor and contemporary with Durham and Dickson would further articulate this view insisting that, "The law given by Moses is usually distinguished into three species: moral (treating of morals or of perpetual duties towards God and our neighbor); ceremonial (of the ceremonies or rites about the sacred things to be observed under the Old Testament); and civil, constituting the civil government of the Israelite people."[54]

---

[52] Ibid., 56.

[53] Dickson, 117-127.

[54] Francis Turretin, *Institutes of Elenctic Theology*, ed. James T. Dennison, Jr., trans. George Musgrave Giger (Phillipsburg: P&R, 1994), 2:145.

3. Love as the Fulfilling of the Law and Christ as the End of the Law

To conclude this chapter, there will be a discussion of two Biblical phrases that require special consideration to avoid misunderstanding. First, the Scriptures clearly teach that "... love *is* the fulfilling of the law" (Rom. 13:10). This principle is erroneously understood by many, both historically and today. One website, which represents the para-Church organization "The Family International," boldly proclaims: "God's Law of Love is the ultimate fulfillment of Biblical law, including the Ten Commandments. ... We therefore believe that through Christ's salvation and His Law of Love, Christians are released from the Mosaic laws in the Old Testament and are no longer required to observe them."[55] This error exists contrary to the Scriptures, and the Westminster divines were very careful to insist upon the specific uses of the Moral

---

[55] The Family International, "What We Believe," accessed May 23, 2018, https://www.thefamilyinternational.org/en/about/our-beliefs/gods-law-love/.

THE NECESSITY OF ABSOLUTES

Law as a standard of behavior for all men instead of such an imprecise ethic. They spoke with great ethical clarity, stating: "The moral law doth for ever bind all, as well justified persons as others, to obedience thereof. ... Neither doth Christ in the gospel any way dissolve, but much strengthen this obligation."[56] The abiding, binding nature of the Moral Law is made abundantly clear in the New Testament Scriptures. The Lord Jesus Christ said, "Think not that I am come to destroy the law, or the prophets: I am not come to destroy, but to fulfil. For verily I say unto you, till heaven and earth pass, one jot or one tittle shall in no wise pass from the law, till all be fulfilled" (Matt. 5:17-18). Paul reiterates this point clearly, with the strongest possible negative, when he asks: "Do we then make void the law through faith? God forbid: yea, we establish the law" (Rom. 3:31). To teach the dismissal of the Moral Law through the institution of an undefined "Law of Love" is un-Biblical because of the clear teaching of Christ and His apostles. It is contrary to the Triune God Who reveals Himself in the

---

[56] *WCF*, XIX.v, 98.

The Nature of Biblical Law

propositions of Scripture, not as the God of confusion and uncertainty, but as the God Who declares what is right and wrong for men. "He hath shewed thee, O man, what *is* good; and what doth the LORD require of thee, but to do justly, and to love mercy, and to walk humbly with thy God?" (Mic. 6:8). The false doctrine that the Moral Law of God has been replaced by a relative "Law of Love" is based upon a misrepresentation of the Biblical definition of love and a misapplication of Christ as the end of the law. It should, however, be noted that there are duties and commands that are relative in their application to some people in differing places and stations. As the divines observe, "That what God forbids, is at no time to be done; what he commands is always our duty; and yet every particular duty is not to be done at all times."[57]

In his highly influential work, *The Practice of Faith, Hope, and Love,* the *Nadere Reformatie* divine, Godefridus Udemans (1581-1649) presents the practice of Biblical Love as obedience to the Law of the Lord. Unlike a vague sense of "love" that rejects

---

[57] *WLC,* Q. 99, par. 5.

the abiding nature of the Moral Law, the seventeenth-century orthodox Dutch divines, in perfect harmony with their English and Scottish counterparts, recognized the abiding obligation of the Moral Law upon humankind—especially the true professors of Jesus Christ. He begins his treatise with the qualification between natural love and spiritual love. The latter is that love which proceeds from God (for God is love, 1 John 4:8) and is imparted within the saints by the indwelling of the Holy Spirit. The first and fundamental Object of spiritual love is God Himself: "God is love, and love flows from Him. Therefore, we must love God, not because of some external benefit outside of God (Job 1:10), but for God's own sake, for He is our highest good (Ps. 16:5)."[58] He goes on to articulate the following premise: "To practice love we should always pay attention to the moral law, which is summarized in the Ten Commandments, for love is the fulfillment of the law (Rom. 13:10)."[59] Udemans' Biblical exegesis exposes the "Law of Love"

---

[58] Godefridus Udemans, *The Practice of Faith, Hope, and Love*, ed. Joel R. Beeke, trans. Annemie Godbehere (Grand Rapids: Reformation Heritage Books, 2012), 27.
[59] Ibid., 194.

The Nature of Biblical Law

eisegesis as he explains from Scripture that love fulfills the Law when the saints observe thankful obedience to God's good Law. Such obedience originates from the heart transformed and implanted with genuine, spiritual love for God as Father and gracious Lord. True Biblical love does not replace the Law—instead, it changes the will of the saints to make them desirous of obedience to the Law (and grieved at their failures), as they aim for the infinite Holiness and Righteousness of God Himself reflected in the Law.

Thomas Watson (1620-86), that great English Puritan of the seventeenth century, was even clearer in his definition of Biblical (spiritual) love. He stated: "[Love] is a holy fire kindled in the affections, whereby a Christian is carried out strongly after God as the supreme good."[60] He went on to insist that this spiritual love is no mere human emotion but is a gift of the Holy Spirit as a result of the gift of knowledge. Rather than born out of feelings, Watson contends that the Scriptures present a love born out of reason. "The antecedent

---

[60] Thomas Watson, *The Ten Commandments*, (Edinburgh: Banner of Truth Trust, 2000/1692), 6.

THE NECESSITY OF ABSOLUTES

of love is knowledge. The Spirit shines upon the understanding, and discovers the beauties of wisdom, holiness, and mercy in God: and these are the loadstone to entice and draw out love to God."[61] Like Udemans, Watson insists that love for God must be preeminent in the Christian heart, else it is no love at all. "We must love God *propter se*, for himself, for his own intrinsic excellencies. … Hypocrites love God because he gives them corn and wine: we must love God for himself: for those shining perfections which are in him."[62] None, however, was so clear as Christ Himself, Who taught His Church, "If ye love Me, keep my commandments" (John 14:15). The beloved disciple, John, spells this out:

> And hereby we do know that we know Him, if we keep His commandments. He that saith, I know Him, and keepeth not His commandments, is a liar, and the truth is not in him. But whoso keepeth His Word, in him verily is the love of God perfected: hereby know we that we are in Him. He that saith he

---

[61] Ibid.
[62] Ibid., 7.

The Nature of Biblical Law

> abideth in Him ought himself also so to walk,
> even as He walked (1 John 2:3-6).

John, by inspiration of the Holy Spirit, makes it abundantly clear that the love of God is made perfect in those who are obedient children to their heavenly Father. As he states elsewhere, "For this is the love of God, that we keep his commandments: and his commandments are not grievous" (I John 5:3). It is evident, then, that obedience as a mark of the new life in Christ is joyous rather than burdensome, and that genuine profession of Christ involves an integral desire for humble, grateful, and joyful obedience to the saint's heavenly Father. While this obedience in the saints, in this life, never attains to the perfect obedience found only in Christ, it always has as its aim the perfection of the Moral Law. What type of self-deceived, carnal "love" must it be that claims to know God and yet rejects and tramples upon His holy commandments? Certainly, men who profess such things are liars.

Second, a word must be said on the principle that "... Christ *is* the end of the law for righteousness to every one that believeth"

THE NECESSITY OF ABSOLUTES

(Rom.10:4). In the ecclesiastical battles of seventeenth-century England, one of the most fundamental and far-reaching was between the orthodox Puritan divines on the one hand and Antinomians on the other. Considering this verse in Romans 10, the Antinomians proposed a form of lawlessness, that somehow through grace, Christ had freed believers from any moral responsibility. Without question, the Puritans agreed that man cannot be saved by the works of the Law. Considered as a covenant of works, the Law can only condemn men. But the Antinomians rejected a right view of the abiding validity of the Moral Law out of a sincere (but sincerely wrong) desire to protect the free grace of God in the salvation of sinners. The disagreement revolved around the correct translation of the Greek word, τέλος. The verse, in the original Greek, reads: τέλος γὰρ νόμου Χριστὸς εἰς δικαιοσύνην παντὶ τῷ πιστεύοντι.[63] The word in particular dispute is τέλος, translated "end" in the Authorized Version.

---

[63] F. H. A. Scrivener, *The New Testament in Greek* (Cambridge: Cambridge University Press, 1881), Rom. 10:4.

The Nature of Biblical Law

Kevan observes: "The Antinomians understood [τέλος] to mean termination, or abolition, and they had no hesitation in affirming that Christ brought the demands of the moral Law to an end."[64]

Anthony Burgess, a great seventeenth-century Puritan divine and member of the Westminster Assembly, combatted this errant translation with its faulty conclusions. He did so, of course, by insisting upon proper exegesis. The word τέλος, according to Burgess, is properly translated in this passage as "the perfection, the fullness of the Law."[65] Burgess goes on to unfold this passage by first dismissing the argument that Paul is referring to the Ceremonial Law. He argues that this is certainly not the case because the Jews looked to the Moral Law as their righteousness—something they never looked to the Ceremonial Law to provide for them. Christ as the end of the Moral Law, therefore, is the only possible exegetical meaning of this

---

[64] Kevan, 137.

[65] Anthony Burgess, *Vindiciae Legis: or, A Vindication of the Moral Law and the Covenants, From the Errors of the* Papists, Arminians, Socinians, *and more especially,* Antinomians, 2nd ed., corrected and augmented, facsimile reprint (Grand Rapids: Reformation Heritage Books, 2011/1647), 265.

THE NECESSITY OF ABSOLUTES

phrase. The question then becomes, in what way is Christ the end of the Moral Law when He Himself made clear: "Think not that I am come to destroy the Law, or the prophets" (Matt. 5:17)? To explain this, Burgess revives an argument from Aquinas; namely, that the end of a thing may either exist as a *natural* end or an *appointed* end. He states: "Now the end of the Law, to which *naturally* [emphasis added] it inclineth, is eternall [sic] life to be obtained by a perfect righteousness in us; but the instituted and *appointed* [emphasis added] end, which God the Lawgiver made in the promulgation of it, was the Lord Christ."[66] Kevan explains Burgess' statement thus:

> ... whatever the Law commanded, promised, or threatened, was so for the purpose of stirring up the covenant people to seek Christ. ... [It] is thus the realization of the end of the Law in both senses proposed by Thomas Aquinas: the 'appointed' end comprehends the 'natural.' The object of the Law is thus fully realized, first as to its natural inclination in the perfect righteousness of Christ, and then as to its appointed end in the salvation of sinners.[67]

---

[66] Burgess, 267.
[67] Kevan, 138-39.

The Nature of Biblical Law

It is also of importance to briefly note that Christ did not create a new law in opposition to the Moral Law of the Decalogue. There is no such thing as a "law of Christ" that stands as a radical dichotomy from the Moral Law. The great *Nadere Reformatie* divine, Wilhelmus à Brakel (1635-1711) addressed this very point when he stated:

> The law of Christ is identical to the law of the ten commandments. Christ did not give another law; Christ gave that law of the ten commandments. To this law He subjected Himself and has perfectly lived according to it, leaving us an example therein. He Himself also is a living law. Christ has never given liberty to transgress any of the ten commandments, be it those that pertain to murder, adultery, or theft, etc. Thus, the law of Christ is the law of the ten commandments.[68]

The Lord Jesus Christ, as the supreme Lawgiver, is also the chief Interpreter of the Moral Law as the great Prophet of God (Hebrews 3:1).

There is a question of the Lord's commandment in John 13:34. Here, the Lord Jesus states to His

---

[68] à Brakel, 3:58.

disciples, "A new commandment I give unto you, That ye love one another; as I have loved you, that ye also love one another." The point of misunderstanding is in the word "new" (καινὴν). The commandment to love one's neighbor was nothing new to the moral precepts of Israel. The LORD had already articulated this principle to Moses, saying, "Thou shalt not avenge, nor bear any grudge against the children of thy people, but thou shalt love thy neighbour as thyself: I *AM* the LORD" (Lev. 19:18). Again, the Lord Jesus Christ articulated this moral principle when asked which was the greatest commandment of all. His response was the summary of both Tables of the Moral Law, quoting from Deut. 6:5 and Lev. 19:18: "… Thou shalt love the Lord thy God with all thy heart, and with all thy soul, and with all thy mind. This is the first and great commandment. And the second *is* like unto it, Thou shalt love thy neighbour as thyself" (Mat. 22:37-39). The Scottish preacher and commentator, George Hutcheson (1615-74), observes:

> … by calling this commandment in special "new," is pointed out … that Christ doth so much and so specially recommend it above

> others, and adds his authority and credit with his disciples to the former injunction of the law, to make it to be studied; and partly, hereby is pointed out that it is "new," in respect that it is urged upon a new ground, and after a new pattern and example; our love to others not being now to be regulated only according to our love to ourselves, as the tenour of the law runs, but a new ground and pattern being laid in Christ's loving of us, which makes the whole complex commandment be "a new commandment."[69]

It thus appears that the "new" commandment given by Christ was not new in substance but "new" in its motive and application, having been renewed by Christ and exemplified by His own perfect demonstration of this moral principle.

---

[69] George Hutcheson, *The Gospel of John* (Edinburgh: Banner of Truth, 1985/1657), 288.

THE NECESSITY OF ABSOLUTES

*****

Christ Jesus was truly the end of the Law for righteousness for His elect by His perfect fulfillment of every jot and tittle of the Moral Law in His perfect obedience. Christ was perfectly obedient to the will of His Father in two ways. First, He was obedient *actively*, whereby He perfectly kept the whole Law of God in a way that no sinful man ever could. He was never tainted with original sin because of His supernatural conception by the Holy Spirit. And, being the Lord from heaven, the perfect Man Christ Jesus kept every letter of the Law in thought, word, and deed. If He is the Lord of the Sabbath (Mat. 12:8), He is Lord of the whole Law. Secondly, He was obedient *passively*, whereby, "... in His death ... having ... felt and borne the weight of God's wrath, He laid down His life an offering for sin, enduring the painful, shameful, and cursed death of the cross."[70] Hence, by His perfect obedience to the Law, Christ established the only and sure means of the sinner's entrance into eternal life. As Stephen Charnock

---

[70] *WLC*, Q.49, 214.

The Nature of Biblical Law

(1628-80) averred: "... the law of God was not abrogated upon the fall of man. ... Since the law is not abrogated, it must be exactly obeyed, the honour of it must be preserved; it cannot be observed by us, it was Christ only who kept it, and never broke it, and endured the penalty of it for us, not for himself."[71] The Moral Law never found its *termination* in Jesus Christ; it found in Christ its true *perfection*. For professors of Christ to reject the Moral Law is to reject their own new nature. "For whom He did foreknow, He also did predestinate *to be* conformed to the Image of His Son, that He might be the Firstborn among many brethren" (Rom. 8:29). Furthermore, the Christian is to be "... renewed in the spirit of your mind; and that ye put on the new man, which after God is created in righteousness and true holiness" (Eph. 4:23-24). While the curse of the Law for the elect has ended in Christ, it remains the pattern for their life and sanctification.

---

[71] Stephen Charnock, *The Complete Works of Stephen Charnock*, vol. 3 (Edinburgh: Banner of Truth, 1986/1865), 519.

Chapter Two

The Moral Law: Perpetuity, Nature, and Uses

> *Think not that I am come to destroy the law, or the prophets: I am not come to destroy, but to fulfill. For verily I say unto you, Till heaven and earth pass, one jot or one tittle shall in no wise pass from the law, till all be fulfilled. ... For I say unto you, That except your righteousness shall exceed* the righteousness of the scribes and Pharisees, ye shall in no case enter into the kingdom of heaven.
>
> (Matt. 5:17-18, 20)

It has already been observed that the Westminster divines adhered to the Divine origin of Biblical Law, that they promulgated the well-established exegetical principle of the tripartite division of the Law, and that they promoted the perpetuity of the Moral Law. Their discussion of the abrogation of the Ceremonial Law and expiration of the Judicial Law will be addressed below. First, however, attention must be paid to the Westminsterian position of the Moral Law. The divines had a very clear understanding of the nature of the Moral Law, its perpetuity and universality, and its abiding use for Christ's Church and people. The matured, Reformation understanding of the Moral Law, expressed by the Assembly, as it was important for the seventeenth century, continues to have abiding relevance for the present-day Church. Many errors in the thesis and application of the Law—past and present—are combatted by the wisdom of the Westminster divines on this issue.

The Moral Law: Perpetuity, Nature, and Uses

1. The Nature, Perspicuity, and Perpetuity of the Moral Law

Beginning its discussion of the Moral Law in good Reformed Scholastic fashion, the Westminster Assembly posits that: "[The moral] law, after his [mankind's] fall, continued to be a perfect rule of righteousness; and, as such, was delivered by God upon Mount Sinai in ten commandments, and written in two tables; the first four commandments containing our duty towards God, and the other six our duty to man."[1] The generous condescension of God extends so far as to prevent humankind from any need to "feel after" a true ethic. In the perspicuous propositions of Scripture, the Lord has made His Mind clear to all mankind, thereby leaving man without excuse for the least disobedience against God's good Law. The Moral Law is indelibly marked on the very nature of man. But, due to the depravity of the whole man, this *natural law* is only sufficient to leave men inexcusable before the great Tribunal of God. Clearly presented in the Pentateuch, and frequently

---

[1] *WCF*, XIX.ii, 96.

THE NECESSITY OF ABSOLUTES

explained and applied throughout the scope of the Scriptures, the Moral Law, in the first place, remains—for all mankind—"a perfect rule of righteousness." God is the three-times Holy God; and He demands righteous obedience from the creature made in His Image.

When the Westminster divines presented their teaching on the Moral Law, they were not producing any novel theology. Rather, they presented the teaching in perfect harmony with the Scriptures and orthodox divines of every age, especially of those leading lights used by God in the revival of the true religion during the Reformation. John Calvin stated:

> [The true knowledge of God ... (and) the knowledge of ourselves] ... the Lord accomplishes in his law. First, claiming for himself the lawful power to command, he calls us to reverence his divinity, and specifies wherein such reverence lies and consists. Secondly, having published the rule of his righteousness, he reproves us both for our impotence and for our unrighteousness. For our nature, wicked and deformed, is always opposing his uprightness; and our capacity,

The Moral Law: Perpetuity, Nature, and Uses

> weak and feeble to do good, lies far from his perfection.[2]

Comparing this quotation with the Confessional statement, there appears a continuation of a high view of the Moral Law in Calvin that is reflected in the work of the Westminster divines and that accentuates their mutual understanding of a Biblical emphasis upon the Majesty of God. Furthermore, while the depraved minds of an "enlightened" society shouted about the "rights of man," the orthodox theologians have always led the way with their insistence upon the right of God as Creator and Governor.

Since the Sovereign God has created and ordered the cosmos on strict, unbreakable *natural* laws, it is consistent with His perfect Nature that He also ordered a system of equally strict and unbreakable *moral* laws governing the thoughts and actions of mankind, which is the sole terrestrial creature made in the Image of God. Nor is it possible to insist that God's Moral Law has somehow simply disappeared or no longer has a binding effect upon redeemed men, due to the Holy

---

[2] Calvin, *Institutes*, I:II.viii.1, 367.

THE NECESSITY OF ABSOLUTES

Majesty of God Himself. Samuel Bolton observed, "For substance, [the moral law] contains such things as are good and holy, and agreeable to the will of God, being the image of the divine will, a beam of His holiness, the sum of which is love to God and love to man."[3] Because God is perfect and infinite Righteousness, and because His Law is a reflection of His holiness, His Standard of righteousness among men as Image-bearers does not and cannot change. The impossibility of any alteration to God's Standard of right and wrong is articulated by Bolton:

> Indeed, the [moral] law, as it is considered as a rule, can no more be abolished or changed than the nature of good and evil can be changed. The substance of the law is the sum of doctrine concerning piety towards God, charity towards our neighbours, temperance and sobriety towards ourselves. And for the substance of it, it is moral and eternal, and cannot be abrogated.[4]

---

[3] Samuel Bolton, *The True Bounds of Christian Freedom* (Edinburgh: Banner of Truth Trust, 1978), 56.
[4] Ibid., 57.

The Moral Law: Perpetuity, Nature, and Uses

It is precisely because of the unchangeable Lawgiver that the Moral Law itself cannot change.

This point led the divines to observe: "The moral law doth for ever bind all, as well justified persons as others, to the obedience thereof; and that not only in regard of the matter contained in it, *but also in respect of the authority of God, the Creator, who gave it* [emphasis added]."[5] God is the Giver of the Moral Law and, being infinite in righteousness and holiness, He could not but give a good Law to man. God made man in His Image as rational creatures and moral agents. It is most fitting, therefore, that the rational creature should reflect the morality of his Creator. Ernest Kevan captures this principle beautifully when he states:

> The moral Law in man is a copy of the Divine nature, and what God wills in the moral Law is so 'consonant to that eternall justice and goodness in himself', that any supposed abrogation of that Law would mean that God would 'deny his own justice and goodnesse.' ... The Law is thus the glorious expression of the glory of God in so far as that glory is to be

---

[5] *WCF*, XIX.v, 98.

THE NECESSITY OF ABSOLUTES

realized by the creatures whom He has made in His own image.[6]

Because man is a moral agent, created in the image of God, it is absurd to justify immoral behavior. It is also absurd to reject the good Moral Law of God in favor of an ethic devised out of the depraved hearts of men. There is one Lawgiver, one Judge; and He has been pleased to give to all men His perfect Standard of right and wrong whereby they will be judged. The Church displays hatred for men, rather than love, when she propagates the myth that relativistic, ever-changing social mores can present a useful ethic that is pleasing to God. Instead, what she does is to blaspheme God, spurn His Law, and lull men into false security; crying, "Peace, peace; when there is no peace" (Jer. 6:14).

The perpetuity of the Moral Law is essential as the Standard given by the eternal Creator and Governor of His creation. A moveable ethic cannot correspond to an eternal Creator. His Moral Law is binding upon all men. It is not

---

[6] Kevan, 63.

The Moral Law: Perpetuity, Nature, and Uses

abrogated in Christ, but rather reinforced in and by Him. As the perfect Example, Christ establishes the Moral Law in His perfect keeping of it. Certainly He brought His elect out from under the Moral Law as a Covenant of Works. But He never, in any way, abrogated the Moral Law as the abiding rule of obedience. He made this point as clearly as possible in the Sermon on the Mount when He instructed His disciples to (as it were) perish the thought that He had come to destroy the Law. In His incarnation, God the Son became truly and really Man, "made under the Law" (Gal. 4:4). This is perhaps one of the most profound mysteries of all of Scripture; namely, that God the Son, the Lawgiver, should become truly Man—God and Man in one Person—in order that He might be *made under the Law*. William Perkins addresses this necessary doctrine when he states:

> ... This may not seem strange, that He which is Lord of the law should be subject to the law. For He must be considered as He is our pledge and surety (Heb. 7:22), and as one that stands in our place, room, and stead, and before God represents the person of all the elect. And in this respect is He subject to the law, not by nature, but by voluntary abasement and

THE NECESSITY OF ABSOLUTES

> condition of will. ... The Son of God was subject to the law ... by the obedience of His passion and by His obedience in fulfilling the law.[7]

Joseph Pipa's comments on this passage are also helpful: "By submitting to the law as the covenant of works, Christ was under contract to obey the law of God perfectly and to bear the curse of any law breaking. In particular, He obeyed the moral commandments perfectly (His active obedience) and He satisfied the curse of God's judgment (His passive obedience)."[8]

The subjection of God the Son to the Law in His incarnation is a matter of great importance to understanding the Westminsterian position. They assert: "This office [of a mediator and surety] the Lord Jesus did most willingly undertake; which, that he might discharge, he was made under the law, and did perfectly fulfill it."[9] This statement contemplates both the active

---

[7] William Perkins, *The Works of William Perkins: Commentary on Galatians* (Grand Rapids: Reformation Heritage Books, 2015), 2:251.

[8] Joseph A. Pipa Jr., *Galatians: God's Proclamation of Liberty*, Focus on the Bible Commentary (Ross-shire, Scotland: Christian Focus Publications, 2010), 147–48.

[9] *WCF*, VIII.iv, 47.

The Moral Law: Perpetuity, Nature, and Uses

and passive obedience of Christ on behalf of His elect. The purchase of salvation was salvation from the *curse* of the Law. This only Christ could do. The precise manner in which He did so was twofold. He perfectly kept the Law *actively*. The definitive Westminsterian statement on His active obedience avers that "Christ humbled himself in his life, *by subjecting himself to the law, which he perfectly fulfilled* [emphasis added]."[10] Christ also completely fulfilled the Law *passively*. The definitive Westminsterian statement on His passive obedience concludes that "Christ humbled himself in his death ... having also conflicted with the terrors of death, and the powers of darkness, *felt and borne the weight of God's wrath, he laid down his life an offering for sin* [emphasis added], enduring the painful, shameful, and cursed death of the cross."[11] Kevan recognizes the far-reaching importance of this doctrine as he summarizes the teaching of the Puritans. The Puritans understood that God requires that man, as a rational and moral agent, must perfectly and completely keep the

---

[10] *WLC*, Q.48, 213.
[11] *WLC*, Q.49, 214.

THE NECESSITY OF ABSOLUTES

whole of the Moral Law, in thought, word, and deed forever. Apart from this "personal, perfect, and perpetual obedience"[12] to the whole Moral Law, there can be no fellowship between God and man, and disobedient man stands condemned before the righteous God. But Adam transgressed the Moral Law in the Garden of Eden, thereby making himself guilty and, as covenant head of all his posterity, corrupted all of his descendants with the guilt of his rebellion. Except for some voluntary condescension on God's part, all of humanity from Adam to the present would be justly cast into everlasting damnation. But God, in His infinite mercy, according to His eternal Covenant of Redemption, was pleased to send His Own Son, God the Second Person, to be that "… Daysman … *that* might lay His Hand upon us both" (Job 9:33). Christ Himself became that "Daysman," the Mediator between the Holy, Righteous God and fallen, sinful man. He did so by becoming truly Man and subjecting Himself to the Law — both actively and passively. Kevan observes:

---

[12] *WLC*, Q.20, 193.

The Moral Law: Perpetuity, Nature, and Uses

"This [Christ did] ... by His obedience, first in a life well-pleasing to the Father, and, secondly, in giving up of Himself to death: these two aspects of His obedience [the Puritans] described as active and passive respectively."[13]

Christ is not only the great Exemplar of Law-keeping, He is the great Lawgiver. To accuse Christ of annulling His own Law is to accuse Him of denying Himself, which is a great evil. This same Law was written on the heart of Adam at creation, known and observed by Abraham (Gen. 26:5), verbally pronounced to the Congregation of Israel at Sinai (Ex. 20:1), twice written with His Own Finger on the tables of stone (Ex. 31:18 and Ex. 34:28), and finally restored and defended during His earthly ministry and through the inspired writings of His apostles. The idea that the Moral Law has ceased to be applicable to human beings since the coming of Christ can only be legitimate if God ceases to be God. But God will not deny Himself. If God can change in such a fashion then simply put, *He is not God*. There are many sincere

---

[13] Kevan, 141.

THE NECESSITY OF ABSOLUTES

lovers of the Lord who yet insist that He has changed His ethic since the coming of Christ. They are sincerely wrong and (unwittingly, no doubt) do despite to the Divine Name, blaspheming the Living God! God annuls His Moral Standard for men only at the moment He ceases to be God. The very perpetuity of the Moral Law, unaltered since the very beginning, testifies to this doctrine. Anthony Burgess is particularly clear upon this point when he maintains that the Moral Law, as written on the heart of Adam in the state of innocency and promulgated to Israel at Sinai, was the *same* as that delivered to the saints prior to the Mosaic administration. He observes:

> And when we say, the law was, before *Moses*, I do not meane only, that it was written in the hearts of men, but it was publikely preached in the ministry that the Church did then enjoy, as appeareth by *Noah*'s preaching to the old world, and Gods striving with men then by his word. So that we may say, the Decalogue is *Adams*, and *Abrahams*, and *Noahs*, and Christs, and the Apostles, as well as *Moses* ... but yet the Law did perpetually found in the Church, ever since it was a Church ... men who speak against the use of the Law, and the preaching

The Moral Law: Perpetuity, Nature, and Uses

> of it, do oppose the universall way of the Church of God in the Old and New Testament.[14]

The Moral Law, pronounced in display of God's Majesty and Power at Sinai, has nothing to do with the Law as a Covenant of Works for God's elect and everything to do with the Moral Law as an integral part of the Covenant of Grace for them. There was a sober reminder of the One with Whom Israel had to do at Sinai, no doubt. But the entire nature of the Divine proclamation of the Moral Law at Sinai is only rightly understood and applied when it is recognized to be King Christ, as *Redeemer*, delivering His good Law to His Church. The Moral Law given at Sinai is, first and foremost, a message of God as the Redeemer of His people. The Sinai transaction understood in this light becomes less the judicial verdict of the Divine *criminal* court, and very much more the proclamation of the Divine *family* court. It is an emancipation ceremony with the terms of freedom from bondage clearly delineated to the household of faith. This is the gracious nature of the Sinai transaction and

---

[14] Burgess, 150.

THE NECESSITY OF ABSOLUTES

explains the condescension of God to His Church ever since. It explains how God pleads and reasons with His people even though it is His Sovereign prerogative to command. It explains why God often condescends to explain Himself, as it were, to His people and to reveal His wisdom to them. God is never required to explain Himself to any creature; and yet, through Christ, to His own adopted family, He often gives reasons in places where He need only command. It is not simply "do this and live" (Deut. 4:1), but "be ye holy, *for* I AM holy" (1 Pet. 1:16). The command is unalterable and immutable, given condescendingly with the reason that the saints are to be a certain way, act a certain way, think and feel a certain way, *because* they are, through Christ, the children of their heavenly Father, His purchased possession.

There is, however, some distinction between the Sinaitic pronunciation of the Moral Law and recapitulation of the same Law in the Sermon on the Mount; namely, that there was, by design, the Presence of the LORD and Lawgiver at Sinai. God the Son, the preincarnate Christ, was at

The Moral Law: Perpetuity, Nature, and Uses

Sinai,[15] pronouncing His Law, in "... thunders and lightnings, and a thick cloud upon the mount, and the voice of the trumpet exceeding loud; so that all the people that *was* in the camp trembled. And mount Sinai was altogether on a smoke, because the LORD descended upon it in a fire: and the smoke thereof ascended as the smoke of a furnace, and the whole mount quaked greatly" (Exod. 19:16, 18). After His incarnation, on the Mount in Matthew 5, the God-Man "... was set ... and He opened His Mouth, and taught them" (Matt. 5:1, 2). It is the very Person of Christ, *Immanuel*, that is the long-promised Daysman to Whom all the Law and the Prophets pointed, and of Whom all who by faith take hold upon Him have the everlasting assurance of their salvation. The Moral Law as administered at Sinai, though it was an administration of the Covenant of Grace, became but a dead letter of condemnation to all who looked to the Law apart from Christ as their means of obtaining a righteous standing with God. This leads Paul, by the inspiration of the Holy Spirit, to insist:

---

[15] See Acts 7:38 and Jn. 1:18.

THE NECESSITY OF ABSOLUTES

> For as many as are of the works of the law are under the curse: for it is written, 'Cursed is every one that continueth not in all things which are written in the book of the law to do them.' But that no man is justified by the law in the sight of God, *it is* evident: for, 'The just shall live by faith.' And the law is not of faith: but, 'The man that doeth them shall live in them.' Christ hath redeemed us from the curse of the law, being made a curse for us: for as it is written, 'Cursed *is* every one that hangeth on a tree:' that the blessing of Abraham might come on the Gentiles through Jesus Christ; that we might receive the promise of the Spirit through faith (Gal. 3:10-14).

It clearly follows, then, that God the Son as the Incarnate Messiah is the One to whom the faithful Hebrews under the Old Testament administration looked for their salvation, and to this same Messiah that all since His coming must look for their salvation; for, there is no way for any man to keep the whole of the Moral Law (or even any part of it), as a covenant of works, in the thought, word, or deed. Such as look to the keeping of the Moral Law as their righteousness cannot but be eternally disappointed, since they will never be able to keep that Law to the perfect

The Moral Law: Perpetuity, Nature, and Uses

standard required by the three-times Holy and Righteous God.

A man will be found righteous before God only insofar as he believes in Jesus Christ, the only perfect and personal Law-Keeper and in Whom alone there is salvation for sinners. One of the most graphic images of this great truth in all of Scripture is to be found in the great Throne Room scene in Revelation 4, where John records: "And immediately I was in the Spirit: and, behold, a throne was set in heaven, and *One* sat on the throne. And He that sat was to look upon like a jasper and a sardine stone: and *there was* a rainbow round about the throne, in sight like unto an emerald" (Rev. 4:2-3). It is an often overlooked portion of Scripture, but has great significance directly pertinent to the subject at hand. The rainbow in the throne room scene, while reminiscent of the rainbow of the Noahic covenant in which God promised never again to destroy the whole earth by a flood, here "… is to relate unto the Covenant of God's Grace through Jesus Christ with His true

THE NECESSITY OF ABSOLUTES

Church."[16] The God, Who cannot even look upon sin or tolerate it in His Presence, brings all of His elect into His very presence through the covenantal application of Christ's salvific cross work. As the apostle Paul states, "For he hath made him *to be* sin for us, who knew no sin; that we might be made the righteousness of God in him" (2 Cor. 5:21). This principle is in keeping with the Westminsterian understanding that the Covenant of Grace was not made with the elect directly but rather that "The covenant of grace was made with Christ as the second Adam, and in him with all the elect as his seed."[17] In and of themselves, the saints are not yet perfected in this life, but Christ's perfect righteousness—His absolute and complete obedience, both actively and passively—is applied, or *imputed*, to the account of His elect.

> Those whom God effectually calleth, he also freely justifieth: not by infusing righteousness into them, but by pardoning their sins, and by accounting and accepting their persons as

---

[16] James Durham, *A Commentary on Revelation*. (Willow Street: Old Paths Publications, 2000), 342.

[17] *WLC*, Q.31, 200.

The Moral Law: Perpetuity, Nature, and Uses

> righteous: not for any thing wrought in them, or done by them, but for Christ's sake alone: not by imputing faith itself, the act of believing, or any other evangelical obedience, to them as their righteousness; *but by imputing the obedience and satisfaction of Christ unto them, they receiving and resting on him and his righteousness by faith* [emphasis added]: which faith they have not of themselves; it is the gift of God.[18]

John Owen captured the essence of the Biblical doctrine of imputation.

> This imputation is *an act of God "ex mera gratia," —of his mere love and grace; whereby, on the consideration of the mediation of Christ, he makes an effectual grant and donation of a true, real, perfect righteousness, even that of Christ himself, unto all that do believe; and accounting it as theirs, on his own gracious act, both absolves them from sin and granteth them right and title unto eternal life.*[19]

In considering this comment, Beeke and Jones observe: "Imputation includes, of course, not only that Christ's righteousness, both active and passive,

---

[18] *WCF*, XI.i, 61.
[19] Owen, *Works*, V:173. [Emphasis Owen's]

THE NECESSITY OF ABSOLUTES

is imputed to believers, but also the sins of believers are imputed to Christ."[20]

---

[20] Joel R. Beeke and Mark Jones, *A Puritan Theology: Doctrine for Life* (Grand Rapids: Reformation Heritage Books, 2012), 499.

The Moral Law: Perpetuity, Nature, and Uses

2. *Natural Law* and Man Left Without Excuse

As long as men remain in rebellion against God and reject salvation through Christ alone, they remain bound under the curse of Adam's rebellion. The Moral Law remains for them a Covenant of Works and, as no man can perfectly keep the whole Law, they are bound to the eternal curse of condemnation of that same Law. The question naturally arises as to how those who have never heard the Word of God proclaimed can be judged by the Moral Law in the Decalogue. But Scripture does not leave this question unanswered. Instead, Scripture is very clear, and it is a vital point in the discussion of Law for the Westminster divines. The very opening paragraph of the *Confession of Faith* speaks to this point when the divines observe: "... The light of nature, and the works of creation and providence, do so far manifest the goodness, wisdom, and power of God, as to leave men inexcusable."[21] Clark observes: "... It would be better to understand this situation in terms of

---

[21] *WCF*, I.i, 3.

THE NECESSITY OF ABSOLUTES

innate or *a priori* ideas. In the act of creation God implanted in man a knowledge of His existence. Romans 1:32 and 2:15 seem to indicate that God also implanted some knowledge of morality. We are born with this knowledge; it is not manufactured out of sensory experience."[22] Paul articulates this principle in these terms: "For the wrath of God is revealed from heaven against all ungodliness and unrighteousness of men, who hold the truth in unrighteousness; because that which may be known of God is manifest in them; for God hath shewed *it* unto them" (Rom. 1:18-19). Simply put, human beings are designed from creation to *think God*. Every culture in the history of the world has been founded upon some religion with the worship of some god or gods—even if the "supreme deity" is understood to be the collective will of the ruling elite or the masses in general. This innate, yet woefully vague, notion of "a god" or "gods," however, falls infinitely below any right understanding of the true God Who is not only the Creator, but Who is the Judge, Lawgiver, and

---

[22] Clark, *What do Presbyterians Believe?*, 11.

The Moral Law: Perpetuity, Nature, and Uses

King (Is. 33:22). In short, this innate, *a priori*, knowledge of God simply leaves man inexcusable before the infinite Tribunal of the Judgment Seat of Christ in his denial of Him.

In addition to *thinking God*, man has an *a priori* knowledge of morality. Paul continues:

> Not the hearers of the law *are* just before God, but the doers of the law shall be justified. For when the Gentiles, which have not the law,[23] do by nature the things contained in the law, these, having not the law, are a law unto themselves: which shew the work of the law written in their hearts, their conscience also bearing witness, and *their* thoughts the mean while accusing or else excusing one another (Rom. 2:13-15).

In his original creation and pristine state, Adam had the entirety of the Moral Law—the same Moral Law as pronounced from Sanai—written on his heart. John Lightfoot (1602-75) states:

> God read a lecture of the Law to him before hee fell, to be a hedge to him to keepe him in Paradise, but when *Adam* would not keepe within compasse, this Law is now become as the flaming sword at Eden gate to keepe him

---

[23] That is, the written Law of Moses, including the Decalogue.

THE NECESSITY OF ABSOLUTES

> and his posteritie out: *Adam* heard as much in the garden, as Israel did at Sinai, but onely in fewer words and without thunder.[24]

In all of its essential qualities, therefore, the Decalogue presents the same Moral Law as that which was initially engraved upon the heart of Adam. Even after the fall, men still have the remnants of this same Moral Law written on their hearts and have a conscious knowledge of God's morality (see Rom. 1:32). The Westminster divines observe: "The rule of obedience revealed to Adam in the estate of innocence, and to all mankind in him ... was the moral law."[25] Not only is man—yes, even man in his state of depravity—designed to acknowledge God, he is also designed to *think morally*. Turretin provides an important definition of natural law, or the light of nature, when he focuses on the essential necessity of it. He states:

> But [natural law] must be drawn from the right of nature itself, founded both on the nature of God, the Creator (who by his holiness must

---

[24] John Lightfoote, *Erubhin or Miscellanies Christian and Judaicall, and others* (London: G. Miller for Robert Swayne and William Adderton, 1629), 182-83.

[25] *WLC*, Q.92, 255.

> prescribe to his creatures the duties founded upon that right), and on the condition of rational creatures themselves (who, on account of their necessary dependence upon God in the genus of morals, no less than in the genus of being, are bound to perform or avoid those things which sound reason and the dictates of conscience enjoin upon them to do or avoid).[26]

Although the guilt of Adam's sin was imputed upon all his posterity proceeding from him by ordinary generation (Christ Himself, therefore, excepted), all men are born guilty sinners. But the natural morality as originally imprinted upon the rational soul of man at creation, though marred by sin, remains an essential part of who he is.

Thomas Ridgeley (1667-1734) is very careful in his use of the expression, "the light of nature." He defines this light of nature as "… God's writing his laws in the hearts of our first parents, or impressing the commands of the moral law on their nature; so that by the power of reasoning with which they were endowed, they might attain to the knowledge of them. Accordingly, man, by the light of nature,

---

[26] Turretin, 2:3.

knew all things contained in the moral law."[27] Hence, the entirety of the Moral Law remains indelibly etched within man's soul so that, even though marred in all his faculties by sin, man remains a rational creature capable of recognizing good and evil but decidedly, without the power to do that which is right and well-pleasing in the Sight of God to salvation. This is because, as Turretin stated above, God is still God Who prescribes His will to the creature, and because man is still man who remains dependent upon God as much for the standard of morality as he depends upon God for his life. Even when a man rejects that he was created by God, his existence proves him a liar. Even when a man rejects God as Lawgiver, he nevertheless devises some form of law as a standard for himself and those around him. Because man is the creature created in the Image of God as a rational being and a moral agent, man simply has no choice but to think morally. It is an essential property of man's humanness.

---

[27] Thomas Ridgeley, *A Body of Divinity* (New York: Robert Carter & Brothers, 1855), II:299.

The Moral Law: Perpetuity, Nature, and Uses

Even though man was designed to think morally, he is left utterly without excuse by the light of nature alone. Robert Shaw observes: "From the light of nature we may learn that there is evil both moral and penal in the world; but as to the question how sin entered into the world, and how deliverance from it may be obtained, the light of nature is entirely silent. It shows men their sin and misery, but it discovers not the plain and certain way of salvation."[28] However, while the fall of Adam plunged himself and all his posterity into this state of sin and misery, along with the corruption of the will and affections of all mankind, it did *not* obliterate man's natural rational faculty. In every nation, the civil magistrate creates and enforces laws for the preservation of peace within its realm. These civil laws are, in the best of nations, but dim and shadowy reflections of the Moral Law. And yet they prove that mankind possesses an innate knowledge of good and evil; that the good is to be encouraged and protected and the evil is to be punished. Indeed, Paul contends that this is the very reason God instituted civil magistracy;

---

[28] Shaw, 5.

namely, to promote what is good and to punish that which is evil, as His minister, or servant (Rom. 13:1-6).

Too often, however, that which is truly good is legislated as if it was evil, and vice versa. "Woe unto them that call evil good, and good evil; that put darkness for light, and light for darkness; that put bitter for sweet, and sweet for bitter! Woe unto *them that are* wise in their own eyes, and prudent in their own sight" (Isa. 5:20-21). The Biblical understanding of the role of the civil magistrate, as evidenced by the light of nature already discussed, is that the civil government has the obligation before God to enforce *both* Tables of the Moral Law or put simply, the whole law as one moral code (see Jas. 2:10-12). Every nation has some set of laws respecting both Tables of the Moral Law, but the manner of their execution in the majority is vastly different than the design of God. In the United States of America, for example, there is the clear recognition that there must be a legislative and judicial statement regarding the worship of God, thereby demonstrating the light of nature with respect to the enforcement of the First Table of

The Moral Law: Perpetuity, Nature, and Uses

the Moral Law. The manner in which the Bill of Rights does this, however, is openly to reject the supremacy of the One, True, and Living God of Scripture and open the way for *every* false religion. "Congress shall make no law respecting an establishment of religion, or prohibiting the free exercise thereof."[29] The same government clearly recognizes the requirement to enforce the Second Table of the Moral Law by forbidding murder. In practice, however, it is questionable whether the violation of this law is justly and universally punished. Even when the death penalty is the stated consequence for murder, murderers are not universally put to death. Those who are sentenced to death may wait years for the sentence to be carried out, or have the sentence reduced, thanks to a legal system that cannot be confused with a justice system. Simultaneously—and even though no law exists permitting it—the judiciary in the United States has "legislated" the wholesale slaughter of

---

[29] "The Bill of Rights of the United States of America (1791)," accessed May 28, 2018, https://www.billofrightsinstitute.org/founding-documents/bill-of-rights/.

millions of unborn children. One cannot look at these atrocities without immediately being aware of the inadequacy of the light of nature to shape the morals of a society.

A further distinction must be offered between the Biblical and Reformed doctrine of natural law and the similar concept as perverted by pagan philosophers. Kevan is correct when he states that

> [The Puritans'] doctrine [of natural law] stands in complete opposition to all naturalistic theories and has no affinities whatsoever with the utilitarian empiricism which seeks to secularize the concept. It is a strictly theological doctrine and perceives the essence of natural Law in the fact of its promulgation by God at the time of man's creation. This alone gives validity to the concept of natural Law and at the same time relates it to man's rational nature.[30]

Consistently in the writings of the leading divines of the First and Second Reformations, is found a resounding emphasis upon the importance of Biblical Law because it aims at the

---
[30] Kevan, 57.

The Moral Law: Perpetuity, Nature, and Uses

Majesty of God. Following the lead of the Westminster divines, Robert Louis Dabney (1820-98) rightly states, "The Law then must remain, under every dispensation, the authoritative declaration of God's character."[31] Man has this natural law bound into his nature, simply because he was created by God after God's own image. The rejection of the living God as Creator, Lawgiver, and Judge is the ultimate blasphemy. Further, it is entirely irrational. Reprobate man's rejection of the God Who has revealed Himself in Scripture in no way affects the Being and Nature of God Himself. God is the Creator of the entire universe and of every man—whether men believe so or not. God is the absolute Lawgiver Who has implanted His good Law in man's heart and mind (Rom. 2:14-15)—whether man submits to the Lawgiver or not. And, all men will stand before the infinite Tribunal of the Godhead on the Day of Judgment, will bow the knee before Him, and will go to their eternal damnation—though they have rejected His sovereign right to rule in this life. The hardness and

---

[31] Robert Louis Dabney, *Systematic Theology* (Edinburgh: Banner of Truth Trust, 1985), 353.

THE NECESSITY OF ABSOLUTES

willful blindness of the reprobate mind does not the slightest injury to God, but it causes everlasting anguish upon himself—soul and body—forever. To reject this natural law is to reject the God Who wrote it in the unbeliever's heart and mind.

The Moral Law: Perpetuity, Nature, and Uses

3. The Three *Uses* of the Moral Law

It has been observed already that God created man with the Law written in his heart and mind. It has been further observed that this natural law, since the fall, is only sufficient to leave men without excuse before God's Judgment Seat. Beyond this natural law, God, in His infinite mercy, has condescended to reveal Himself, His good Law, and the way of salvation in the Person and Work of His Son, the Lord Jesus Christ, through the propositions of Scripture. While the Moral Law cannot save any man, it remains vitally *useful*. But there is one area in which the Moral Law is of no use to man since the fall; namely, in the matter of justification. Man *cannot* be justified by the works of the Moral Law. Paul is explicit and unwavering on this point: "Therefore by the deeds of the law there shall no flesh be justified in [God's] sight" (Rom. 3:20). Thomas Ridgeley comments:

> But it is impossible for fallen man thus to obey. How perfect soever his obedience may be for the future, it is supposed, from the nature of the thing, that it cannot be sinless, after sin has been committed; and it would be a reflection on the justice and holiness of God, for us to

THE NECESSITY OF ABSOLUTES

> conclude that he will accept of imperfect obedience, instead of perfect. It follows that a right to life is not to be expected from our imperfect obedience to the law.[32]

It is impossible that any man, born of ordinary generation, could ever perfectly keep the whole of the Moral Law in thought, word, or deed. And even if such a man could be found, the very fact that he is "shapen in iniquity" and conceived in sin (Ps. 51:5) would make his obedience to the Moral Law to fall infinitely below the standard of absolute perfect righteousness that God requires, for man has "... come short of the glory of God," (Rom. 3:23). Even though man, since his fall in Adam, cannot keep the Moral Law perfectly, yet that same Moral Law remains eminently useful to all men everywhere. It is, as Thomas Boston (1676-1732) observes, "An universal law, binding all men, in all places, and at all times. ... It is a perfect law, comprehending the whole of man's duty to God, and to his neighbour. ... It is indispensable and

---

[32] Ridgeley, II:302.

The Moral Law: Perpetuity, Nature, and Uses

perpetual."[33] The fall of man did not eradicate man's moral duty before God, nor did it remove the usefulness of God's Moral Law.

The Westminster divines recognized the abiding usefulness of the Moral Law and, in keeping with the consistent pattern of the orthodox Reformed position on the subject, demonstrated that there are primarily three uses of the Moral Law, dependent upon the state of man. These three uses were first articulated by Philip Melanchthon (1497-1560) in the 1535 edition of his seminal work, *Loci Communes*.[34] Shortly thereafter, Calvin presented the mature thought on the subject in his *Institutes of the Christian Religion*, arguing for a *pedagogical* use, a *civil* use, and a *normative* use of the Moral Law. Calvin defined the *pedagogical* use of the Law as that function in which, "... while it shows God's righteousness, that is, the righteousness alone acceptable to God, it warns, informs, convicts, and

---

[33] Thomas Boston, *The Complete Works of the Late Rev. Thomas Boston, Ettrick*, vol. 2, ed. Samuel M'Millan (Stoke-on-Trent: Tentmaker Publications, 2002), 62.

[34] Melanchthon, Philip. *Loci Communes Theologici*. Edited by Wilhelm Pauck. In *The Library of Christian Classics: Melanchthon and Bucer*: 1-152. (Louisville, KY: Westminster John Knox Press, 1969), 49-57.

THE NECESSITY OF ABSOLUTES

lastly condemns, every man of his own unrighteousness."[35] It is this property of the Moral Law that Paul refers to as leaving all men without excuse (Rom. 1:20). The second, or *civil*, use of the Law was, for Calvin, that property whereby "... at least by fear of punishment to restrain certain men who are untouched by any care for what is just and right unless compelled by hearing the dire threats in the law."[36] Of the third, or *normative*, use of the Law, Calvin writes:

> The third and principal use, which pertains more closely to the proper purpose of the law, finds its place among believers in whose hearts the Spirit of God already lives and reigns. For even though they have the law written and engraved upon their hearts by the finger of God [Jer. 31:33; Heb. 10:16], that is, have been so moved and quickened through the directing of the Spirit that they long to obey God, they still profit by the law in two ways.[37]

The first of these ways, Calvin argues, is more and more each day to teach the believer the will of God and deepen his understanding of His

---

[35] Calvin, *Institutes*, II:II.vii.6, 354.
[36] Ibid., 358.
[37] Ibid., 360.

The Moral Law: Perpetuity, Nature, and Uses

good will. Second, however, the Moral Law in the heart of the believer is used by the Holy Spirit to teach him greater obedience and make him more vigilant to withstand temptations.[38] The impact of Calvin's treatment of the three uses of the Moral Law cannot be overemphasized, especially with regard to the *Third Use* of the Moral Law. Any right understanding of the Divine work of Sanctification will have as a central part of the doctrine the *normative* use of the Moral Law.

Turretin presents the same substance as Calvin respecting the usefulness of the Moral Law, but he explains it using a different formula. He divides the subject into a twofold use of the Moral Law: an "absolute" use and a "relative" use. Turretin's "absolute" use equates to the *civil* use and is binding upon all men of every nation throughout the history of the world. It is this use which sets forth God's universal standard for man's conduct toward God and toward his neighbor. The "relative" use varies depending upon the state of man. Turretin's discussion of the "relative" use

---

[38] Ibid., 360-61.

THE NECESSITY OF ABSOLUTES

equates to both the *pedagogical* and the *normative* uses of the Moral Law, since he subdivides the "relative" use into the three states of man in this life. The first of these is the relation of Adam in his pristine state after creation and before the fall. It was at that point the Covenant of Works and life and happiness would have been obtained by the keeping of the Moral Law, had Adam not rebelled. The second "relative" state aligns precisely with the *pedagogical* use of the Law whereby unregenerate man is convicted of his sinfulness, restrained from utter lawlessness by the threat of punishment, and finally, upon hardening himself to the sovereignty of God, stands condemned by the same Moral Law that he hated and rejected throughout his life. The third "relative" state is the same as the *normative* use of the Moral Law whereby the Law, in the Hand of the Holy Spirit, convinces a man of his utter helplessness and hopelessness in his fallen estate and points him to Christ as the only Savior of men.[39]

---

[39] Turretin, II:137-39.

The Moral Law: Perpetuity, Nature, and Uses

The Westminster divines present the three uses of the Moral Law in a slightly different way, by presenting the universal application of the Moral Law to all men, the particular use of the Moral Law for the unregenerate, and the particular use of the Moral Law for the regenerate. First, they maintained that

> The moral law is of use *to all men* [emphasis added], to inform them of the holy nature and the will of God, and of their duty, binding them to walk accordingly; to convince them of their disability to keep it, and of the sinful pollution of their nature, hearts, and lives: to humble them in the sense of their sin and misery, and thereby help them to a clearer sight of the need they have of Christ, and of the perfection of his obedience.[40]

This statement addresses the evangelical use of the Moral Law. It is of great interest to note with what succinctness and perspicuity, yet with what completeness, the divines present this first use of the Moral Law. First and foremost, the Moral Law informs man of God's holy nature and sovereign

---

[40] *WLC*, Q.95, 256-57.

THE NECESSITY OF ABSOLUTES

will. As has already been stated, God created man to *think morally*—it is an essential part of man's nature. Though his corrupt nature runs from God and strives to throw off God's Law, man can no more escape God's design of obedience than he can his own physical, genetic structure. This is precisely the meaning of Paul when he states that those Gentiles who were without the written Moral Law yet became a "law unto themselves" (Rom. 2:14). Men love to legislate, even though they despise the Lawgiver and His perfect Law.

The recognition of evil is also universal. Unregenerate men love to play semantic games to avoid terms like "sin" and "evil," and they create entire systems of pseudo-science to excuse wicked conduct. They lament the "problems" in society and look for every possible windmill to attack as the true source of all of society's ills, refusing to look to themselves as sinners and the source of their own civil disease. Yet, the restraining use of even the shadow of the Moral Law in civic legislation is evident by the majority of a society that outwardly abides by the general principles of the Second Table of the law, if for

The Moral Law: Perpetuity, Nature, and Uses

no other reason than their fear of reprisal by the civil magistrate. It is this function that Paul addresses in his description of the purpose of the civil magistrate: "... If thou do that which is evil, be afraid; for [the civil magistrate] beareth not the sword in vain: for he is the minister of God, a revenger to *execute* wrath upon him that doeth evil" (Rom. 13:4). But, while all men are conceived and born in sin, the elect are, in time, regenerated. The Holy Spirit works in the hearts of the unregenerate elect to convict them to acknowledge that higher and purer Law, reflective of the Holy God in Whose image they were created. They begin to recognize that their outward obedience to the civil magistrate is vain and self-serving, falling woefully short of the glory of the One Who is King of kings and Lord of lords. And, clearly recognizing the inescapable condemnation that sin deserves, they look to Christ, the great Law-keeper, as their true and only hope for escape from that just damnation. As Ridgeley summarizes:

> Hence arises a clear sight of the need which persons have of Christ, and of the perfection of his obedience. When we find that we are condemned by the law, and that righteousness

> is not to be attained by our own obedience to it, we are led to see our need of seeking it elsewhere; and when the gospel gives us a discovery of Christ, as ordained by God to procure for us righteousness, or a right to eternal life by his obedience, we see the need we have of faith in him, whereby we derive from him that which could not be attained by our own conformity to the law.[41]

Second, the divines asserted that "The moral law is of use *to unregenerate men* [emphasis added], to awaken their consciences to flee from the wrath to come, and to drive them to Christ; or, upon their continuance in the estate and way of sin, to leave them inexcusable, and under the curse thereof."[42] Morton Smith succinctly summarizes this use of the Moral Law when he states that "It is God's ordained means of bringing sinners face to face with their sin and their need of a savior."[43] Boston equates the Law in this capacity as a "looking-glass"[44] wherein

---

[41] Ridgeley, II:303.
[42] *WLC*, Q.96, 258.
[43] Morton Smith, *Systematic Theology* (Greenville: Greenville Seminary Press, 1994), 2:622.
[44] Boston, II:63.

The Moral Law: Perpetuity, Nature, and Uses

unregenerate men see their sinfulness, its odiousness to the Holy God, and the certainty of their just damnation so long as they remain in that sin and thus under a guilty sentence before the Divine Tribunal. Although varied in their reactions between men, there are only two responses to this use of the Moral Law. Elect individuals understand their complete inability to alter their course to destruction and, regenerated by the Holy Spirit, are driven to Christ as their only Savior and perfect Sacrifice. The reprobate, more hardened than ever in their hatred for the Divine Judge, plunge themselves into deeper condemnation by looking to every vain imagination they can devise as a means of escape—even if for a moment—rather than turning in submission to the foot of Christ's cross.

Third, the Westminster divines concluded that there is a special use of the Moral Law with respect to the regenerate. They wrote:

> Although *they that are regenerate* [emphasis added], and believe in Christ, be delivered from the moral law as a covenant of works, so as thereby they are neither justified nor condemned; yet, besides the general uses

THE NECESSITY OF ABSOLUTES

> thereof common to them with all men, it is of special use, to show them how much they are bound to Christ for his fulfilling it, and enduring the curse thereof in their stead, and for their good; and thereby to provoke them to more thankfulness, and to express the same in their greater care to conform themselves thereunto as the rule of their obedience.[45]

This "Third Use" of the Moral Law addresses its *normative* function. The Moral Law is of use in this sense only for the regenerate. Joel Beeke contends that the Third Use of the Moral Law is an entirely Biblical concept, one of the central themes of the Psalter, Christ's Sermon on the Mount, and the ethical portions of the Pauline epistles. He states:

> The directions contained in these portions of Scripture are intended primarily for those already redeemed, and seek to encourage them to reflect a theology of grace with an ethic of gratitude. In this ethic of gratitude, the believer lives out of and follows in the footsteps of his Savior, who was Himself the Servant of the Lord and Law-Fulfiller, daily obeying all His Father's commandments throughout His earthly sojourn.[46]

---

[45] *WLC*, Q.97, 258.

[46] Joel Beeke, *Puritan Reformed Spirituality* (Darlington: Evangelical Press, 2006), 118.

The Moral Law: Perpetuity, Nature, and Uses

The Westminster divines rightly emphasized the fact that the regenerate are no longer under the Moral Law as a covenant of works. This is really the only possible way of understanding such passages that state that all those in Christ are, in some way, freed from the law. When Paul says "... for ye are not under the law, but under grace" (Rom. 6:14) and "... ye also are become dead to the law by the body of Christ" (Rom. 7:4), he is emphasizing the very principle that he clearly spells out in Galatians where he writes, "Christ hath redeemed us from the curse of the law, being made a curse for us" (Gal. 3:13). Because Scripture makes clear that all men, without exception, remain under the Moral Law, the serious Christian is led to question in what way he, as a regenerate man, can be freed from the law.[47] The straightforward answer is that the Moral Law remains the abiding, unwavering, unassailable standard of the living God, binding upon all men; but the manner of that standard differs in the nature of the men to whom it applies. To the unregenerate, the Moral Law remains a

---

[47] See Rom. 1:18-32; 2:14-15; and Gal. 3:10-12.

THE NECESSITY OF ABSOLUTES

covenant of works, binding them to perfect, personal, and perpetual obedience upon pain of everlasting damnation for the breaking of it. To the regenerate, however, the Moral Law is no longer a covenant of works; for Christ his Savior has freed him from the curse of that Law by taking upon Himself the curse due to His elect and fulfilling its righteous terms in their stead. Being freed from the curse of the Moral Law, however, does not free the regenerate man from the abiding authority of the Moral Law as a *rule of obedience*. Having been freed from the curse of the Law by Christ and regenerated by the Holy Spirit, the redeemed man now looks with undying gratitude upon his Master and Lord. Obedience to the Moral Law, then, rather than being a means to a man's salvation—which it could never be—becomes a joyful duty of praise for that salvation already accomplished and applied. Boston states:

> [The Moral Law is] a rule of life unto them [that are in Christ], wherein they may express their gratitude by obeying the law of Christ. So the law leads to Christ as a Redeemer from its curse and condemnation, and he leads back to the

The Moral Law: Perpetuity, Nature, and Uses

> law as a directory, the rule and standard of their obedience to him.[48]

When Christians are once again reminded that the Moral Law is a gift from a gracious and loving God, a reflection of His own holiness and righteousness, and the light burden of the Covenant of Grace, then the Church will once again be filled with Godly men and women who are thankful and faithful to Christ their Savior and who demonstrate that gratitude by framing their lives after His commandments. In this light, "… The third use of the law promotes *love*. … It is not a cruel or hard taskmaster for those who are in Christ. … God's people treasure the law as the gift of a loving God (Ps. 147:19, 20; Rom. 9:4)."[49]

It has already been established (and cannot be stressed enough) that the keeping of the Moral Law has no place in the justification of sinners. The Law, however, is a vital part of the process of sanctification. Rousas Rushdoony argued, "Man's *justification* is by the *grace* of God in Jesus Christ;

---

[48] Boston, II:64.
[49] Beeke and Jones, 570; Authors' emphasis.

man's *sanctification* is by means of the *law* of God."⁵⁰ In the interest of Christian charity, one may hope that Rushdoony meant to say that sanctification is a work of God's grace, whereby the Holy Spirit graciously *uses* the Law as an integral part of the whole-life transformation of the saints. The statement, as it stands, is patently false because all parts of a man's salvation—including both justification and sanctification—are the products of the free grace of God. Furthermore, the Law, in and of itself, can neither justify nor sanctify any man. Paul negates the very possibility of justification by the Law in Romans 3:20, and again he observes, "Be it known unto you therefore, men *and* brethren, that through [Jesus] is preached unto the forgiveness of sins: and by him all that believe

---

⁵⁰ Rousas J. Rushdoony, *The Institutes of Biblical Law*, vol. 1 (Kindle, Vallecito, CA: Chalcedon Foundation, 2012), loc. 393; Rushdoony's emphasis. Rushdoony's statement is directly contrary to the Westminsterian statement on sanctification, which begins with the words, "Sanctification is a work of God's grace" [*WLC*, Q.75, 238]. To make a statement that justification is by grace, but sanctification is by the law, is to insist upon a false juxtaposition between these two gracious effects of God's free grace alone.

The Moral Law: Perpetuity, Nature, and Uses

are justified from all things, from which ye could not be justified by the law of Moses" (Acts 13:38-39). The Law, in and of itself, is also completely incapable of sanctifying any man, "For the law made nothing perfect" (Heb. 7:19). The Moral Law does, however, remain the ethical Standard of God and cannot be disannulled as the foundation of behavior required by the One Who is infinite Holiness and Righteousness. Further, our best works are imperfect and tainted with sin (see *WLC* Q.78). The Law, therefore, continues as a vital and integral part of the life of the saints—but never as a covenant of works, whereby they are justified; nor even, in itself, is the Law the means whereby they are sanctified.

At this point, the Westminster divines provide a very important definition of sanctification which clarifies the Third Use of the Moral Law.

> Sanctification is a work of God's grace, whereby they whom God hath, before the foundation of the world, chosen to be holy, are in time, through the powerful operation of his Spirit, applying the death and resurrection of Christ unto them, renewed in the whole man after the image of God; having the seeds of repentance unto life, and all other saving

THE NECESSITY OF ABSOLUTES

> graces, put into their hearts, and those graces so stirred up, increased, and strengthened, as that they more and more die unto sin, and rise unto newness of life.[51]

It is evident, then, that the work of sanctification is both a definitive and an ongoing process by the Holy Spirit within the "whole man" of believers. This blessing is given by Christ to His people, in accordance with His promise of the Holy Spirit; this supports the abiding importance of the Moral Law in sanctification.

> If ye love Me, keep My commandments. And I will pray the Father, and He shall give you another Comforter, that He may abide with you for ever; *even* the Spirit of truth; Whom the world cannot receive, because it seeth Him not, neither knoweth Him: but ye know Him; for He dwelleth with you, and shall be in you. I will not leave you comfortless, I will come to you (John 14:15-18).

The Moral Law is the scalpel in the Hands of the Holy Spirit Who, as an infinitely skillful Surgeon, excises the cancerous tumors and

---

[51] *WLC*, Q.75, 238.

The Moral Law: Perpetuity, Nature, and Uses

gangrenous putrefaction of sin from the believer's whole person, giving ample room for the growth of holy tissue and newness of life. God's people are thereby progressively conformed to the Image of Jesus Christ, the perfect Law-Keeper; and these adopted children are recreated into truly new creatures, set apart to a holy dedication to God, and fitted for an eternity in His Presence.

The Holy Spirit does not work unilaterally in this process, however. He equips the saints with newly renovated wills to work with Him in this gracious process of being fitted for heaven. Paul demonstrates the beautiful cooperation between the Holy Spirit and the saint in this process of progressive sanctification when he writes: "Wherefore, my beloved, as ye have always obeyed, not as in my presence only, but now much more in my absence, work out your own salvation with fear and trembling. For it is God which worketh in you both to will and to do of *His* good pleasure" (Phil. 2:12-13). This is a special work of the Holy Spirit, accompanied by faith, as he elsewhere observes: "... God hath chosen you to salvation through sanctification of the Spirit and belief of the truth" (2 Thess. 2:13).

THE NECESSITY OF ABSOLUTES

James Durham distinguishes the Third Use of the Moral Law, and its role in the process of sanctification in the lives of believers, from the keeping of the Law as a covenant of works. He states that they differ in four specific areas: in the end for which those duties are performed (as already observed, not in order to be justified, but because of redemption already accomplished and applied); in the strength whereby obedience is performed (by the strength of grace and not by any natural ability on the part of the regenerate); in the manner in which the imperfect but conscientious obedience to the Law is accepted by God (accepted by God upon the merits of Christ alone); and, in the saint's motive for Law-keeping (from the motive of love and thankfulness). Durham explains the last two differences this way:

> ... The acceptation of our performances, prayers, praises, are founded on Christ's righteousness, and God's mercy in him, in whom only they are sweet-smelling sacrifices, and accepted as our persons are. For the great motive of our obedience in the covenant of

The Moral Law: Perpetuity, Nature, and Uses

> grace ... is love and gratitude, and that not simply to God as Creator, but as Redeemer.[52]

The whole-life transformation of the redeemed engenders a new motivation. Rather than being consumed with the "self" and the lusts of this fleeting world, the saint focuses his life on the beauty, glory, and majesty of God as Redeemer. Through Christ, God the Father is *"our* Father;" God the Son, *"our* Savior and Elder Brother;" God the Holy Spirit, *"our* Comforter." The infinite holiness of this great Redeemer-God still produces a fear in the hearts of Christians. But it is not the fear of condemned men who dread their rightful Judge, nor the fear of a slave toward a master, but a Godly, reverential, familial fear of children who love their Father and fear doing anything to displease Him. John Calvin gives a fitting summary of the transformative aspect of the Third Use of the Moral Law when he states:

---

[52] Durham, 54.

THE NECESSITY OF ABSOLUTES

Now the great thing is this: we are consecrated and dedicated to God in order that we may thereafter think, speak, meditate, and do, nothing except to his glory. We are not our own. ... Conversely, we are God's: let us therefore live for him and die for him. We are God's: let his wisdom and will therefore rule all our actions. We are God's: let all the parts of our life accordingly strive toward him as our only lawful goal.[53]

---

[53] Calvin, *Institutes*, I:III.vii.1, 690.

The Moral Law: Perpetuity, Nature, and Uses

*****

In this chapter, it has been demonstrated that the Moral Law of God is still very much in force for all mankind. It remains God's Standard for all men governing their inclinations, affections, wills, and actions. The Moral Law does not cease to exist because man rebels against it. Nor does the Moral Law disappear with the coming of the Savior, the Lord Jesus Christ. Certainly, Christ took upon Himself the *curse* of the Law on the behalf of His elect. But by removing the curse, He never removed the validity or perpetually binding nature of the Law for all. God could no sooner remove the relevance of the Law than He could cease to be God; for the Moral Law is the very reflection of the absolute holiness and righteousness of God. All men, therefore, remain bound to the Moral Law as the alone—and unalterable—Standard for their duty to God and their fellow men. However, there is this striking difference: for the unregenerate, the Moral Law *remains* a covenant of works; but, for the regenerate, it is a rule of obedience. Those who reject Christ will be judged according to the principle of the Law, "for as many as have sinned without law shall also perish without law: and as

THE NECESSITY OF ABSOLUTES

many have sinned in the law shall be judged by the law ... in the day when God shall judge the secrets of men by Jesus Christ according to my gospel" (Rom. 2:12, 16). For the regenerate, however, the Moral Law is no longer a covenant of works whereby they are either justified or condemned. Christ, having taken the just wrath of God due to sinners upon Himself, has freed all of His elect from the curse of the Law and provided for right standing in the heavenly court. This infinite grace and mercy does not, however, free the saints from obedience (see Romans 6:1-4). Indeed, the responsibility of obedience is even greater for the saints, because they have been made new creatures in Christ and are being sanctified by the inner working of the Holy Spirit. For Christ's people, the Moral Law is now the rule of obedience, practiced in the whole man out of hearts filled with love and thanksgiving.

Chapter Three

The Moral Law: Presented in Two Tables

> What shall we say then? Shall we continue in sin, that grace may abound? God forbid. How shall we, that are dead to sin, live any longer therein? Know ye not, that so many of us as were baptized into Jesus Christ were baptized into his death? Therefore we are buried with him by baptism into death: that like as Christ was raised up from the dead by the glory of the Father, even so we also should walk in newness of life.
>
> (Rom: 6.1-4)

One of the largest sections of the *Westminster Larger Catechism* undertakes a thorough discussion of the Moral Law (Questions 91-148). Intended for Christians, the primary purpose of the *Catechism* is

THE NECESSITY OF ABSOLUTES

to address what true professors of Christ are to believe and the manner in which they are to act. Even a cursory review of this section of the *Catechism* reveals the diligent labors of a body of men deeply committed to the practice of the Third Use of the Moral Law. This chapter will summarize the Westminsterian presentation of this Law, including the "rules for right understanding," the Preface, the First Table of the Decalogue, the Second Table of the Decalogue, and the Christian's inability to perfectly keep the Moral Law.

The Moral Law: Presented in Two Tables

1. Rules for the Right Understanding of the Ten Commandments

The Decalogue is a *summary* of the Moral Law. As Watson observes: "In the commandments there is a *synechdoche*, more is intended than is spoken."[1] It was delivered, knowing the frame of man, as a brief and memorable framework. The scope of the entire Scripture is brought to bear in order to understand fully the details of each of the Commandments and the right manner in which the Law is to be kept. The Westminster divines put their considerable talents into presenting a literary output that would aid the Christian in his daily walk before his King and Savior with the design of presenting the best human summary of what the Scriptures principally teach. In the *Larger Catechism*, they include a remarkable and very important section immediately preceding the details of the Moral Law; namely, a list of "… rules [that] are to be observed for the right understanding of the ten commandments."[2] These rules are of

---

[1] Watson, 45; Watson's emphasis.
[2] *WLC*, Q.99, 260. [The actual question.]

THE NECESSITY OF ABSOLUTES

immeasurable benefit because, with this Biblical framework for understanding of the Commandments in hand, the Christian is able to rightly comprehend what is the actual duty that God requires of him.

Often, when a Christian defends the abiding, binding nature of the Moral Law, he is met with the objection, "But I keep the law! I haven't killed anyone!" This objection is based upon a faulty view of the Moral Law and the spiritual, whole-life encompassing nature of that Law. Unless a man is convicted by the Holy Spirit that the Moral Law is the objective standard of righteousness as ordained by God and that the comparison is never between man and man but between the perfect Example of Christ and man, he will never understand how utterly he violates the *whole* of the Law in thought, word, and deed, and that daily.

First, then, the divines observe "that the law is perfect, and bindeth everyone to full conformity in the whole man unto the righteousness thereof, and unto entire obedience forever; so as to require the utmost perfection of every duty, and to forbid the least degree of

The Moral Law: Presented in Two Tables

every sin."³ Believers, especially, having been recreated in the Image of Christ by the regenerative power of the Holy Spirit, willingly strive for complete obedience to the whole Moral Law. This is, by no means, attainable in this life. The prophet Isaiah complained, "But we are all as an unclean *thing*, all our righteousnesses *are* as filthy rags; and we all do fade as a leaf; and our iniquities, like wind, have taken us away" (Isa. 64:6). The fact that it is unattainable, however, does not negate the responsibility and desire for Christians to strive for full obedience. Christ's mandate is clear: "Be ye therefore perfect, even as your Father which is in heaven is perfect" (Mt. 5:48). à Brakel maintains that

> Perfection is the goal which is held before man. God stirs His children up to strive for this. He who approximates this as much as possible is in the best condition. This however is not to suggest that man can attain to the highest level of perfection in this life. A godly person will most certainly attain to this perfection held

---

³ *WLC*, Q.99.1, 261.

THE NECESSITY OF ABSOLUTES

before him – however, not here, but after this life.[4]

Paul explains this principle when he states, "Not as though I had already attained, either were already perfect: but I follow after, if that I may apprehend that for which also I am apprehended of Christ Jesus" (Phil. 3:12). The regenerated heart does not seek to keep the Law as a covenant of works whereby he merits favor with God, nor does he expect obedience in his own strength. Instead, he trusts in the merits of Christ alone.

> Blessed *be* the God and Father of our Lord Jesus Christ, Who hath blessed us with all spiritual blessings in heavenly *places* in Christ: according as He hath chosen us in Him before the foundation of the world, that we should be holy and without blame before Him in love: having predestinated us unto the adoption of children by Jesus Christ to Himself, according to the good pleasure of His will, to the praise of the glory of His grace, wherein He hath made us accepted in the Beloved," (Eph. 1:2-6).

---

[4] À Brakel, 3:77.

The Moral Law: Presented in Two Tables

And he looks to Christ alone for his renovation, Who, "... being made perfect, He became the Author of eternal salvation unto all them that obey Him" (Heb. 5:9), and looks to God through Christ for his ultimate success, knowing that "... it is God which worketh in you both to will and to do of *His* good pleasure" (Phil. 2:13).

Second, the divines maintain "that [the Moral Law] is spiritual, and so reacheth the understanding, will, affections, and all other powers of the soul; as well as words, works, and gestures."[5] Paul avers, "For we know that the law is spiritual" (Rom. 7:14). A mere outward keeping of the Ten Commandments is neither intended by, nor acceptable to, God. To be genuinely spiritual and truly acceptable to God, the indwelling Holy Spirit must be the primary Mover in the obedience of the saints: "*This* I say then, walk in the Spirit, and ye shall not fulfil the lust of the flesh" (Gal. 5:16). This is the fulfillment of the Covenant promise of God: "A new heart also will I give you, and a new spirit will I put within you: and I will take away the

---

[5] *WLC*, Q.99.2, 261.

stony heart out of your flesh, and I will give you an heart of flesh. And I will put My Spirit within you, and cause you to walk in my statutes, and ye shall keep My judgments, and do *them*" (Ezek. 36:26-27). Christ fulfilled this promise after His ascension; as He said, "It is expedient for you that I go away: for if I go not away, the Comforter will not come unto you; but if I depart, I will send Him unto you" (John 16:7). It was attested to by a multitude of witnesses on the day of Pentecost when Peter explained, "Therefore being by the right Hand of God exalted, and having received of the Father the promise of the Holy Ghost, [Jesus] hath shed forth this, which ye now see and hear" (Acts 2:33).

Being spiritual, obedience to the Moral Law rises out of a heart filled with genuine spiritual love for the Triune God Who has redeemed it. This makes the keeping of the Law not only a rule of obedience for the believer, but an obedience borne out of a thankful and willing heart. Anything less than this genuine love for God, and desire for His honor and glory alone, results in obedience that is merit-based, and this

The Moral Law: Presented in Two Tables

is not only futile, but also openly and eternally rejected by God. Boston summarizes:

> In short, all true and acceptable obedience to the will of God flows from a right principle, that of faith and love in the heart. Faith is the hand that unites the soul to Christ, and obedience to God is the fruit of that union. Love is the spring and source of it; for he that loveth Christ, keepeth his commandments. And it must be directed to a right end, namely, the glory of God. We are not to obey God, in order to stop the mouth of a natural conscience, or gain applause among men, but to grow more like God, and bring more honour and glory to him.[6]

Third, the divines observe "that one and the same thing, in divers respects, is required or forbidden in several commandments."[7] Paul states, "Mortify therefore your members which are upon earth; fornication, uncleanness, inordinate affection, evil concupiscence, and covetousness, which is idolatry" (Col. 3:5). Here, it is clear that Paul equates covetousness not only with a violation

---

[6] Boston, II:55.
[7] *WLC*, Q.99.3, 262.

THE NECESSITY OF ABSOLUTES

of the Tenth Commandment, but also as a violation of the First Commandment, since it is both a discontentment with what the Lord has been pleased to give to men, and because it is born out of the heart a kind of self-love which cannot coexist with a genuine love for God.

The violation of any or all of Commandments Two through Ten is a violation of Commandment One. Man violates God's Law because he places self above, or before, the LORD his God. Elsewhere, Paul writes, "For the love of money is the root of all evil: which while some coveted after, they have erred from the faith, and pierced themselves through with many sorrows" (1 Tim. 6:10). In this verse it is the *love* of money that is framed as the root of evils—not money, in and of itself. First, the love of anything more than God is a violation of the First Commandment. Second, those who have an inordinate love for gain are covetous, thereby violating the Tenth Commandment. Third, this love of money often leads to dishonesty in gaining the desired object (a violation of the Eighth Commandment), deprives others of their livelihood whereby they maintain their life and

The Moral Law: Presented in Two Tables

health (a violation of the Sixth Commandment), and entices a man away from right Biblical doctrine and genuine Christian living (violations of the First and Second Commandments).

Fourth, they teach "that as, where a duty is commanded, the contrary sin is forbidden; and, where a sin is forbidden, the contrary duty is commanded: so, where a promise is annexed, the contrary threatening is included; and, where a threatening is annexed, the contrary promise is included."[8] Being mindful that the Decalogue is by design exhaustive in principle but brief in particulars, the divines were right to insist upon this useful rule. This principle is clearly articulated in the Scripture. For instance, the Fifth Commandment positively commands: "Honour thy father and thy mother" (Exod. 20:12). Elsewhere, the "contrary sin" is forbidden: "For every one that curseth his father or his mother shall be surely put to death: he hath cursed his father or his mother; his blood *shall be* upon him" (Lev. 20:9). Another example is the Eighth Commandment that

---

[8] *WLC*, Q.99.4, 262.

THE NECESSITY OF ABSOLUTES

teaches theft as a forbidden sin. Paul demonstrates the contrary duty when he states: "Let him that stole steal no more: but rather let him labour, working with *his* hands the thing which is good, that he may have to give to him that needeth" (Eph. 4:28). Considering the Fifth Commandment again, there is a promise annexed: "… that thy days may be long upon the land which the LORD thy God giveth thee" (Exod. 20:12). Elsewhere, violators are assured of the "contrary threatening:" "The eye *that* mocketh at *his* father, and despiseth to obey *his* mother, the ravens of the valley shall pick it out, and the young eagles shall eat it" (Pro. 30:17).

Fifth, they aver, "That what God forbids, is at no time to be done; what he commands, is always our duty; and yet every particular duty is not to be done at all times."[9] As was discussed in the previous rule, the remedy for theft is lawful employment (Eph. 4:28). Nevertheless, all men are required by the Fourth Commandment to keep the Sabbath Day holy by *not* laboring on that day. Thus, while gainful employment in a

---

[9] *WLC*, Q.99.5, 263.

The Moral Law: Presented in Two Tables

lawful calling is a wonderful gift from God, and being lawfully employed is an act of obedience, that same gift becomes a curse and a snare to so many professing Christians who attempt to justify their violation of the Fourth Commandment (or other Commandments) in their keeping of the Eighth Commandment.

Sixth, they further observe "that under one sin or duty, all of the same kind are forbidden or commanded; together with all the causes, means, occasions, and appearances thereunto."[10] The Fourth Commandment directs men to sanctify the Sabbath Day (the duty commanded), which forbids the practice of anything that might prevent the Sabbath's sanctification (the sin forbidden). The Lord Jesus Christ, in His Sermon on the Mount, demonstrates this rule with memorable clarity. Considering the Sixth Commandment, He said, "Ye have heard that it was said by them of old time, 'Thou shalt not kill' ... but I say unto you, that whosoever is angry with his brother without a cause shall be in danger of the judgment" (Matt.

---

[10] *WLC*, Q.99.6, 264.

THE NECESSITY OF ABSOLUTES

5:21-22). The Lord teaches that unjustified hatred can be heart-murder, as hatred is inevitably the motivation for murder. Again, Christ explains the Seventh Commandment when He states: "Ye have heard that it was said by them of old time, 'Thou shalt not commit adultery:' but I say unto you, that whosoever looketh on a woman to lust after her hath committed adultery with her already in his heart" (Matt. 5:27-28). The Lord God is not concerned only with the outward keeping of His Law. He would have His people to be heart-keepers of the Law. The affections (motivations and underlying emotions) precede the actions. Sinful behavior does not originate in the hands and the feet, but in the heart or mind. Therefore, Paul commands the Church, "Abstain from all appearance of evil. And the very God of peace sanctify you wholly; and *I pray God* your whole spirit and soul and body be preserved blameless unto the coming of our Lord Jesus Christ" (1 Thess. 5:22-23). If the appearance of evil is forbidden, then all occasions to sin are forbidden as well.

Seventh, they teach "that what is forbidden or commanded to ourselves, we are bound,

The Moral Law: Presented in Two Tables

according to our places to endeavour that it may be avoided or performed by others, according to the duty of their places."[11] One of the more difficult responsibilities of Christians is to assist others in their obedience before the Lord. Yet, Scripture teaches that Christ's people are to assist one another in their faithfulness, with respect to each believer's station and lawful calling. "Thou shalt in any wise rebuke thy neighbour, and not suffer sin upon him" (Lev. 19:17). There is an urgency in the Letter to the Hebrew Christians concerning this principle of assisting one another. To avoid the danger of a heart hardened against the great Prophet Jesus Christ, the author in one place exhorts: "But exhort one another daily, while it is called To day; lest any of you be hardened through the deceitfulness of sin" (Heb. 3:13). Hardness of heart arises, in part, out of a sluggish or defiant spirit that refuses to be obedient to Christ's commands. Another source of hard-heartedness is when Christians do not avail themselves of the means of grace. This is exceptionally prevalent in

---

[11] *WLC*, Q.99.7, 265.

THE NECESSITY OF ABSOLUTES

the modern day when Church attendance is considered to be optional. Hence, the strong exhortation is given: "And let us consider one another to provoke unto love and to good works: not forsaking the assembling of ourselves together, as the manner of some *is*; but exhorting *one another*: and so much the more, as ye see the day approaching" (Heb. 10:25). In His infinite wisdom, Christ has provided an instrument within the framework of the Church to assist Christians in aiding one another through mutual admonition and exhortation so that the saints can encourage one another in walking humbly and obediently before the Lord.

Finally, they state "that in what is commanded to others, we are bound, according to our places and callings, to be helpful to them; and to take heed of partaking with others in what is forbidden them."[12] The first part of this rule reinforces the scope of its predecessor. An excellent Biblical example of the saints being helpful to others in their obedience is

---

[12] *WLC*, Q.99.8, 265.

The Moral Law: Presented in Two Tables

demonstrated in the role of ecclesiastical office. Paul demonstrates precisely what it means to be an officer in the Church when he states, "Not for that we have dominion over your faith, but are helpers of your joy: for by faith ye stand" (2 Cor. 1:24). When men, called and ordained to the office of Preaching Elder "preach the word; be instant in season, out of season; reprove, rebuke, exhort with all longsuffering and doctrine" (2 Tim. 4:2) it is a precious gift of the King and Head of the Church for the maintenance and growth in grace of His people in the wilderness of this life, which ought not to be neglected nor abused. The second portion of this rule warns against "peer pressure." Believers often fall into grave temptation when they lack wisdom in selecting the company they keep or the type of example they provide to others. It is a serious danger that so many fall into when they think that, as Christians, they can habitually congregate with unbelievers and bring them to Christ. The exact opposite is more likely. "When thou sawest a thief, then thou consentedst with him, and hast been partaker with adulterers" (Ps. 50:18). Paul observes: "Be not deceived: evil communications corrupt good manners" (1 Cor.

THE NECESSITY OF ABSOLUTES

15:33). Christians—especially Covenant children and those newly regenerated—must often be advised of this rule for the proper understanding of the Moral Law and its application in their lives.[13] But even older, more mature believers have often stumbled in their walk before the Lord because of their negligence in considering the company they keep. Each one must strive to grow and mature both for his own growth in grace and in his role of being a leader to others in what is defined by Scripture as good in the Eyes of God.

---

[13] The Book of Proverbs, in its entirety, is an excellent compendium on holy living.

The Moral Law: Presented in Two Tables

2. The Preface to the Ten Commandments

After presenting the rules for the right understanding of the Decalogue, the Westminster divines proceed with an examination of the Commandments. They begin with the Preface to the First Commandment: "And God spake all these words, saying, I AM the LORD thy God, which have brought thee out of the land of Egypt, out of the house of bondage" (Exod. 20:1-2). One of the most important emphases of the First and Second Reformation periods was the centrality of the Bible as the very Word of God, and that the whole of Scripture—both Old and New Testaments—is a genuinely Christian Document. The importance of this point is evident in their observations upon the Ten Commandments, including its Preface. While there was an immediate, historical context to the Old and New Testament Scriptures, being the very Word of God they remain equally relevant to every age—including the modern era and beyond. Many errors that have infested the Church throughout the ages are combatted by the right understanding that the Word of God remains *current* in every age and that there is specific application, in all of its parts,

THE NECESSITY OF ABSOLUTES

to every generation of the Church. So, while the immediate context of the Lord's proclamation at Sinai was Israel's exodus out of the bondage of Egypt, it is of immediate relevance to every generation of those who have been freed from the bondage of sin and death through the salvific cross work of the Lord Jesus Christ and the regenerative power of the Holy Spirit.

Two doctrines are observed in the Preface by the Westminster divines. The first doctrine emphasized in the Preface is the identification of the Person and Nature of the LORD, JEHOVAH, Who gave His good Law to His people. The divines observe: "[In the Preface] God manifesteth his sovereignty, as being JEHOVAH, the eternal, immutable, and almighty God; having his being in and of himself, and giving being to all his words and works."[14] The Lord God identifies Himself in the words, "I *AM* the LORD," (אָנֹכִי יְהוָה),[15] that is, "I,

---

[14] *WLC*, Q.101, 266.

[15] All Hebrew quotations taken from *Biblia Hebraica Stuttgartensia: With Werkgroep Informatica, Vrije Universiteit Morphology; Bible. O.T. Hebrew. Werkgroep Informatica, Vrije Universiteit* (Bellingham, WA: Logos Bible Software, 2006).

The Moral Law: Presented in Two Tables

JEHOVAH." The LORD identifies Himself to His people as the almighty, self-sufficient, eternal, unchangeable, and true God. The One with whom Israel has to do is eternally the same. Elsewhere the immutability of God is specifically tied to the pronunciation of the Divine Name. "And God said unto Moses, 'I AM THAT I AM': and He said, 'Thus shalt thou say unto the children of Israel, I AM hath sent me unto you'" (Exod. 3:14). Again, "For I *AM* the LORD, I change not" (Mal. 3:6). Thomas Watson observes that "by this great name God sets forth his majesty ... it signifies God's self-sufficiency, eternity, independency, immutability, Mal. 3:6."[16] In the article on the Divine Name, M'Clintock and Strong explain: "Here the Almighty makes known his unchangeable character, implied in his eternal self-existence, as the ground of confidence for the oppressed Israelites to trust in his promises of deliverance and care respecting them."[17] In this identification of Himself as the Creator God and

---

[16] Watson, 16.

[17] "Jehovah," in *Cyclopædia of Biblical, Theological, and Ecclesiastical Literature*, prepared by John M'Clintock and James Strong (New York: Harper & Brothers, 1891), 810–11.

absolute Sovereign over all of His creation, the LORD makes evident to the Israelites that the One Who commands them is the only One with the infinite power and right to do so. He is the Creator of man and so has the intrinsic right to legislate His will to men.

The Lord Jesus Christ takes the same Title to Himself during His earthly ministry. While the significance does not come across as clearly in the English translation, He definitively refers to Himself as JEHOVAH before the Jews who, in response, take up stones to put Him to death for blasphemy. "Jesus said unto them, 'Verily, verily, I say unto you, before Abraham was, I AM'" (John 8:58). John later records the words of the glorified Christ identifying Himself as JEHOVAH when He says, "I AM Alpha and Omega, the beginning and the ending, saith the Lord, which is, and which was, and which is to come, the Almighty" (Rev. 1:8). The Psalmist makes a clear reference to eternality of the Son as truly JEHOVAH when he writes: "Of old hast Thou laid the foundation of the earth: and the heavens *are* the work of Thy hands. They shall perish, but Thou shalt endure: yea, all of them

The Moral Law: Presented in Two Tables

shall wax old like a garment; as a vesture shalt Thou change them, and they shall be changed: but Thou *art* the same, and Thy years shall have no end" (Ps. 102:25-27). The writer to the Hebrews quotes this passage to demonstrate the genuine Godhood of Christ (Heb. 1:10-12) and, later, concludes: "Jesus Christ the same yesterday, and to day, and for ever" (Heb. 13:8).

The second doctrine emphasized in the Preface is an encouragement to God's people to obey His good Law. The nature of this encouragement is remarkable indeed for all of the elect in every age. He is JEHOVAH, the one and only God, the Creator of all things and Governor of all that He has created. But, He is also the God Who *is in Covenant* with Christ and His elect. He states: "I *AM* the LORD **thy God**" (אֱלֹהֶיךָ). Boston, in keeping with the consistent, Reformed understanding of the Decalogue, recognizes that the giving of the Ten Commandments at Sinai is integral to the Covenant of Grace and is not a recapitulation of the Covenant of Works. He argues: "Not as if obedience to the commands were conditions of that covenant; that is the nature of the covenant of works. For mark, God tells them he is their God before ever he proposes one commandment to them; and for God to be the God of a people in the sense of the promise made to Abraham, includes the assurance of their complete salvation."[18] By the Covenant of Redemption from eternity, and through the salvific cross work of Christ in the fullness of time, the LORD, JEHOVAH, is the God of His people. And Christ's vicarious, propitiatory atonement in time was efficient for the salvation of all of His elect, including the saints of the Old Testament economy who predated the coming of Christ. Watson explains the ramifications of this precious truth when he writes:

> Had God only called himself Jehovah, it might have terrified us, and made us flee from him, but when he said, 'thy God,' this may allure and draw us to him; this, though a preface to the law, is pure gospel. This word *Eloeha*, 'thy God,' is so sweet, that we can never suck out all the honey in it. 'I am thy God,' not only by creation, but by election. This word, 'thy God,' though it was spoken to Israel, is a charter which belongs to all the saints.[19]

---

[18] Boston, II:86.
[19] Watson, 17.

The Moral Law: Presented in Two Tables

Through Christ, the LORD redeems His elect in every age, even more surely and no less miraculously than He did when He delivered the physical Israelites out of the bondage and servitude to their cruel Egyptian masters.

Through Christ, God is the Father of His people. Moses made this abundantly clear to Israel of old. "Ye *are* the children of the LORD your God" (Deut. 14:1). The same principle applies to the saints in the New Testament period: "And I will be a Father unto you, and ye shall be My sons and daughters, saith the Lord Almighty" (2 Cor. 6:18). Christ makes this abundantly clear to His Church when He encourages His people that "'I ascend unto My Father, and your Father; and *to* My God, and your God'" (John 20:17). The Fatherly care of God to His people is beyond the scope of human understanding and provides an infinite peace to the people of God in this life. But the LORD is also the Husband of His people. "For thy Maker *is* thine Husband; the LORD of hosts *is* His Name; and thy Redeemer the Holy One of Israel" (Isa. 54:5). Paul speaks specifically of Christ being the Husband of His bride, the Church, when he states: "For the husband is the head of the wife, even as Christ is

THE NECESSITY OF ABSOLUTES

the Head of the church. ... Husbands, love your wives, even as Christ also loved the church, and gave Himself for it" (Eph. 5:23, 25). The Preface to the Decalogue, then, serves as a powerful and tender encouragement for the people of God to willingly submit to the authority and the commands of their Sovereign Creator-Redeemer God Who has condescended to covenant with them in Christ. It is both His right to command as Creator and King and His privilege to command as Redeemer, Father, and Husband.

The Moral Law: Presented in Two Tables

3. The First Table of the Decalogue

In a treatise of this nature, it is impossible to examine fully each point of the Westminster Standards with reference to the Moral Law, its meaning, and its application to believers. At the same time, in order to appreciate completely the Westminsterian position on Biblical Law, a brief examination of their treatment of each of the Commandments is necessary so that the clarity and relevance of their position may be set before the Church for God's own glory and the edification of His people. The Westminster divines worked within a scholastic framework that rationally discusses the scope of Scripture in an orderly fashion. They were not, however, "scholastics" in the Medieval sense of the word. For the divines, the scholastic method was a useful tool that organized Biblical principles so that Christians would be able to understand the Scriptures and to apply them in their daily lives. To the twenty-first century mind, the Westminster exposition of the Moral Law may appear archaic and "wordy," but if studied carefully the currency and applicability of these principles become apparent to the believing mind.

THE NECESSITY OF ABSOLUTES

Since the Moral Law remains the rule of obedience for the saints in every age, the Westminsterian treatment of the Law is very important for the modern Church.

The divines present the Decalogue in two tables. This was, by no means, a novel approach. The two table "model" is evident in the original giving of the Ten Commandments on Sinai, written with the Finger of God[20] on two tables of stone (Deut. 9:10). Moses summarized the First Table thus, "Hear, O Israel: the LORD our God *is* one LORD: and thou shalt love the LORD thy God with all thine heart, and with all thy soul, and with all thy might" (Deut. 6:4-5). God summarized the Second Table of the Law in these words: "Thou shalt not avenge, nor bear any grudge against the children of thy people, but thou shalt love thy neighbour as thyself: I *AM* the LORD" (Lev. 19:18). Christ summarized the two Tables quoting from these two portions of Scripture: "Thou shalt love the Lord thy God with all thy heart, and with all thy soul, and with

---

[20] In Scripture, the term "Finger of God" refers to the work of the Holy Spirit. Compare Mt. 12:28 and Lk. 11:20.

The Moral Law: Presented in Two Tables

all thy mind. This is the first and great commandment. And the second *is* like unto it, Thou shalt love thy neighbour as thyself. On these two commandments hang all the law and the prophets'" (Matt. 22:37-40).

The First Table of the Decalogue, consisting of the first four Commandments, summarizes the duty that man owes to God,[21] while the last six Commandments summarize the duty which each man owes to his fellow man under God.[22] In their summary of the First Table of the Decalogue, the divines pay particular attention to the duties required and the sins forbidden in each Commandment, and they also address any promises, threatenings, and reasons provided, or "annexed." Committed to the Biblical principle that God's commands are never about merely the outward performance of a duty, the divines rightly look to the whole of Scripture to analyze each of the Commandments so that Christians can strive for a whole-man obedience to God "... with all thy heart,

---

[21] *WLC*, Q.102, 267.
[22] Ibid., Q.122, 303.

THE NECESSITY OF ABSOLUTES

and with all thy soul, and with all thy mind" (Matt. 22:37).

At first blush, the First and Second Commandments appear to be quite similar. There is a distinct difference between them, however. The First Commandment is the fundamental dictate of God regarding the sole Object of worship; namely, the Triune God, JEHOVAH, Who has revealed Himself in the propositions of Scripture. The Second Commandment specifically addresses the only acceptable manner in which the true God will be worshiped. The Third Commandment also focuses upon the right worship of God, in the sense that "… we are commanded to worship [God] with that frame of spirit which is suitable to the greatness of the work, and the majesty of him with whom we have to do."[23] The Fourth Commandment specifically designates one day in seven to be wholly dedicated to the worship of God. While all of the Commandments are universal in scope, they have a specific propriety for believers.

---

[23] Ridgeley, II:335.

The Moral Law: Presented in Two Tables

[I] The divines begin their list of the duties required by the First Commandment with the words, "The duties required in the first commandment are, the knowing and acknowledging of God to be the only true God, and our God."[24] The Psalmist exhorts the saints in every age: "O come, let us worship and bow down: let us kneel before the LORD our Maker. For He *is* our God; and we *are* the people of His pasture, and the sheep of His Hand" (Ps. 95:6-7). Because the LORD is both Creator of all things and the Redeemer of His people, Christians are specially to focus their entire lives—thoughts, words, and actions; at home and abroad—to acknowledge, worship, obey, profess, and defend the Name of the LORD, with genuine love for Him, humility in living before Him, and a holy zeal for His honor and glory. Put simply, "Man's chief end is to glorify God, and to enjoy him forever."[25] Too often, Christians are exceedingly timid before unbelievers in defense of the LORD as the one, true God. When Christians place something before the Lord God—whether in

---

[24] *WLC*, Q.104, 267.
[25] *WSC*, Q.1, 421.

THE NECESSITY OF ABSOLUTES

their thoughts (e.g., by being distracted while worshiping God) or in their actions (e.g., by giving precedence to any activity over the worship of God, such as absenting oneself from Sabbath worship for any reason other than a providential hindrance) — they have violated the First Commandment. When professing Christians give place to the false deities of unbelievers (including false impressions of the true God professed by monotheists like Jews and Muslims — for there is no right apprehension of the LORD apart from Christ and the Biblical doctrine of the Trinity), they are violating this Commandment. It is never admissible for the people of God to give the false impression that a person's chosen deity (other than the true God) is as good as the true and living God or that one's personal religion is as good as the true religion of the Scriptures. This is both a violation of this First Table (by not having a genuine love and zeal for the LORD) and also of the Second Table (by not loving one's neighbor as oneself), and suffering sin upon them (Lev. 19:17).

The First Commandment obligates men to own the LORD as *their* God. The divines teach

The Moral Law: Presented in Two Tables

these other duties inculcated herein include, "… our knowing and acknowledging of God to be the only true God, and our God; and to worship and glorify him accordingly."[26] As previously observed, all men, by design, have an innate awareness of God. The majority of mankind acknowledges a deity (or deities) of some kind. According to God in this Commandment, however, all men are required to know *only* the true God. All false religions are, from their foundation, atheistic. Unless someone knows, acknowledges, and worships the true God of Scripture, he is functionally an atheist. Beyond the denial of the existence of false gods, he must *acknowledge* the God of Scripture. The modern conception of religion is that a person's faith is a personal choice, and every religion is equally valid. This is certainly the legal statement on the matter in the United States. For a civil magistrate to declare that he will not promote and defend the true faith to the exclusion of all others, but will allow for tolerance of every religious belief, is tantamount to an open rejection of genuine religion, for: "Thou

---

[26] *WLC*, Q.104, 267.

shalt have no other gods before Me," says the LORD. Even more pronounced is the requirement to *worship* and *glorify* the true God alone.

In addition to the duties commanded, the divines summarize the sins forbidden in this Commandment. The long list of sins forbidden by this Commandment in the *Larger Catechism* can be summarized under two primary heads: atheism and idolatry. Atheism is the refusal to acknowledge God as God, while idolatry is the practice of offering acknowledgement, worship, and service to anything other than the one true God alone. There are very few actual professing atheists in society, although there are vast numbers who are atheists in practice, even among professing Christians. It is sobering to realize that many false doctrines in the broader Church are principial denials of the true God. A fundamental error of Roman Catholicism is ascribing veneration and service to the creature that belongs exclusively to God Himself; be that to Mary, the saints, angels, or the papal antichrist. Other doctrines that violate this commandment include Arminianism, which is

The Moral Law: Presented in Two Tables

all too prevalent in Evangelicalism today. Ridgeley describes, as an act of practical atheism,

> To maintain corrupt doctrines and dangerous heresies, subversive of the fundamental articles of faith and contrary to the divine perfections. Of this kind are those doctrines which militate against his sovereignty and dominion over the wills, consciences, and affections of men ... [and] when, in order to magnify his mercy, we disregard his holiness or justice, and so presume that we shall be happy without being holy.[27]

The chief source of practical atheism among Christians is ignorance. "For My people *is* foolish, they have not known Me; they *are* sottish children, and they have none understanding: they *are* wise to do evil, but to do good they have no knowledge" (Jer. 4:22). So deadly is ignorance that the Lord repeatedly speaks against it in His Word.

> Hear the word of the LORD, ye children of Israel: for the LORD hath a controversy with the inhabitants of the land, because *there is* no truth, nor mercy, nor knowledge of God in the land. My people are destroyed for lack of

---

[27] Ridgeley, II:319.

THE NECESSITY OF ABSOLUTES

> knowledge: because thou hast rejected knowledge, I will also reject thee, that thou shalt be no priest to me: seeing thou hast forgotten the law of thy God, I will also forget thy children (Hosea 4:1, 6).

Christians should study the Scriptures diligently and seek to understand the pure Word of God without the compromise of atheistic doctrines (see Acts 17:10-11). Christians must understand that obedience to this Commandment may require that they seek a truly Biblical Church to attend, even if that means that they have to relocate in order to join a consistently Reformed Church where they will be taught Biblical doctrine, have the keys of the Kingdom administered properly, and be led to worship the Lord only in Spirit and in truth (cf. John 4:23). Further, worse than the natural ignorance of depraved humanity is the willful ignorance of those who have been exposed to the Scriptures yet shut their eyes and hearts to the preaching of the whole counsel of God.

Idolatry takes many forms in the world at large. But sadly it also creeps into the professing Church by offering worship and service to anything other than the one true God alone. The

The Moral Law: Presented in Two Tables

idolatry spoken against here is manifested most prevalently when Christians neglect to worship God as God alone. This is a subtle sin among many professing Christians, as they often violate this mandate unwittingly. The Christian violates this Commandment when he trusts in anything more than, or equally as much as, God Himself; whether that be a trust in his occupation, his wealth, or his abilities—all which are gifts from God alone. This is a matter of great ingratitude among those who profess Christ. Slips of the tongue often reveal the secret idols of men's hearts such as, for example, the oft-repeated phrase, "Good luck!" Beside the sovereign God there is no destiny, luck, or fate that exists and certainly nothing that has any control over the affairs of men in this life or the next. Very few believers actually realize the danger and blasphemy of such non-existent things.

Even more prevalent is the love of self, loved ones, and the world in the Christian's life. Modern American society actually promotes the love of self to the point that a person is considered seriously flawed if he does not love himself enough. Yet this is precisely what the Lord abhors, which is why He has taken care to warn His Church of this

THE NECESSITY OF ABSOLUTES

dangerous idolatry. "[M]en shall be lovers of their own selves, covetous, boastful, proud, blasphemers, disobedient to parents, unthankful, unholy," etc. (2 Tim. 3:2). The warning comes to the Church not because it is a danger with the world in general, but because it becomes prevalent among professing Christians to the point that "… all seek their own, not the things which are Jesus Christ's" (Phil. 2:21). In a generation inundated with "social media" and radically liberal education, it is no surprise that self-love has become one of the favored idols in the Church.

Another violation of this Commandment that walks peacefully together with love of self is love of the world. The Lord exhorts His people: "Love not the world, neither the things *that are* in the world. If any man love the world, the love of the Father is not in him. For all that *is* in the world, the lust of the flesh, the lust of the eyes, and the pride of life, is not of the Father, but is of the world" (1 John 2:15-16). And the Lord has been pleased to give the remedy for both self-love and worldly love: "Set your affection on things above, not on things on the earth. … Mortify

The Moral Law: Presented in Two Tables

therefore your members which are upon earth ..." (Col. 3:2, 5). When faithful ministers return to preaching the Law of God, Christians will become more mindful of the fact that when they trust anything more than God, love anything more than God, rely upon anything more than God, they are violators of His Law and have committed the idolatry referred to in this First Commandment.

[II] The Second Commandment addresses the fundamental, but too often neglected, duty of worshiping the LORD according to His commands. In other words, the only "... acceptable way of worshipping the true God is instituted by himself, and so limited by his own revealed will, that he may not be worshipped according to the imaginations and devices of men, or the suggestions of Satan, under any visible representation, or any other way not prescribed in Holy Scripture."[28] The Second and Fourth Commandments are unique within the Decalogue because, within each of these Commandments,

---

[28] *WCF*, XXI.1, 110-11.

THE NECESSITY OF ABSOLUTES

there is a reason given by God to reinforce man's obedience. It is a demonstration of the marvelous condescension of God that He would provide His own reasoning with His commands, even though it is His Divine prerogative to command only and require unwavering obedience without any further explanation. Durham answers the question as to why these two Commandments have reasons added to them, when he states:

> Because all the other commandments are by the law of nature determined in men's consciences, and the sins against them are by nature's light seen to be evil; but the substance of these two, to wit, what way he will be worshipped in externals, and on what day is the solemn time of worship, being determined by God's positive law, they are not so impressed on men's consciences as the duties required in the other commandments are.[29]

In addition to the command itself, and the reason added by the LORD, the Second Commandment also has a promise and a threatening added to it.

---

[29] Durham, 71.

The Moral Law: Presented in Two Tables

The divines observe several important duties in the Second Commandment. Their general statement upon the subject is: "The duties required in the second commandment are, the receiving, observing, and keeping pure and entire, all such religious worship and ordinances as God hath instituted in his word."[30] Perhaps even more forcefully, they state elsewhere:

> The acceptable way of worshiping the true God is instituted by himself, and so limited by his own revealed will, that he may not be worshipped according to the imaginations and devices of men, or the suggestions of Satan, under any visible representation, or any other way not prescribed in the Holy Scripture.[31]

There is little question that the majority of innovations in worship among Reformed and Evangelical Churches in modern society are based upon good intentions. Nevertheless, the Biblical testimony of God's displeasure over any addition to His revealed order of worship demonstrates that proper motivations and sincerity are still odious to the three-times Holy God when His people of

---

[30] *WLC*, Q.108, p. 276.
[31] *WCF*, XXI.i, 110-11.

THE NECESSITY OF ABSOLUTES

themselves fabricate means and modes of worship that have not been commanded by Him. In moments of honest Scriptural reflection, those who add their inventions to Divine worship must admit that they have exchanged the worship of the true God for a worship according to their own wills. Under the Old Testament economy, the minute details of the Ceremonial Law are clearly set forth throughout the entire corpus. Neither do the New Testament Scriptures leave the Church of this age to wonder how to worship God aright after the fullness of Christ has been revealed. The abolition of the positive precepts of the Ceremonial Law were promised in the Old Testament economy: "And [the Messiah] shall confirm the covenant with many for one week: and in the midst of the week He shall cause the sacrifice and the oblation to cease, and for the overspreading of abominations He shall make *it* desolate, even until the consummation, and that determined shall be poured upon the desolate" (Dan. 9:27). The Lord Jesus Christ, during His earthly ministry, emphasized the imminent change in the positive precepts of Divine

The Moral Law: Presented in Two Tables

worship, when He articulated the abolition of the Ceremonial Law in both its mode and location. He stated: "'Woman, believe Me, the hour cometh, when ye shall neither in this mountain, nor yet at Jerusalem, worship the Father" (John 4:21). The abolition of worship "at Jerusalem" could only mean the abrogation of the entire Old Testament Ceremonial Law, which was ordained by God to center around the temple as the central and exclusive place of ceremonial worship. "But unto the place which the LORD your God shall choose out of all your tribes to put His Name there, *even* unto His habitation shall ye seek, and thither thou shalt come" (Deut. 12:5). God's positive precept for Biblical worship in the New Testament Church is, by its very design, more spiritual in nature with significantly fewer outward forms and ceremonies. Paul articulates the radical difference between Old and New Testament worship with the abolition of the ceremonies when he writes:

> For [Christ] is our peace, Who hath made both one, and hath broken down the middle wall of partition *between us*; having abolished in His flesh the enmity *even* the law of commandments *contained* in ordinances; for to

THE NECESSITY OF ABSOLUTES

> make in Himself of twain one new man, *so* making peace; and that He might reconcile both unto God in one body by the cross, having slain the enmity thereby. (Eph. 2:14-16).

It would be inaccurate to say that an attachment to ceremonies, *per se*, is a valid definition of legalism. The faithful worshiper under the Old Testament economy properly used the Divinely prescribed ceremonies. During the digression of the Second Temple era, however, the rabbinic leaders made the Biblical ceremonies and all other Jewish rites genuinely legalistic, especially as embodied in circumcision. In fact, since Christ's institution of the simpler, more spiritual form of Biblical worship under the New Testament economy, any return to such rudiments as the forms or ceremonies similar to that of the Old Testament economy is a clear violation of the Second Commandment and a rejection of the finished work of Christ. Paul is unwavering in this point: "Behold, I Paul say unto you, that if ye be circumcised, Christ shall profit you nothing. For I testify again to every man that is circumcised, that he is a debtor to do the whole law. Christ is

The Moral Law: Presented in Two Tables

become of no effect unto you, whosoever of you are justified by the law; ye are fallen from grace" (Gal. 5:2-4). Durham concludes: "But the ceremonial law is *mortifera*, deadly, and cannot be revived without falling from grace."[32] Anything beyond these elements articulated in the New Testament Scriptures goes beyond the scope of the Church's authority, violates the Second Commandment, and lays snares for the people of God.

The catechetical work of the Westminster divines provides a well-reasoned list of sins forbidden in the Second Commandment, which is designed to demonstrate that only that which is commanded in the Scriptures is to be done in Divine worship. It remains only to consider the duties required now under the New Testament economy. Here, the divines list the following:

> [1] Prayer, with thanksgiving ... made in the name of the Son, by the help of the Spirit, according to his will. ... [2] The reading of the Scriptures with godly fear, [3] the sound preaching and conscionable hearing of the word ... [4] singing of psalms with grace in the heart; as also [5] the due administration and

---

[32] Durham, 56.

> worthy receiving of the sacraments instituted by Christ, are all parts of the ordinary religious worship of God.[33]

In addition to these five ordinary elements, they also list the following occasional elements of worship: "... religious oaths and vows, solemn fastings, and thanksgivings upon special occasions."[34]

The Westminsterian position on the right understanding and application of the Second Commandment, therefore, attains the high-water mark of Reformed thought on the subject and presents the Biblical doctrine of worship with a perspicuity and scope unparalleled since the days of the apostles. Taking to their hearts the sober warning of Scripture that, when the Church worships God "what thing soever I command you, observe to do it: thou shalt not add thereto, nor diminish from it" (Deut. 12:32), the divines here establish the definitive presentation of the Regulative Principle of Worship. When succeeding generations of

---

[33] *WCF*, XXI.3 & 5, 112 & 114 [numbering added].
[34] Ibid., 114.

The Moral Law: Presented in Two Tables

Reformed ministers and theologians have consistently eroded this fundamental principle, they have done nothing less than to despise the Word of God and have infected Christ's Church with gross error. The Lord Jesus Christ addresses this error when He condemns the Pharisees for abandoning the Biblical doctrine of worship for their spurious traditions. He soundly rebukes them, saying, "Ye hypocrites, well did Esaias prophesy of you, saying, 'This people draweth nigh to Me with their mouth, and honoureth Me with *their* lips; but their heart is far from Me. But in vain they do worship Me, teaching *for* doctrines the commandments of men'" (Matt. 15:7-9). The seriousness of the issue prevents the preceding observation from being anything more than a sane and sober assessment of what has occurred in present-day Reformed bodies. Abandoning the Second Commandment as rightly understood and applied by the Westminster divines has resulted in a dramatically diminished Reformed presence in Western civilization. Should the Reformed Church desire to regain her role as the true messenger of King Jesus Christ in a sinful and darkened world, she first must restore this Regulative Principle of

THE NECESSITY OF ABSOLUTES

Worship and return to a humble and faithful approach to the thrice Holy God Who alone can determine the way in which He is to be worshiped.

Should anyone question the preceding statement, one needs only to look upon the clear face of the LORD's reason and His threat that are added to this Commandment and to the general scope of the Scriptures on the subject. When JEHOVAH sent Israel into the land of promise to possess it, He clearly instructed them through Moses that they should utterly destroy the cultic worship of the Canaanites and kill every living soul among the inhabitants of the land. This is exceedingly clear in the passage that follows:

> When the LORD thy God shall cut off the nations from before thee, whither thou goest to possess them, and thou succeedest them, and dwellest in their land; take heed to thyself that thou be not snared by following them, after that they be destroyed from before thee; and that thou enquire not after their gods, saying, 'How did these nations serve their gods? Even so will I do likewise.' Thou shalt not do so unto the LORD thy God: for every abomination to the LORD, which He hateth, have they done unto their gods; for even their sons and their

The Moral Law: Presented in Two Tables

> daughters they have burnt in the fire to their gods. What thing soever I command you, observe to do it: thou shalt not add thereto, nor diminish from it (Deut. 12:29-32).

The history of successive generations of the Old Testament Church shows the radical manner in which they openly rebelled against this precept. That many rejected the true religion and adopted the cults of surrounding nations is evident. But, there was a much subtler manner in which they rebelled, and were equally condemned for it. When they utterly rejected the warning of the LORD through Moses and adopted the *mode* of worship from heathen religions, they applied it in the worship of the true God: "Nevertheless the people did sacrifice still in the high places, *yet* unto the LORD their God only" (2 Chron. 33:17). In the First Commandment the LORD reveals that He alone is to be worshiped. But, in the Second Commandment He insists that He will be rightly worshiped *only* according to the manner that He commands. To add to worship what "seems best" to men, with no further justification than their own ill-advised fervor, is open idolatry against the one, true God Who requires absolute obedience to His command.

THE NECESSITY OF ABSOLUTES

As Durham explains, "Now, it is sin not only to worship false gods, but to worship the true God in a false way; and it is a duty also to worship him rightly, according as he has appointed in his Word."[35]

The LORD gives for a clear reason for this Commandment regarding worship by saying, "… for I the LORD thy God *AM* a jealous God" (Exod. 20:5). The Lord God is jealous for the purity of His worship, and he accounts all those who worship Him in a manner of their choosing, rather than of His design, to be spiritual adulterers. "… The Lord [will] have his people carry so to him, as a wife should carry to a jealous husband, with such circumspection as he may not have any occasion of suspicion."[36] Again, "God will have his spouse to keep close to him, and not go after other lovers. … He cannot bear a rival."[37] So forceful is the Lord's reason on this matter that he adds a threat and a promise. He threatens all who violate this

---

[35] Durham, 93.
[36] Ibid., 145.
[37] Watson, 64.

The Moral Law: Presented in Two Tables

Commandment—even though they give lip-service to being worshipers of the true God—to pour out His wrath upon them, and upon the third and fourth generation of their children who follow in the idolatrous practices of their fathers. God pronounces this sentence against them because He accounts all who practice open idolatry, or invented worship of the true God, as "them that hate Me" (Exod. 20:5). But to all who will worship the LORD and Him alone (the First Commandment) according to His direction for Divine worship, and that without compromise (the Second Commandment), He "[will shew] mercy unto thousands[38] of them that love Me, and keep My commandments" (Exod. 20:6). One of the fundamental errors of the Christian Church today is the prevalence of the willful violation of the Second Commandment. Even in many Reformed Churches, while the true Triune God is professed

---

[38] In the Hebrew, this word (לַאֲלָפִים) is pregnant and refers to a thousand *generations*, as: "Know therefore that the LORD thy God, He *is* God, the faithful God, which keepeth covenant and mercy with them that love Him and keep His commandments to a thousand (לְאֶלֶף) generations" (Deut. 7:9).

and acknowledged, the mode of worshiping Him is full of human inventions.

[III] The Third Commandment enforces the jealousy that God has for His own Name and declares that He places a specific duty upon all men to honor His Name and inculcates using It with fear and reverence, especially in worship. As with the other Commandments, the Westminster divines searched the Scriptures to explain this precept and provide specific application to the lives of Christians. Like the other First Table Commandments, the modern Church has largely taken a very lax view of the manner in which the Name of God is used by its members—in worship and in daily conversation. The God Who warned the Church in the Old Testament that "… the LORD will not hold him guiltless that taketh His Name in vain" (Exod. 20:7) is the same LORD that will not tolerate the mishandling or misusing of His Name today. Too often in Evangelical (and, sadly, even in some Reformed) circles, so much emphasis has been placed upon the Lord Jesus Christ as "our Friend" that genuine reverence for

The Moral Law: Presented in Two Tables

His absolute Majesty has been dismissed. It has been forgotten, or ignored, that "... our God *is* a consuming Fire" (Heb. 12:29). The Church today needs to be reminded of the fact that the LORD takes the use of His Name with the utmost seriousness and that the consequences of using His Name lightly are severe. "If thou wilt not observe to do all the words of this law that are written in this book, that thou mayest fear this glorious and fearful Name, THE LORD THY GOD; then the LORD will make thy plagues wonderful, and the plagues of thy seed, *even* great plagues, and of long continuance, and sore sicknesses, and of long continuance" (Deut. 28:58-59). Elsewhere, the LORD commands that blasphemers receive capital punishment at the hands of the Congregation: "And thou shalt speak unto the children of Israel, saying, Whosoever curseth his God shall bear his sin. And he that blasphemeth the Name of the LORD, he shall surely be put to death, *and* all the congregation shall certainly stone him: as well the stranger, as he that is born in the land, when he blasphemeth the Name *of the LORD*, shall be put to death" (Lev. 24:15-16). The warning needs to be oft-repeated to this "casual" Church age that the LORD continues to have a complaint against His people, for: "A son honoureth *his* father, and a servant his master: if then I *be* a Father, where *is* Mine honour? And if I *be* a Master, where *is* My fear? Saith the LORD of hosts unto you, O priests, that despise My Name" (Mal. 1:6). Instead, "... the name of God, his titles, attributes, ordinances, the word, sacraments, prayer, oaths, vows, lots, his works, and whatever else there is whereby he makes himself known, [must] be holily and reverently used in thought, meditation, word, and writing; by an holy profession, and answerable conversation, to the glory of God, and the good of ourselves, and others."[39]

The divines give a thorough listing of sins forbidden by this Commandment. Reformed pastors should make a careful study of these in order to aid their congregations better to keep the LORD's Name holy in their daily lives. A few of these, however, call for special notice, simply because they are prevalent among modern

---

[39] *WLC*, Q.112, 285.

The Moral Law: Presented in Two Tables

Christians. In common conversations, it has sadly become unusual *not* to hear the Name of God used flippantly. It is not only the heathen that do this, but many Christians throw God's Name about as if it were simply a part of normal and accepted common speech. Watson states: "We take God's name in vain ... when we use God's name in idle discourse. He is not to be spoken of but with a holy awe upon our hearts."[40] Perhaps far more common is the questioning of God's providential dealing with His people. Instead of leading to self-examination, these events often evoke complaints from God's people. It is one thing to examine one's own life, confess and repent of any sin, and humbly pour out one's complaints before the throne of grace, through Christ, with a prayer for relief; it is quite another to go about complaining about one's "bad luck." This is a denial of the sovereign providence of God and a questioning of His governance over the creature. Another far too common misuse of the Name of God that is seldom addressed is when Christians live in worldliness. They will gladly make a verbal profession that they

---

[40] Watson, 85.

THE NECESSITY OF ABSOLUTES

are "Christians," but in conduct they live as the world does. It must be remembered that the obvious root of "Christian" is "Christ." Therefore, when a "Christian" conducts himself wickedly before the world, in addition to the sinful conduct, he is also taking the LORD's Name in vain by making the living God a Party to his own sins before the world. Paul makes this abundantly clear: "Thou that makest thy boast of the law, through breaking the law dishonourest thou God? For the Name of God is blasphemed among the Gentiles through you, as it is written" (Rom. 2:23-24). This is a very common form of blasphemy. Another common form of blasphemy is the ascription to the creature an attribute that rightly belongs exclusively to God. How often in conversation does the term "Awesome" get tossed about. But only the living God should inspire genuine awe in the hearts of men, for God alone is Awesome. The perfections of God belong to Him alone and should never be ascribed to the creature. Another prevalent form of blasphemy is blaming God rashly or ascribing to Him a censure for His sovereignty. The Pharisees were blasphemers against the LORD

The Moral Law: Presented in Two Tables

when they accused Christ of casting out demons in the name of the devil (cf. Matt. 12:22-24). Men violate this Commandment in various other ways, such as taking rash oaths and making frivolous vows. Self-examination is essential to identifying and rectifying the misuse of the Name of God, especially those common colloquialisms of daily speech which are so often fraught with vain oaths.

[IV] The Fourth Commandment is often overlooked in the Church today. The Scriptures demonstrate, however, that this Commandment is very precious in the Sight of the LORD. It is both a *creation* ordinance and a *redemptive* ordinance and, like the rest of the Moral Law, it remains binding upon all men and especially upon the people of Christ. The very nature of this Commandment is evident from the unique wording and position of the Sabbath ordinance in the Decalogue. Instead of beginning with either "Thou shalt" or "Thou shalt not," the Fourth Commandment begins with the word "Remember" in Exodus 20:8 and "Keep" (or

THE NECESSITY OF ABSOLUTES

"Observe") in Deuteronomy 5:12.[41] Nicholas Bownd remarks: "... to this [commandment] He puts an especial mark, saying *Remember*. That is, 'think of it aforehand.' For indeed the want of remembering it in due time is many times one cause that it is no better observed when it comes."[42] The LORD reasons with humankind in this precept more than in any other. First, He demonstrates His own generous nature of affording six days for man's labor and recreation, requiring only one in seven days to be dedicated wholly to His worship and service ("Six days shalt thou labor, and do all thy work ..." (Exod. 20:9)). Second, He puts Himself as the perfect Example of the holy rest enjoined, since He rested from His creative labors on the first Sabbath after creation ("For ... the LORD ...

---

[41] See Gen. 2:1-3, 4:3, and Ex. 16:23 as just a few examples of the Sabbath Commandment prior to the giving of the Fourth Commandment at Sinai. Hence, the LORD commands His people to "Remember" that principle of the Sabbath because it is a creation ordinance and no new Commandment.

[42] Nicholas Bownd, *Sabbathum Veteris Et Novi Testamenti: or The True Doctrine of the Sabbath*, ed. Chris Coldwell (Dallas and Grand Rapids: Naphtali Press and Reformation Heritage Books, 2015), 36. [It is not unreasonable to posit that Bownd's work is *the* definitive Puritan treatment of the Sabbath.]

The Moral Law: Presented in Two Tables

rested the seventh day" (Exod. 20:11)). Third, the LORD demonstrates that He blesses and consecrates the Sabbath, above all the other days of the week ("... wherefore the LORD blessed the Sabbath day, and hallowed it" (Exod. 20:11)). In the recapitulation of the Law in Deuteronomy, a fourth reason is given; namely, that the Sabbath Commandment is *redemptive* in nature ("... remember that thou was a servant in the land of Egypt, and *that* the LORD thy God brought thee out thence through a mighty Hand and by a stretched out arm: therefore the LORD thy God commanded thee to keep the Sabbath day" (Deut. 5:15)).

The Westminster divines took note of all of these reasons and summarized the great importance of truly *remembering* the Sabbath day. They wrote:

> The word *Remember* is set in the beginning of the fourth commandment, partly, because of the great benefit of remembering it, we being thereby helped in our preparations to keep it, and, in keeping it, better to keep all the rest of the commandments, and to continue a thankful remembrance of the two great benefits of creation and redemption, which contain a short abridgement of religion; and partly, because we are very ready to forget it, for that there is less light of nature for it, and yet it restraineth

THE NECESSITY OF ABSOLUTES

> our natural liberty in things at other times lawful; that it cometh but once in seven days, and many worldly businesses come between, and too often take off our minds from thinking of it, either to prepare for it, or to sanctify it; and that Satan with his instruments much labour to blot out the glory, and even the memory of it, to bring in all irreligion and impiety.[43]

A common objection against the Fourth Commandment is that it is actually a part of the Ceremonial Law and, as such, is abrogated in Christ. Even in the best of hands, this is a presumptuous and un-Biblical argument. To begin with, it is irrational to assume that the LORD would present only *nine* moral Commandments and then haphazardly insert an unrelated *ceremonial* statute in the middle of the Moral Law. Moses was very clear on this point in his final address to Israel. He states: "And [the LORD] declared unto you His covenant, which He commanded you to perform, *even* ten commandments; and He wrote them upon two tables of stone. And the LORD commanded me at that time to teach you statutes and judgments,

---

[43] *WLC*, Q.121, 301.

The Moral Law: Presented in Two Tables

that ye might do them in the land whither ye go over to possess it" (Deut. 4:13-14). There is an obvious distinction between the Moral Law presented in the Decalogue as the perpetually binding Divine Standard for the actions of men and the "statutes and judgments" (the Ceremonial and Judicial laws) that were given to the Old Testament Church to be performed "in the land." Bownd observes:

> ... this commandment is properly and truly moral as well as the rest, and not ceremonial. For the moral law is that which does properly and of itself inform men's manners, as the word itself imports; inform, I say, and certify them either concerning the true religion towards God, or in their duties to men. But [the] ceremonial is that which is added for a time, in some respect, to some persons, for a help to that which is moral.[44]

From the time of creation until the resurrection of the Lord Jesus Christ, the specific day for the keeping of the Sabbath was the seventh day of the week. Since Christ's resurrection, however, the

---

[44] Bownd, 69.

positive element of this portion of the Moral Law has changed, by God's direction, from the seventh to the first day of the week. In the *Confession*, the divines explain this principle when they observe that

> ... [in] his word, by a positive, moral, and perpetual commandment, binding all men in all ages, [God] hath particularly appointed one day in seven for a sabbath, to be kept holy unto him: which, from the beginning of the world to the resurrection of Christ, was the last day of the week; and, from the resurrection of Christ, was changed into the first day of the week, which in Scripture is called the Lord's day, and is to be continued to the end of the world, as the Christian Sabbath.[45]

À Brakel defends the perpetual and binding nature of Sabbath observance as a commandment of the moral—rather than the ceremonial—law by proving from the Scriptures that Christ, His apostles, and the entire early Church faithfully kept the Sabbath Day. There was, however, one distinct difference; namely, the institution by Christ at His resurrection, and

---

[45] *WCF*, XXI.7, 118.

The Moral Law: Presented in Two Tables

by His and His apostles' examples, of the *first* day of the week—rather than the *seventh* day—as the Christian Sabbath, also known as the Lord's Day. Quoting such familiar passages as John 20:26 (where the Lord Jesus appeared to His disciples on the *first day of the week*), Acts 20:6-7 (where Paul observed the Christian Sabbath on the *first day of the week*), I Corinthians 16:1-2 (where Paul enjoins the bringing in of the collection into the Church upon the *first day of the week*), and Revelation 1:10 (where the ascended Christ reveals His Revelation to John on the *first day of the week, which is the Lord's Day*), à Brakel sets forth the Biblical principle of the perpetuity of the Sabbath Day with the change from the seventh to the first day of the week following the resurrection of Christ.[46] He then adds to the Biblical testimony the witness of early Church fathers including Irenaeus, Basilius, Epiphanius, Athanasius, Eusebius, Augustine, Justin Martyr, Chrysostom, and Constantinus Magus. His conclusion of this section is that the commandment itself, being given before the fall

---

[46] À Brakel, 3:162-164.

THE NECESSITY OF ABSOLUTES

(and therefore not ceremonial), having been codified with the other nine in the Ten Commandments (and thus necessarily moral), which Christ declared could not pass away so long as the earth endures and therefore remains binding upon all of His people, having been faithfully observed by Christ, His apostles, and the early Church, must, of necessity, remain an integral part of the Church of the Lord Jesus Christ throughout every age. "How can anyone therefore reject this day with good conscience? Ought not everyone to be convinced of the eternal duration of the Sabbath, be ashamed over his unsteadfastness and grieve over its desecration, and furthermore, be stirred up to a conscientious observance?"[47]

One particular reason for the keeping of the Fourth Commandment is given in these words: "For *in* six days the LORD made heaven and earth, the sea, and all that in them *is*, and rested the seventh day: wherefore the LORD blessed the sabbath day, and hallowed it" (Exod. 20:11).

---

[47] Ibid.

The Moral Law: Presented in Two Tables

The Sabbath Commandment, then, is a creation ordinance and binding upon all mankind. A particular notice must be paid to the reason given in the restatement of the Fourth Commandment in Deuteronomy. Moses reminds Israel: "And remember that thou wast a servant in the land of Egypt, and *that* the LORD thy God brought thee out thence with a mighty Hand and by a stretched out Arm: therefore the LORD thy God commanded thee to keep the sabbath day" (Deut. 5:15). While the keeping of the Sabbath is a creation ordinance and binding upon all mankind, in a very special way, it is also a redemptive ordinance.

Because of the very nature of this specific day—the *only* Biblically ordained holy day for the New Testament Church—all Christians should take special notice of those duties required of them for a proper *Remembrance* of the Sabbath. The proper keeping of the Sabbath requires preparation before the day begins. Christians should put a close to the labor of their lawful callings on the seventh day in order to prepare their hearts—and the hearts of their families—for the keeping of the Sabbath on the first day of the week. While those works of necessity and mercy are not only allowed but

THE NECESSITY OF ABSOLUTES

encouraged on the Lord's Day,[48] all other work is strictly forbidden. Watson explains: "To do secular work on this day is to follow the devil's plough; it is to debase the soul. God made this day on purpose to raise the heart to heaven, to converse with him, to do angels' work; and to be employed in earthly work is to degrade the soul of its honour. God will not have his day entrenched upon, or defiled in the least thing."[49] To sanctify the Lord's Day truly, and enjoy it Biblically as the true delight of one's soul, the head of the household should prepare his own heart, and the hearts of his family, on the night before the Lord's Day begins. On Lord's Day morning, attention should be paid to a continued spiritual preparation from the night before and, if preparations have been properly made, little more will be required before the family goes together to spend the larger part of the day in the corporate worship of the Church. Upon their return, the family continues with private and

---

[48] See Mt. 12:1-14.
[49] Watson, 99.

The Moral Law: Presented in Two Tables

personal worship until the end of the day.[50] It is by these means that a family is able to keep the whole Lord's Day with "... an holy resting all the day ... and [make] it our delight to spend the whole time ... in the public and private exercises of God's worship."[51]

The Scriptures record that the LORD is very jealous for His Sabbath, just as He is for every other Commandment with respect to the duty which man owes to God. In the wilderness, when a man was found gathering sticks on the Sabbath day, he was brought before Moses to determine his punishment. The LORD responded: "The man shall be surely put to death: all the congregation shall stone him with stones without the camp" (Num. 15:35). Despite the clear teaching of Scripture on the sanctity and purpose of the Sabbath, there are many in the Church today—including within Reformed circles—who agree that work is not to be done, but yet insist that recreation is perfectly acceptable. Again, the LORD does not leave His

---

[50] See *WCF*, XXI.8, 119.
[51] *WLC*, Q.117, 296-97.

THE NECESSITY OF ABSOLUTES

people to wonder about His position on recreation on the Lord's Day.

> If thou turn away thy foot from the Sabbath, *from* doing thy pleasure on my holy day; and call the Sabbath a delight, the holy of the LORD, honourable; and shalt honour Him, not doing thine own ways, nor finding thine own pleasure, nor speaking *thine own* words: then shalt thou delight thyself in the LORD; and I will cause thee to ride upon the high places of the earth, and feed thee with the heritage of Jacob thy father: for the Mouth of the LORD hath spoken *it* (Isa. 58:13-14).

Bownd contends that, since God forbids the labor of lawful occupations on the Sabbath day, much more should Christians abstain from recreational activities that are lawful on the other six days. Beyond the Biblical instruction on the subject, Bownd rightly concludes that these recreations are clearly inconsistent with a Godly keeping of the Sabbath day, "because we cannot have the present delight in the use of them, and yet at the same time be occupied in hearing of

The Moral Law: Presented in Two Tables

the Word, and such other parts of God's holy worship and service."[52]

There is a clear promise of blessing to all those that keep the Sabbath (Isa. 56:2) in contrast to those who desecrate it. It is a perpetually binding moral Commandment that originated at the creation, was spoken verbally by the LORD from Sinai and written on the tables of stone with His own Finger, was attested to by Christ—Who "… came not to destroy the law," (Matt. 5:17)—was reinforced by the apostles and the early Church, and remains a perpetual ordinance until the consummation. More than this, the Christian Sabbath is a delight to all of the saints. It is a precious gift from the King and Head of the Church that, when properly *remembered*, yields timeless blessings and unending spiritual delights. For the Puritan divines, it was a great day of spiritual resting from the cares of this life and a day wherein the Lord prepares His people for a faithful witness in their daily labors before the world of men. John Willison encouraged the Church with these words:

---

[52] Bownd, 268.

THE NECESSITY OF ABSOLUTES

> As for the minor proposition, that the work of the Sabbath is so great and necessary, it is plain, if we consider that the Sabbath is the great market day of heaven: upon which we ought to take in and lay up provision for our souls for the rest of the week, yea, for eternity itself. It is the usual day of sinners' conversion and acquaintance with God: It is the day wherein we have our sins to bewail, our needs to get supplied, our hard hearts to get melted, our dead affections to get raised, our guilty conscience to get disburdened, our dark minds to get enlightened, our weak graces to get strengthened.[53]

John Dod agreed, stating: "Make the Sabbath the Market-Day for thy Soul: Lose not one Hour, but be either praying, conferring, or meditating: Think not thy own Thoughts."[54] The right understanding of the Biblical Commandment regarding the Sabbath Day, when applied in the believer's heart and family, is the great delight of this present life and the chief preparation for the eternal Sabbath to come.

---

[53] John Willison, *A Treatise Concerning the Sanctification of the Lord's Day* (Albany: J. Boardman, 1820/1712), 93.

[54] *Gleanings of Heavenly Wisdom: or, The Sayings of John Dod, M.A., and Philip Henry, M.A.*, compiled by John Bickerton Williams (London: T. Nelson and Sons, 1851), 13.

The Moral Law: Presented in Two Tables

[Summary of the First Table] All of humanity, having been created by the Triune God in His own Image, are designed by their Creator to recognize and obey Him as the absolute Authority. Because of Adam's rebellion, the whole nature of man has been marred by sin so that his conception of God is, by nature, inherently flawed. "Because that, when they knew God, they glorified *Him* not as God, neither were thankful; but became vain in their imaginations, and their foolish heart was darkened" (Rom. 1:21). The clarity and force with which the LORD has been pleased to reveal Himself in His Word remains the perpetually binding Standard for mankind. The First Table of the Law demonstrates, in perspicuous detail, the one true and living God Who alone is to be worshiped, the manner in which He will be worshiped, the sanctity of His Name, and the holy day upon which He will be worshiped. Nothing is left to man's vain imagination with respect to His honor and glory. Sadly, the mass of fallen humanity continues to produce lifeless and dumb idols, bowing themselves before and serving the creature rather than the Creator. Worse, the Christian Church in Western civilization has devolved from

THE NECESSITY OF ABSOLUTES

the pinnacle of the Reformation and has ensconced a watered-down theology (proper) and doctrine of worship. Rather than being transformed by the whole Word of God, the modern Church has conformed to the world. The Biblically mandated remedy to this downward spiral is to return to the unadulterated, uncompromising, and unashamed practice and preaching of the First Table of the Moral Law.

The Moral Law: Presented in Two Tables

4. The Second Table of the Decalogue

Considering that man is a creature and wholly dependent upon his Creator for every breath, it would seem that human beings would place their highest priority upon the right worship of the Triune God. As has been shown above, this is by no means the case. Beyond this, one might assume that men would strive to be in harmony with his fellow man, since the very nature of society demands a close proximity to one another. But this, too, is by no means the case. The Westminster divines, recognizing the universal scope of the effects of the fall, looked to Scripture for the Standard directing all relationships between man and man. As with the First Table of the Law respecting right worship, they discovered in the Second Table of the Decalogue the design of God for interpersonal relationships and societal mores. "The sum of the six commandments which contain our duty to man, is, to love our neighbour as ourselves, and to do to others what we would have them to do to us."[55] Watson, with his usual insightful eloquence, states:

---

[55] *WLC*, Q.122, 303.

THE NECESSITY OF ABSOLUTES

> The commandments may be likened to Jacob's ladder: the first table respects God, and is the top of the ladder that reaches to heaven; the second respects superiors and inferiors, and is the foot of the ladder that rests on the earth. By the first table, we walk religiously towards God; by the second, we walk religiously towards man. He cannot be good in the first table that is bad in the second.[56]

Watson has emphasized the key to the whole Moral Law in this observation. Humankind was not designed to operate within a purely utilitarian framework but, rather, to "walk religiously" both toward God and toward his fellow man. All men owe acknowledgment, obedience, and reverence to God their Creator. But they also owe respect, service, and kindness to their fellow man because human beings are the Image bearers of God. Disrespect and abuse toward the Image bearer is a direct attack against the Creator in Whose Image man is made. James addresses this principle with reference to the inconsistent manner in which even Christians use their tongues. He writes: "But the tongue can no man tame; *it is* an unruly evil, full of deadly

---

[56] Watson, 122.

The Moral Law: Presented in Two Tables

poison. Therewith bless we God, even the Father; and therewith curse we men, which are made after the similitude of God" (James 3:8-9). A Biblical walking before God is obedience to His Law with *consistency*. One simply cannot make a consistent Biblical *con*fession with his tongue apart from a consistent Biblical *pro*fession with his deeds.

[V] In keeping with the exegetical framework of the Reformation, the Westminster divines understood that the Fifth Commandment is a brief summary of the duties required by God within human society. There is significantly more in this Commandment than obedience toward one's biological father and mother. "The general scope of the fifth commandment is, the performance of those duties which we mutually owe in our several relations, as inferiors, superiors, or equals."[57] Once again, the divines recognized that while the foundational precept is given in the Decalogue, the whole of Scripture must be brought to bear for a right understanding and application of the duties required and sins forbidden in the Commandment;

---

[57] *WLC*, Q.126, 305.

THE NECESSITY OF ABSOLUTES

for God does not leave man with a need to speculate as to what He requires of them in this duty. Durham remarks:

> ... this command in its scope respects the duty that we owe to all relations, whether they be above us, inferior to us, or equal with us. This is clear from Christ's summing all the second table ... *Thou shalt love thy neighbor as thyself*; and therefore our neighbor in general must be the object of this command, as well as of the rest. And so it takes in all the duties of honor that everyone owes to another, whatever be their place. There is a duty of honor and respect called for from everyone to everyone.[58]

In an age where society teaches that God does not exist, that human beings are merely highly evolved animals, and that there is no absolute standard of good and evil apart from what seems right in the eyes of the individual (subject to change at any given moment without warning), it is little wonder that there is a radical hatred against, and general disrespect for, all in authority—whether in the home, the Church, or the civil magistracy. The general rebellion

---

[58] Durham, 295.

The Moral Law: Presented in Two Tables

against authority in the American society is directly attributable to a rejection of the absolute authority of God and His Word. This has been programmed into generations of American young people in the systematic destruction of the fundamental Biblical structure of the family by the satanic institutions of the socialistic, atheistic public education system and the hedonistic entertainment industry. Self-love and love of pleasures have become the highest ideals of the modern world; sadly, however, the mainstream evangelical Church in this nation has either openly rejected or hidden the solution by rejecting the abiding relevance and universal applicability of the Moral Law while embracing these same worldly principles herself. It is imperative that the true Church in this nation continue to defend the fundamental building block of society by instructing her people of the primacy of the family as the God-ordained school in which children are supposed to be trained in love, submission, and obedience to the Lord God and His Commandments above all, then to everyone in authority over them through honor and obedience to their parents and the Eldership in the Church, and a genuine love for one another among their

THE NECESSITY OF ABSOLUTES

siblings and fellow Covenant children in the Church, all in accordance with His word. With the blessing of God, such a truly Biblical education would contribute to young men and women in society who are submissive in the Lord to those in authority at every level, humble before their equals, and Christ-like toward their subordinates.

Paul refers to this Fifth Commandment when he states: "Children, obey your parents in the Lord: for this is right. Honour thy father and mother; (which is the first commandment with promise;) that it may be well with thee, and thou mayest live long on the earth" (Eph. 6:1-3).[59] While the temporal blessings for obeying this command may well have been more readily apparent to the Old Testament Church where the physical land of Canaan was given to the Church as the Land of Promise, there is yet a

---

[59] It is of note that Paul speaks of the this as the "first commandment with promise," even though there is a clear promise of blessing attached to the Second Commandment (as noted above). This is another Biblical demonstration that the saints have always understood that there are two Tables to the Moral Law, for Paul was referring in this passage to the first Commandment of the Second Table.

The Moral Law: Presented in Two Tables

continuing applicability to the saints in the present age. The divines observe that this reason, annexed to the Commandment, "… is an express promise of long life and prosperity, as far as it shall serve for God's glory and their own good, to all such as keep this commandment."[60] Boston concurs with the divines and their judicious statement regarding the promise and he explains it thus:

> [This promise] is to be understood, as all other temporal promises are, not absolutely, as if in no case it could be otherwise; but with these two limitations: (1.) As far as it shall serve for God's glory; and God may be more glorified in their early death than their long life. The honour of God is the immoveable rule by which these things must be all measured. (2.) As far as it shall serve for their good; and so it may be a greater mercy to them to be hid in the grave, than to be left on earth; and surely it is no breach of promise to give one what is better than what was promised. And these two are not to be separated, but joined together; for whatever is most for God's honour, is most for the godly man's good.[61]

---

[60] WLC, Q.133, 315.
[61] Boston, II:259.

THE NECESSITY OF ABSOLUTES

[VI] As with all the Commandments, the Westminster divines look not upon the bare words of the prohibition in the Sixth Commandment, but upon the scope of Scripture regarding the requirement to preserve human life along with the prohibition to take the life of any man unjustly. The seat of murder begins in the heart, as Christ so graphically portrayed when He stated, "… whosoever is angry with his brother without a cause shall be in danger of the judgment: and whosoever shall say to his brother, Raca, is in danger of the council: but whosoever shall say, Thou fool, shall be in danger of hell fire" (Matt. 5:22). John summarizes: "Whosoever hateth his brother is a murderer: and ye know that no murderer hath eternal life abiding in him" (1 John 3:15). If the Lord is so adamantly opposed to hatred because it is heart-murder, He will certainly pour out His just judgment upon those who commit murder willfully against a neighbor. He makes this abundantly clear throughout the Scriptures, and the Lord has not changed this Standard since the very beginning. "Whoso sheddeth man's blood, by man shall his blood be shed: for in the image

The Moral Law: Presented in Two Tables

of God made He man" (Gen. 9:6). It is as the Image-bearers of God that human beings have their real worth, and the willful taking of a human life—by open murder, by the abomination of abortion, or any other way—is repugnant to God in every age. Therefore, the divines were right to emphasize the heart of this Commandment as a positive command to preserve human life—whether the life of another person or one's own life—and not simply as a prohibition against murder. In their statement regarding the sins forbidden by this Commandment, they profess: "The sins forbidden in the sixth commandment are, all taking away the life of ourselves, or others, *except in case of public justice, lawful war, or necessary defence* [emphasis added]."[62] Again, this begins in the heart. For if an individual believes that human beings are nothing more than "highly evolved animals," then he will not think twice about killing a man under any pretence whatsoever. However, for those transformed by the regenerative power of the Holy Spirit, the eyes are opened. The saints understand that man is *not* an animal, but a human being made

---

[62] *WLC*, Q.136, 320.

THE NECESSITY OF ABSOLUTES

in the Image of God; and God abhors those who unlawfully kill His Image-bearers.

[VII] The Seventh Commandment forbids all sexual immorality of every kind, including the act of adultery wherein the marriage bond is broken. But the almost endless list of sexual sins committed in modern American culture could be completely overcome by the simple positive duty of "… chastity in body, mind, affections, words, and behaviour; and the preservation of it in ourselves and others; [with] watchfulness over the eyes and all the senses."[63] Like the prohibition against murder that precedes it, the sins forbidden in this Commandment originate in the heart. As Christ states, "… whosoever looketh on a woman to lust after her hath committed adultery with her already in his heart" (Matt. 5:28). The wicked heart of man has a tendency to go after the things that appear desirable in his depraved eyes. Therefore, the believer, being a new creature in Christ, is to guard his eyes and to monitor the activities he

---

[63] Ibid., Q.138, 323.

The Moral Law: Presented in Two Tables

attends, the places he goes, and the situations in which he places himself in order to guard against the remnants of depravity that remain within him until his full sanctification after his death. This means that Christians are to know their own hearts, their own cherished lusts, and die to those choice sins to preserve their purity before the Lord their King and Head.

[VIII] The Eighth Commandment, rightly understood from the scope of Scripture, does more than forbid the theft of anything not belonging to oneself. The divines recognized the reach of this Commandment when they emphasized full contentment with God's providential provision and diligent labor in a lawful calling. Further, this Commandment establishes the rights and responsibilities of proprietorship. As such, each person is responsible before God, as a steward, for all that has been given to him in trust. But this leads to the realization that everything men have—their property, lives, and even time—are all gifts given by God, with each individual responsible before God to give an account for how he has wisely used, or foolishly misused, what He entrusted to him.

THE NECESSITY OF ABSOLUTES

This directly relates also to the business dealings between man and man. All such dealings must be open, fair, and honest. Christians, especially, should be very careful to practice absolute integrity in business transactions, since they know Who the Judge is Who will require an account of their activities. Truly here, loving one's neighbor as oneself, and treating others even in business transactions, drives to the heart of this Commandment. Hence,

> The duties required in the eighth commandment are, truth, faithfulness, and justice in contracts between man and man ... a provident care and study to get, keep, use, and dispose those things which are necessary and convenient for the sustentation of our nature, and suitable to our condition ... and an endeavour, by all just and lawful means, to procure, preserve, and further the wealth and outward estate of others, as well as our own.[64]

[IX] The Ninth Commandment requires the preservation of the truth, at all times, and in all situations, especially when called to testify before any proper judicatory. The LORD

---

[64] *WLC*, Q.141, 328.

The Moral Law: Presented in Two Tables

requires honesty in all of men's relations with one another and hates those who lie. God is the God of Truth (cf. Jn. 1:5, 9; 17:3; 1 Jn. 5:20) and so He will not tolerate falsehood. As John Murray observes: "It is because untruth is the contradiction of the nature of God that it is wrong. Truth and untruth are antithetical because God is truth."[65] Honesty is especially incumbent upon those who have been regenerated, because they have been redeemed from the ways of the old man and have been recreated in the Image of Christ. Because Jesus Christ is "... the Way, the Truth, and the Life" (John 14:6) and His people are being conformed to His perfect example, Paul exhorts the saints: "Lie not one to another, seeing that ye have put off the old man with his deeds; and have put on the new *man*, which is renewed in knowledge after the image of Him that created him" (Col. 3:9-10). He elsewhere confirms this: "Wherefore putting away lying, speak every man truth with his neighbor" (Eph. 4:25). There is, therefore, a decided emphasis upon

---

[65] John Murray, *Principles of Conduct: Aspects of Biblical Ethics* (Grand Rapids: William B. Eerdmans Publishing Company, 1957), 148.

THE NECESSITY OF ABSOLUTES

love to God in this Commandment, for God is the God of Truth. But there is also a strong emphasis of love toward one's fellow man in this Commandment. Believers are required to look out for the good of their neighbor and seek the best for him in all his lawful endeavors. The divines state: "The duties required in the ninth commandment are, the preserving and promoting of truth between man and man, and the good name of our neighbour, as well as our own ... a charitable esteem of our neighbours; loving, desiring, and rejoicing in their good name."[66] Genuine Biblical love for others demands that men seek the best for their fellow men as well as the good for themselves and their own families. As such, the Ninth Commandment covers a wide range of words and actions, the heart of each one being honesty and truthfulness.

[X] As the First Commandment is the central Commandment for the whole Moral Law, but especially for the First Table, so the Tenth

---

[66] *WLC*, Q.144, 335.

The Moral Law: Presented in Two Tables

Commandment is central to the Second Table of the Law. As Boston observes: "The scope of this command is to strike at the root and first risings of sin in the heart, in the desires going out of their right line of purity and equity. It is a strict boundary set to the unbounded desires of the heart."[67] Paul so fully recognized the fundamental nature of covetousness in a man's sinful disposition and conversation that he equates it with idolatry: "Mortify therefore your members which are upon the earth; fornication, uncleanness, inordinate affection, evil concupiscence, and covetousness, which is idolatry: for which things' sake the wrath of God cometh on the children of disobedience" (Col. 3:5-6). It is the discontentment with one's personal status and estate that leads to a wandering eye towards those things that rightly belong to one's neighbor. James is very clear on this point when he states, "Ye lust, and have not: ye kill, and desire to have, and cannot obtain: ye fight and war, yet ye have not, because ye ask not. Ye ask, and receive not, because ye ask amiss, that ye may consume *it* upon your lusts" (James 4:2-3). The

---

[67] Boston, II:332.

THE NECESSITY OF ABSOLUTES

divines observe, therefore, that "The duties required in the tenth commandment are, such a full contentment with our own condition, and such a charitable frame of the whole soul toward our neighbour, as that all our inward motions and affections touching him, tend unto, and further all that good which is his."[68] A renewed heart trusts implicitly in the good providence of his God and Father Who provides all good and necessary things for his spiritual and physical estates. It is very difficult for men to be content with what God has given to them, and covetousness continues to be a constant temptation in the hearts of even regenerated men. But the sanctifying work of the Holy Spirit is able to generate such an unquestioning trust in the Lord that the Christian will be content in his condition and "… exercise a composure of mind, acquiescing in the divine dispensations in every condition of life."[69]

---

[68] *WLC*, Q.147, 345.
[69] Ridgeley, II:416.

The Moral Law: Presented in Two Tables

5. Indwelling Sin and the Christian's Inability to Keep the Law Perfectly

Sin is the great evil in the world today, just as it has been since Adam's rebellion in the Garden of Eden and just as it shall be until the consummation of the ages when the King and Judge will return. In the hearts of Christ's people, though regenerated by the power of the Holy Spirit, sin remains a constant sorrow. In reflecting upon the holy Law of God, there must also be the discussion of sin. For, "Sin is any want of conformity unto, or transgression of, any law of God, given as a rule to the reasonable creature."[70] The least sin is a rebellion against God, and He will not wink at sin. Elsewhere, the divines articulate the Biblical fact that some sins are "more heinous" than others; and many sins are aggravated by the status of the person committing the offense, the parties offended by the sin, the nature of the offense itself, and the timing of the sin committed.[71] Nevertheless, the very nature of sin as an affront to the absolute

---

[70] *WLC*, Q.24, 195.
[71] These points are discussed in *WLC*, Q.150 & 151, 348-58.

THE NECESSITY OF ABSOLUTES

holiness of God makes every sin odious and hateful in His sight—regardless of how seemingly small it may appear to men. To the Church of the Old Testament economy, the Lord God said,

> Ye shall not make yourselves abominable with any creeping thing that creepeth, neither shall ye make yourselves unclean with them, that ye should be defiled thereby. For I *AM* the LORD your God: ye shall therefore sanctify yourselves, and ye shall be holy; for I *AM* holy: neither shall ye defile yourselves with any manner of creeping thing that creepeth upon the earth. For I *AM* the LORD that bringeth you up out of the land of Egypt, to be your God: ye shall therefore be holy, for I *AM* holy (Lev. 11:43-45).

Even though the dietary restrictions impressed upon the Church under age have been abrogated along with the entirety of the Ceremonial Law, the requirement for the saints to be holy has not changed one *iota*. Peter quotes from this Levitical passage when he instructs the New Testament Church:

> Wherefore gird up the loins of your mind, be sober, and hope to the end for the grace that is

The Moral Law: Presented in Two Tables

> to be brought unto you at the revelation of Jesus Christ; as obedient children, not fashioning yourselves according to the former lusts in your ignorance: but as He which hath called you is holy, so be ye holy in all manner of conversation; because it is written, 'Be ye holy; for I AM holy' (1 Pet. 1:13-16).

And Paul continues the category of uncleanness in the New Testament, modified to a moral import. God will not look favorably upon the sins of men. It is contrary to the absolute perfection of His Divine Nature to ignore sin because it constitutes an open rebellion against His absolute sovereignty and holiness, and violates His perfect Law, which is the Standard He has ordained for men as the reflection of His own eternal holiness. The Scriptures explain this with abundant clarity when the Holy Spirit through the prophet writes: "*Thou art* of purer eyes than to behold evil, and canst not look on iniquity" (Hab. 1:13). With this awful fact in mind, it is incumbent upon faithful pastors to exhort and admonish their congregations of the terrible evil of evils, the sinfulness of sin, as an open rebellion against the three-times holy God, Who will not look upon sin, let alone allow it in His righteous Presence.

THE NECESSITY OF ABSOLUTES

There is an all too common misconception that Christians are either "perfected" in this life or, recognizing the impossibility of obedience to the Moral Law, that Christians are exempted from obedience to the Moral Law. Both ideas are entirely un-Biblical. First, there is no perfection in this life. Boston explains this point when he states, "The law is perfect, and requires a full conformity thereto. It requires the utmost perfection in every duty, and forbids the least degree of every sin. So that life and salvation are absolutely unattainable by it, since no man can perform such an obedience to it as it requires."[72] As the Westminster divines aver: "No man is able, either of himself, or by any grace received in this life, perfectly to keep the commandments of God; but doth daily break them in thought, word, and deed."[73] These statements are entirely consonant with the Scriptures. John writes: "If we say that we have no sin, we deceive ourselves, and the truth is not in us. ... If we say that we have not sinned, we make Him a liar,

---

[72] Boston, II:73.
[73] *WLC*, Q.149, 347.

The Moral Law: Presented in Two Tables

and His Word is not in us" (1 John 1:8, 10). As Solomon, under the inspiration of the Holy Spirit, authoritatively declared, "For *there is* not a just man upon earth, that doeth good, and sinneth not" (Eccles. 7:20). Quoting from Psalm 14, Paul was even bolder and plainer when he stated: "As it is written, 'There is none righteous, no, not one: there is none that understandeth, there is none that seeketh after God. They are all gone out of the way, they are together become unprofitable; there is none that doeth good, no, not one'" (Rom. 3:10-12). This deliberately universal language applies equally to the believer and to the reprobate alike, with the noted caveat that the believer, having been regenerated by the power of the Holy Spirit, is further being sanctified by Him and will be, upon his death, made completely sinless.

But there is another difference between the believer and the reprobate—indeed the *fundamental* difference. That difference is the Person and Work of Christ applied to the account of the believer and the Holy Spirit sent in infinite power to work in the heart and life of the believer. The Moral Law remains the absolute, unwavering Standard of the three-times Holy God for all of mankind—

THE NECESSITY OF ABSOLUTES

redeemed and reprobate alike. The reprobate are bound to the Moral Law as a Covenant of Works which, upon their inability to obey the law perfectly, they stand everlastingly condemned before God. The believer has the same Moral Standard in the Law, and he is still bound to obedience to it. But it is Christ Who has perfectly kept the Law on behalf of His elect people, and they are accepted before the Father *through* Christ *by* His perfect obedience alone. The only Way that the Christian's poor service is accepted by God, therefore, is in and through the Mediator, the Lord Jesus Christ. Watson observed:

> To obey the law in a legal sense—to do all the law requires—no man can ... but in a true gospel-sense, we may so obey the moral law as to find acceptance. This gospel obedience consists in a real endeavour to observe the whole moral law ... not, I have done all I should do, but I have done all I am able to; and wherein my obedience comes short, I look up to the perfect righteousness and obedience of Christ, and hope for pardon through his blood. This is to obey the moral law evangelically;

The Moral Law: Presented in Two Tables

which, though it be not to satisfaction, yet it is to acceptation.[74]

Apart from Christ and His righteousness and obedience applied to the sinner's account, there is only utter and everlasting damnation. "Every sin, even the least, being against the sovereignty, goodness, and holiness of God, and against his righteous law, deserveth his wrath and curse, both in this life, and that which is to come; and cannot be expiated but by the blood of Christ."[75]

No man can perfectly keep the Moral Law, and even the saints break the Law every day in thought, word, and deed. But they are not condemned by the Law since Christ has taken their curse upon Himself and has imputed His righteousness to their account before His Father. As such, while the Moral Law no longer remains a Covenant of Works for the redeemed man, it does still abide as a Rule of Obedience, from a newly recreated heart filled with love for God and thanksgiving for the "so great salvation"[76] applied to His account by Christ. "That

---

[74] Watson, 16.
[75] *WLC*, Q. 152, p. 359.
[76] See Heb. 2:3.

THE NECESSITY OF ABSOLUTES

we may escape the wrath and curse of God due to us by reason of the transgression of the law, he requireth of us repentance toward God, and faith toward our Lord Jesus Christ, and the diligent use of the outward means whereby Christ communicates to us the benefits of his mediation."[77] Christ's specific role as Mediator was designed by God so that, as the Mediator of the Covenant of Grace, in the unity of His Theanthropic Person, He might sustain His perfect manhood by His eternal Divinity, perfectly keep the whole of the Law of God, have the full wrath and justice of God poured out upon Himself in His manhood, and to do so in such a way that "… the proper works of each nature might be accepted of God for us, and relied on by us, as the works of the whole person."[78] Boston summarizes this beautiful comfort from Scripture when he writes: "Our salvation is suspended in obedience to the law; which since we cannot perform, let us be induced to betake ourselves to the obedience

---

[77] *WLC*, Q.153, 360.
[78] *WLC*, Q.40, 207 (along with Q.36-39, 204-207).

The Moral Law: Presented in Two Tables

and satisfaction of Christ, by which the law is magnified and made honourable, and with which God is well pleased; and will be pleased with every sinner that takes the benefit thereof."[79]

---

[79] Boston, II:73.

THE NECESSITY OF ABSOLUTES

*****

Even this brief and somewhat cursory review of the Westminsterian view of the Decalogue demonstrates several key points that the faithful Church must keep in mind. Acknowledging that the Decalogue is the *summary* of the Moral Law, given by God in a simple and easily remembered form, and that the whole of Scripture must be examined for the right application of the Moral Law in a believer's life, it becomes apparent that there is significantly more to these Commandments than external obedience or abstention to the Law. The Law is spiritual; and the keeping of the Law must originate in the heart, which is the essence of a man's being. Only a heart purified by faith (Heb. 9:13-14; 1 Pet. 1:22) and a life that is being sanctified can even begin to approach God's perfect Standard through the daily mortification of the *old man* and putting on of the *new man* that is created in the Image of Jesus Christ. At its heart, the Law is the Law of Love—first to God and then to one's fellow man. This love is no mere emotion but is an active love that "… is a holy fire kindled in the affections, whereby a Christian is carried out

The Moral Law: Presented in Two Tables

strongly after God as the supreme good."[80] With the right Biblical frame of reference, the Christian will begin to understand that the Moral Law has application to every area of his life (Ps. 119:96). The LORD God is jealous for His Moral Standard, and He demands a holiness and righteousness in His people that transcends the "moralism" of the world. Rather than a simple list of "dos" and "don'ts," the Decalogue reveals the requirement by the Holy God that His people become a truly holy people from their hearts, with His glory as their primary aim, and not merely in their actions. Furthermore, the Moral Law is not a subjective ideal that can be bent to fit the state of a man's outward estate. It is, rather, the objective Standard of the living God, Who is the Judge of all men and angels and to Whom each man—even, and especially, each Christian—must give an account. As Dabney observes:

> Christ, in His Sermon on the Mount, then, and other places, rebukes and corrects, not the [moral] law itself, nor the Old Testament interpretations of the law, but the erroneous

---

[80] Watson, 6.

THE NECESSITY OF ABSOLUTES

and wicked corruptions foisted upon it by traditions and Pharisaic glosses. The moral law could not be completed, because it is as perfect as God, of whose character it is the impress and transcript. It cannot be abrogated or relaxed, as it is as immutable as He.[81]

Unless the Church returns to the Biblical and Westminsterian teaching of the Moral Law, there is little hope for righteous living in the Church and even less hope for the darkened world to which the Church has been called to be a light and reflection of the thrice Holy God.

---

[81] Dabney, 357.

Chapter Four

The Ceremonial Law Abrogated and Judicial Law Expired

> And you, being dead in your sins and the uncircumcision of your flesh, hath he quickened together with him, having forgiven you all trespasses; blotting out the handwriting of ordinances that was against us, which was contrary to us, and took it out of the way, nailing it to his cross; *and* having spoiled principalities and powers, he made a shew of them openly, triumphing over them in it. Let no man therefore judge you in meat, or in drink, or in respect of an holyday, of the sabbath *days*: which are a shadow of things to come, but the body **is** of Christ.
> (Col: 2.13-17)

THE NECESSITY OF ABSOLUTES

Having considered the Moral Law as God's abiding, binding moral Standard for all men in every age, it is necessary to consider the other two divisions of Biblical Law. To be clear, these laws—whether ceremonial or judicial—were also breathed out by God and have been preserved by Him in His infallible and sufficient word. As such, they remain a relevant part of the Christian life for a number of important reasons. But their application was only temporary by God's own design so that to insist that they have an abiding, binding nature to the New Testament Church is a grave error. The Ceremonial Law was *primarily* the application of the First Table of the Moral Law in the religious life of Israel as the Church in the Old Testament economy. The Judicial Law was *primarily* the application of the Second Table of the Moral Law in the civil life of Israel as a distinct nation-state under the authority of JEHOVAH. The Ceremonial Law, pointing to Christ and having been completely fulfilled in Him, is now abrogated. The Judicial Law, applying distinctly to Israel as a nation of old, ceased to have binding authority upon other nations, except insofar as the general, or moral, equity of those laws is applicable to every nation as accountable to the sovereign King of kings and Lord of lords.

THE NECESSITY OF ABSOLUTES

1. The Ceremonial Law and Its Abrogation in Christ

Heinrich Bullinger referred to the Ceremonial Laws as

> ... holy rites and actions ordained and delivered by God himself to the people of Israel until the time of amendment, partly to represent, and in a shadow to shew, the mysteries of God; and partly to worship God by them, and also with them to keep the people of God in a lawful religion, and in the society of one ecclesiastical body.[1]

Bolton summarized the nature and position of the Ceremonial Law for the New Testament Church when he stated,

> The ceremonial law was an appendix to the first table of the moral law. It was an ordinance containing precepts of worship for the Jews when they were in their infancy, and was intended to keep them under hope, to preserve them from will-worship, and to be a wall of separation between them and the Gentiles. This law, all agree, is abrogated both in truth and in fact.[2]

---

[1] Bullinger, III:126.
[2] Bolton, 56.

The Ceremonial Law Abrogated and Judicial Law Expired

The following statement on the Ceremonial Law presented by the Westminster divines is a definitive summary of the subject. They state:

> Besides this law, commonly called moral, God was pleased to give to Israel, as a church under age, ceremonial laws containing several typical ordinances; partly of worship, prefiguring Christ, his graces, actions, sufferings, and benefits; and partly holding forth divers instructions of moral duties. All which ceremonial laws are now abrogated under the New Testament.[3]

Unlike the Moral Law, summarized in the Ten Commandments, which were given orally to Israel by God Himself, then preserved on tablets of stone written with the Finger of God and preserved in the Ark of the Covenant until the time of the Babylonian captivity, the Ceremonial Law was given to Moses while on Sinai then distributed by him—both orally and in writing—to the congregation of Israel.[4] With this differing manner of delivery, there also came a difference in the

---

[3] *WCF*, XIX.3, 97.

[4] See Ex. 24:12-31:18 and Dt. 4:14ff; 14:1-18:22.

THE NECESSITY OF ABSOLUTES

duration of the Ceremonial Law. As Bownd observed,

> ... the Sabbath and moral law were given to the people immediately by God; but the other festival days, as the whole ceremonial law also, first to Moses, and then by his ministry unto the people. So it seemed, that the Lord Himself also distinguished them even in nature; and look what difference there is between the nature of the moral and ceremonial law, the same is between the Sabbath, and new moons and other Jewish festivals.[5]

Even from the giving of the Law to Israel through Moses, there was a distinction between the binding, abiding, and universal application of the Moral Law and the temporary and isolated nature of the Ceremonial and Judicial Laws to Israel. The writer to the Hebrews makes this abundantly clear when he states:

> ... the first *covenant* had also ordinances of divine service, and a worldly sanctuary. ... The Holy Ghost this signifying, that the way into the holiest of all was not yet made manifest, while as the first tabernacle was yet standing:

---

[5] Bownd, 117.

> which *was* a figure for the time then present, in which were offered both gifts and sacrifices, that could not make him that did the service perfect, as pertaining to the conscience; *which stood* only in meats and drinks, and divers washings, and carnal ordinances, imposed *on them* until the time of reformation. But Christ being come an high priest of good things to come, by a greater and more perfect tabernacle, not made with hands, that is to say, not of this building; neither by the blood of goats and calves, but by his own blood he entered in once into the holy place, having obtained eternal redemption *for us* (Heb. 9:1, 8-12).

The *Annotations* is an important work for understanding the mind of the divines on specific portions of the Scriptures because the editors took the reasoning of the Westminster divines and expressed them in a commentary on the whole of the Scriptures. Commenting on Hebrews 9:10, they state that

> ... of Christ's coming, who should and did reform the carnal rites, or ceremonies and services of the Law, by fulfilling them; exhibiting the truth and those spiritual blessings typified and signified by them; and by instituting a more simple and spiritual worship. This is what is meant, when God promises to create new heavens, and a new

THE NECESSITY OF ABSOLUTES

earth, Esay 65.17. and when S. Paul saith, *All things are made new*, 2 Cor 5.17.[6]

Reflecting on the Mosaic institution as a whole, in light of this very passage in Hebrews, Philip Ross concludes that the Ceremonial Laws were from their very institution designed to be temporary, especially since the center of Old Testament worship focused on the tabernacle (and later temple), which was itself a "pattern" of that which God displayed to Moses in Mount Sinai (cf. Exod. 25:9, 40). Hence, he refers to the Ceremonial Laws as "pattern laws," designed from the outset to point to Something else in the future, rather than being the permanent design of Biblical worship from that time until the Consummation.[7]

The divines, as has been seen, speak to this point directly in their statement regarding the abrogation of the Ceremonial Law, because it was given to Israel "... as a church under age." Calvin explains that "... the Jews were kept

---

[6] Heb. 9:10 in *Annotations Upon all the Books of the Old and New Testaments* (London: Evan Tyler, 1657), pages not numbered.

[7] See Ross, 110-15.

under the charge of a 'tutor' [Gal. 3:24] until the seed should come for whose sake the promise had been given. For, since they had not yet come to know Christ intimately, they were like children whose weakness could not yet bear the full knowledge of heavenly things."[8] Commenting on Galatians 3:24, specifically the phrase, "the law was our schoolmaster," the editors of the *Annotations* observe that the Law was

> a means and instrument to rule and regulate our minds and actions agreeable to the infancy of the Church with a great deal of austerity. The Jews under the law here are compared to children, and the faithful under the Gospel to men of riper years that need no school-master ... the Ceremonial Law also brings us unto Christ; because the same not onely covinceth men of sin, but also exhibiteth types and figures of Christ and his benefits: and teacheth that whatsoever was shadowed out by them, was truly to be found in Christ.[9]

In commenting upon the Epistle to the Galatians, Perkins considers the following verses: "Wherefore the law was our schoolmaster *to bring us* unto

---

[8] Calvin, *Institutes*, II:II.7.2, 350.
[9] Gal. 3:24 in *Annotations*.

THE NECESSITY OF ABSOLUTES

Christ, that we might be justified by faith. But after that faith is come, we are no longer under a schoolmaster" (Gal. 3:24-25). Perkins notes:

> The ceremonial law is that which prescribed rites and gestures in the worship of God in the time of the Old Testament. Ceremonies are either of figure and signification or of order. The first are abrogated at the coming of Christ, who was the accomplishment of them all (Col. 2:17). The second being ceremonies of particular order to the times of the Old and New Testament concern not us.[10]

The Substance and Object of faith unto salvation, being Christ Jesus Himself, has never changed since the *protevangelium* given in the Garden at the time of the fall (Gen. 3:15). But until the time of His incarnation, and the completion of His salvific cross work, His Church was kept under the Ceremonial Law as a vibrant and sensible means for pointing to Him as their only Savior from the fallen estate. While the outward forms of worship have changed with the coming of Christ, being changed from a more sensible to a more spiritual form of worship, the central focus of both forms of worship remains

---

[10] Perkins, *Works*, II:206.

unchanged, namely, the worship of the Triune God Who has revealed Himself in the propositions of Scripture, through the Mediation of Jesus the Messiah and Mediator of the Covenant of Grace.

The Mosaic period of the Church, therefore, must never be considered to have been a radically different institution than the New Testament Church. There has only ever been one Church since its institution in the Garden of Eden with the establishment of the Covenant of Grace. There have, however, been various administrations of that Church with the greatest distinction appearing at the institution of the New Testament Church with Christ's ministry and (especially after His ascension and the outpouring of the Holy Spirit) that of His apostles. John Ball, therefore, maintained that the Mosaic institutions were a part of the Covenant of Grace, identical in spiritual substance as the Covenant of Grace administered under the New Testament economy. The difference between the Mosaic and the Christian institutions, rather than being one of substance, was only a difference in administration—the external ordinances differed while the substance remained the same. In defense of his position, he referred to

THE NECESSITY OF ABSOLUTES

Hebrews 10:1, "For the law having a shadow of good things to come, and not the very image of the things, can never with those sacrifices which they offered year by year continually make the comers thereunto perfect." From this passage Ball commented:

> It may be said the Apostle sheweth the former Covenant to be faultie, or that another Covenant was lacking. But that is not mentioned to prove the Covenants to be two in substance opposite one to the other: but because the first Testament did not containe the Image of the things themselves, and therfore was not to be rested in, as if we could be justified by the workes of the Law, or ceremoniall observances annexed: but must be used as an introduction to leade us unto Christ, who is the very Image of the things themselves. This first Covenant therefore could not be fulfilled or effectuall, but by the bringing in of a second, which was prefigured thereby.[11]

Christ was the Substance to Whom the Ceremonial Law pointed. It must be remembered that the saints of the Old Testament

---

[11] John Ball, *A Treatise of the Covenant of Grace* (London: Simeon Ash, 1645), 118-19.

economy were just as dependent upon faith in Christ Jesus (the Messiah then to come) as the saints of the New Testament economy are. Trusting in the sacrificial system was as futile to the Israelite as trusting in his own righteousness is for the modern Church member. It is faith in Christ and embracing His finished salvific cross work on behalf of His elect that is the *alone* means of justification before God. Ridgeley observes: "... the design of [the ceremonial laws] was to lead [the Israelites] into the knowledge of Christ, and the way of salvation by him, then to come."[12] Hence, the ordinances under the sacrificial system were "typical," as the divines observe; that is, they typified Christ and His Sacrifice. Because Christ has come, the divines insist that the Ceremonial Law, in its entirety, has been "abrogated."

The term "abrogation" requires particular attention. It is a legal term, utilized judiciously in this place by the divines. A definitive definition of the term is "to repeal (as a law, or established usage), to annul, to abolish authoritatively or

---

[12] Ridgeley, II:308.

THE NECESSITY OF ABSOLUTES

formally, to cancel."[13] Burgess explained the term in this manner:

> *Abrogation* is then properly, when a Law is totally taken away. And this Abrogation ariseth sometimes from the expresse constitution at first, which did limit and prescribe the time of the lawes continuance: sometimes by an expresse revoking and repealing of it by that authority which made it: sometimes by adding to that repeale and expresse law commanding the contrary. Now it may be easily proved, that the Ceremoniall ... lawes they are abrogated by expresse repeale.[14]

Since the accidents of the Ceremonial Law have been annulled with the coming of Christ, it is essential that the New Testament Church never seek to revive any of the aspects of the old Ceremonial Law. Having already observed the temporary nature of the Judicial Law, Durham continues by considering the temporary nature of the Ceremonial Law. He states:

> The *ceremonial law* is in ceremonies, types and shadows, pointing at a Savior to come. This is

---

[13] "Abrogate," in *A New English Dictionary on Historical Principles* (Oxford: Clarendon Press, 1901), I:34.

[14] Burgess, 211.

The Ceremonial Law Abrogated and Judicial Law Expired

> also abrogated, the substance being come. But there is this difference, that the judicial law is but *mortua*, dead; and may, where it is thought fit, with the foregoing caution, be used under the New Testament. But the ceremonial law is *mortifera*, deadly, and cannot be revived without falling from grace (Gal. 5:2, 4).[15]

Because Christ was the very Substance to Whom the entirety of the Ceremonial Law pointed and of Whom it was but a pale shadow, now that this Substance has come, it is the height of rebellion for the Church to attempt to recapitulate the ceremonialism of the Old Testament economy. The Ceremonial Law prefigured Christ, and Christ perfectly fulfilled the entirety of that salvation which was foreshadowed in the Ceremonial Law. With the coming of Christ, there *must* be a cessation of the old Levitical forms. As Daniel prophesied: "And he shall confirm the covenant with many for one week: and in the midst of the week he shall cause the sacrifice and the oblation to cease, and for the overspreading of abominations he shall make *it* desolate, even until the consummation, and that determined shall be poured upon the desolate"

---

[15] Durham, 55-56.

THE NECESSITY OF ABSOLUTES

(Dan. 9:27). According to this passage, not only would Christ abolish the Old Testament religious ceremonies (causing "... the sacrifice and oblation to cease ..."), He would do so in such a permanent manner that they will never be revived, ("... even until the consummation ..."). Paul states this quite clearly when he says, "Let no man therefore judge you in meat, or in drink, or in respect of an holyday, or of the new moon, or of the sabbath *days*: which are a shadow of things to come, but the body is of Christ" (Col. 2:16-17). The first General Synod in Jerusalem was convened in order to consider this very point and determined that the Gentile Christians should not be subjected to the Ceremonial Law. Peter proclaims: "Now therefore why tempt ye God, to put a yoke upon the neck of the disciples, which neither our fathers nor we were able to bear?" (Acts 15:10). With the consensus of the Commissioners, the assembly sent a written proclamation to the Presbyteries that "... it seemed good to the Holy Ghost, and to us, to lay upon you no greater burden than these necessary things; that ye abstain from meats offered to idols, and from blood, and from things strangled, and from fornication: from which if ye keep yourselves, ye

The Ceremonial Law Abrogated and Judicial Law Expired

shall do well" (Acts 15:28-29; 16:4). Thence, by the Divine decree and the determination of this counsel, the Ceremonial Law was expressly abrogated. It was against the return to these ceremonial ordinances that Paul so sharply exhorted the Galatian Christians.

The Scriptures of the New Testament are very clear that the ceremonies of the Old Testament economy passed away with Christ's completed work. The striking passage in the Gospel account is well worth noticing: "Jesus, when He had cried again with a loud voice, yielded up the ghost. And, behold, the veil of the temple was rent in twain from the top to the bottom; and the earth did quake, and the rocks rent" (Matt. 27:50-51). Calvin comments:

> Nor was it proper that the *vail* should be *rent*, until the sacrifice of expiation had been completed; for then Christ, the true and everlasting Priest, having abolished the figures of the law, opened up for us by his blood the way to the heavenly sanctuary, that we may no longer stand at a distance within the porch, but may freely advance into the presence of God. For so long as the shadowy worship lasted, a *vail* was hung up before the earthly sanctuary, in order to keep the people not only from

THE NECESSITY OF ABSOLUTES

> entering but from seeing it, (Exod. 26:33; 2 Chron. 3:14.) Now Christ, by *blotting out the handwriting which was opposed to us*, (Col. 2:14,) removed every obstruction, that, relying on him as Mediator, we may all be *a royal priesthood*, (1 Pet. 2:9). Thus the *rending* of the *vail* was not only an abrogation of the ceremonies which existed under the law, but was, in some respects, an opening of heaven, that God may now invite the members of his Son to approach him with familiarity. ... Meanwhile, the Jews were informed that the period of abolishing outward sacrifices had arrived, and that the ancient priesthood would be of no farther use; that though the building of the temple was left standing, it would not be necessary to worship God there after the ancient custom; but that since the substance and truth of the shadows had been fulfilled, the figures of the law were changed into spirit.[16]

Through Christ's completed cross work, the fullness of the Gospel was revealed and, through His apostles, was no longer isolated to the physical nation of the Israelites but was spread throughout the world to every nation, tribe, and

---

[16] John Calvin, *Commentary on a Harmony of the Evangelists Matthew, Mark, and Luke*, vol. 3, trans. Rev. William Pringle (Bellingham, WA: Logos Bible Software, 2010), 323–324.

The Ceremonial Law Abrogated and Judicial Law Expired

tongue. The elect of every nation belong to God through Christ and have been completely freed from the shadowy rudiments of the Ceremonial Law now that the Substance Himself has come and accomplished that for which He was sent. A. A. Hodge confirms this point when he remarks: "The instant of Christ's death, the veil separating the throne of God from the approach of men 'was rent in twain from the top to the bottom' (Matt. xxvii. 50, 51), thus throwing the way open to all, and dispensing with the priests and their ceremonies for ever."[17]

The importance of the Westminsterian view of the abrogation of the Ceremonial Law, coupled with their view of the regulative principle of worship,[18] cannot be overstated. The subject of worshiping God is of such central importance to the

---

[17] A. A. Hodge, *The Westminster Confession: A Commentary* (Edinburgh: Banner of Truth Trust, 2002/1869), 256.

[18] "But the acceptable way of worshipping the true God is instituted by himself, and so limited by his own revealed will, that he may not be worshipped according to the imaginations and devices of men, or the suggestions of Satan, under any visible representation, or any other way not prescribed in the Holy Scripture." *WCF*, Ch. XXI.i, 110.

THE NECESSITY OF ABSOLUTES

very purpose of man that Calvin went so far as to aver that the manner of worshiping God was the primary catalyst and justification for the Protestant Reformation.[19] The Old Testament Scriptures record, in minute detail, the manner which God prescribed for His worship under that economy of the Church. Those various ceremonial institutions all pointed toward Christ and found their fulfillment in Him. Seeing that Christ as the Substance has come and accomplished everything to which the Ceremonial Law pointed, it has been abrogated and completely removed from the Church in the New Testament.

---

[19] Calvin states: "If it be inquired, then, by what things chiefly the Christian religion has a standing existence amongst us and maintains its truth, it will be found that the following two not only occupy the principal place, but comprehend under them all the other parts, and consequently the whole substance of Christianity, viz., a knowledge, first, of the mode in which God is duly worshipped; and, secondly of the source from which salvation is to be obtained. When these are kept out of view, though we may glory in the name of Christians, our profession is empty and vain." John Calvin, "The Necessity of Reforming the Church," in *Tracts and Letters of John Calvin*, vols. 1-7 (Edinburgh: Banner of Truth Trust, 2009), I:126.

Underlying the Ceremonial Law, however, is a moral element that is often overlooked. Viewed only as a set of obligatory observances and rituals, the Ceremonial Law has no binding force on Christians. The underlying moral element continues to obligate the Church under the administration of the New Testament. With respect to this moral element, Turretin insists: "...with regard to doctrine and signification ... We confess that it still remains and is useful in many ways among Christians; and that the mystical truth, hidden under this shell, is always the same and of perpetual necessity."[20] Ridgeley, in his detailed exposition of the *WLC*, identifies six major headings of the Ceremonial Law. Under each of these heads he presents the underlying moral element that remains binding upon Christians. As an example, Ridgeley avers that "...the principal design of [circumcision] was, that it might be a sign or seal of the blessings of the covenant of grace, in which God promised that he would be 'a God to them;' and by observing this rite, they were to own

---

[20] Turretin, 2:158.

THE NECESSITY OF ABSOLUTES

themselves as his people (Gen. 17.7, 10)."[21] Ridgeley goes on to identify the underlying moral elements in each of the remaining five heads wherein he demonstrates that the many detailed laws of cleansing demonstrate the sinfulness of sin and the extent to which Christians must learn to hate it, how the temple prefigured Christ Who is "God with us," that the priestly office with all of its elegant trappings pointed to Christ as the Great High Priest, that the many sacrifices and offered gifts were but types of the perfect Sacrifice of Christ Who is accepted by God on behalf of His elect people, and that each of the annual feasts foreshadowed specific significance for Christians with respect to Christ and His finished cross work.[22] Each of these symbolic rituals has been abrogated for the New Testament Christian. But the underlying significance of these Ceremonial Laws should have an even greater impact on Christians than the ancient Church precisely because Christ the Substance has come.

---

[21] Ridgeley, II:309.
[22] Ibid., II:309-311.

The Ceremonial Law Abrogated and Judicial Law Expired

God, as the sole Object of man's worship, remains the only One Who can dictate the manner in which He will be worshiped. With the abrogation of the Old Testament ceremonies, God is no longer to be worshiped by outward signs and shadowy elements. The worship of the Church since Christ and to the consummation has significantly less outward show but significantly more spiritual reality. When the Westminster divines reduce the Divinely appointed elements of New Testament worship to prayer, the reading of the Scriptures, the preaching of the Word, singing of Psalms, the due administration of the Sacraments of Baptism and the Lord's Supper, as the only regular elements in worship (beside the occasional elements of lawful oaths and vows, fastings, and thanksgivings), it is precisely because only these elements can be found expressly set down in the New Testament Scriptures in light of the abrogation of the Ceremonial Law. The modern Church—even the larger part of the Reformed Churches—has multiplied these elements and added to them according to expediency or "tradition." Sadly, the primary reason for the continuation of Christ's Church apart from Rome

THE NECESSITY OF ABSOLUTES

in the sixteenth century Reformation has been largely abandoned with the addition of these additional elements. In essence, the Protestant Church has increasingly returned to the papal antichrist of Rome and ought to repent of her error of corrupting the Biblical worship of God. There must, then, for the modern Reformed pastor, be a renewed practice of Biblical worship as set forth in the New Testament Scriptures and summarized so completely and eloquently by the Westminster divines.

2. The Judicial Law and Its Expiration with the New Testament Church

The Westminster divines move from their discussion of the abrogation of the Ceremonial Law to their presentation that the Old Testament Judicial Laws have expired. Their comments are quite brief: "To them also as a body politic, he gave sundry judicial laws, which expired together with the state of that people, not obliging any other now, further than the general equity thereof may require."[23] The argument is quite simple: God provided, through Moses, various laws concerning the government of Israel as a body politic, along with rules of jurisprudence. With the dissolution of Israel as a nation in 70 AD due to their rejection of the Messiah, all of the particular political laws also expired. Ridgeley summarizes:

> It cannot be supposed that so great a people, so much interested in the care of God, to whom he condescended to be their king, should be without a body of laws for their government. Accordingly, there were some given them by

---

[23] *WCF*, XIX.iv, 97.

> him, which were founded in and agreeable to the law of nature and nations. ... Moreover, there were other judicial laws given to Israel, which had a more immediate tendency to promote their civil welfare, as a nation distinguished from all others in the world; which laws expired when their civil polity was extinct.[24]

Commenting upon this paragraph in the light of its treatment by Bolton, Beeke and Jones remark, "The ceremonial law was abolished, so the judicial law became 'an appendix to the second table' concerning civil government in Israel to give a rule of public justice, to distinguish Israel from others, and to be a type of Christ's government. Insofar as the judicial law is 'of common and general equity,' it remains in force; otherwise, it too has ceased."[25] It is precisely this use of the term "equity" that has caused so many questions among Reformed theologians in the present day.

Before proceeding to discuss the meaning of "general equity," there should be some clarification with reference to the distinction

---

[24] Ridgley, II:307–8.
[25] Beeke and Jones, 563.

made by Bolton that the Judicial Law is "an appendix to the second table."[26] While the civil magistrate has the duty before God to oversee the physical wellbeing of his subjects, he is not limited to the enforcement of the Commandments of the Second Table of the Law. Because the civil magistrate is "... ordained of God ..." and is "... the minister of God to thee for good" (Rom. 13:1, 4), it is incumbent upon him that he enforce God's Moral Law (both Tables of it) upon the population over whom he has been appointed by God. Every magistrate, of every nation—both Christian and pagan—will give account to the righteous Judge for his enforcement of the whole Moral Law, in both Tables (see Psa. 2:10-12). It is of particular importance to understand that, for the divines of the First and Second Reformations, this duty was especially inculcated upon the Christian magistrate as one particularly equipped and duty-bound to this function. Martin Bucer, that great light of the First Reformation, in humbly advising the Christian magistrate, insisted that a primary part of his responsibility was the protection of the Church

---

[26] Bolton, 56.

THE NECESSITY OF ABSOLUTES

by enforcing measures against all who would violate the First Table of the Moral Law. He went so far as to state:

> Accordingly, in every state sanctified to God capital punishment must be ordered for all who have dared to injure religion, either by introducing a false and impious doctrine about the worship of God or by calling people away from the true worship of God ... for all who blaspheme the name of God and his solemn services ... who violate the Sabbath ... who rebelliously despise the authority of parents and live their own life wickedly ... who are unwilling to submit to the sentence of a supreme tribunal ... who have committed bloodshed ... adultery ... rape ... kidnapping ... who have given false testimony in a capital case. ... In these sanctions of God, we see that he judges that the death penalty should eliminate from his people whoever has openly defected from him or held him in contempt or persuades others to do the same, to the betrayal and vitiation of true religion ....[27]

As this discussion progresses, two points should be borne in mind from this quotation:

---

[27] Martin Bucer, *De Regno Christi*, ed. Wilhelm Pauck, in *The Library of Christian Classics: Melancthon and Bucer* (Louisville: Westminster John Knox Press, 1969), 378-79.

first, Bucer was addressing a Christian magistrate in a professedly Christian nation (this address in 1550 was addressed to King Edward VI of England); second, he emphasized the importance of the Christian magistrate to enforce the First Table—not only the Second Table—of the Moral Law. This bears particularly on the subject of the place of the Judicial Laws in modern Christian societies because, while the *particular* equity of the Judicial Laws, with their express penalties, have expired, the *general* equity of those Laws remain binding upon all civil magistrates, especially those professing Christian magistrates governing professing Christian nations. The Westminster divines articulated this point when they averred,

> The civil magistrate ... hath authority, and it is his duty, to take order, that unity and peace be preserved in the church, that the truth of God be kept pure and entire, that all blasphemies and heresies be suppressed, all corruptions and abuses in worship and discipline prevented or reformed, and all ordinances of God duly settled, administered, and observed.[28]

---

[28] *WCF*, XXIII.iii, 128-29.

THE NECESSITY OF ABSOLUTES

The magistrate has, therefore, a specific interest in considering his duty to the preservation and promulgation of the Moral Law in his land for the preservation of the civil estate from God's judgment and destruction.

3. The Principle of *General Equity*

At the time of the Westminster Assembly, the seat of controversy concerning the Law had to do primarily with the relationship of the Christian to the Moral Law.[29] As such, there was little debate over the abrogation of the Ceremonial Law and the expiration of the Judicial Law. In the twentieth century, however, a lasting controversy arose with the formation of Reconstructionism and Theonomy. Among professing Confessional Christians, much of the controversy during the later twentieth century developed out of a misunderstanding of the definition of *general equity*. The term *equity*, in English, developed from the Latin term *aequitas*, which

> ... was somewhat influenced in meaning by being adopted as the ordinary rendering of the Gr. εφπιειϖκεια ... which meant reasonableness and moderation in the exercise of one's rights, and the disposition to avoid insisting on them too rigorously. ... In Jurisprudence. ... The recourse to general principles of justice (the *naturalis aequitas* of the

---

[29] Ibid.

THE NECESSITY OF ABSOLUTES

> Roman jurists) to correct or supplement the provisions of the law. *Equity of a statute*: the construction of a statute according to its reason and spirit, so as to make it apply to cases for which it does not expressly provide.[30]

Thus, when the Westminster divines speak of the Judicial Law as "... expired ... not obliging any other now, further than the general equity thereof may require," they mean that the details of the Judicial Law have little explicit application to any nation apart from the ancient nation of Israel (now extinct), *except* insofar as those Biblical Judicial Laws present the "general principles of justice" as given by God in His Moral Law. Calvin writes:

> It is a fact that the law of God which we call the moral law is nothing else than a testimony of natural law and of that conscience which God has engraved upon the minds of men. Consequently, the entire scheme of this equity of which we are now speaking has been prescribed in it. Hence, this equity alone must be the goal and rule and limit of all laws.[31]

---

[30] "Equity," in *New English Dictionary*, III:2, 262.
[31] Calvin, *Institutes*, II:IV.20.16, 1504.

The universal or Moral basis of this principle can be seen in the use of interchangeable phrases such as *moral equity, common equity,* and *natural equity* (instead of, or in addition to, *general equity*) by many of the Reformers, Puritans, Presbyterian divines of the sixteenth and seventeenth centuries in the literature of the period.[32] An excellent illustration of the three types of Biblical Law in a single example is presented by the great Puritan divine (and member of the Westminster Assembly), William Gouge. In his commentary on the Book of Hebrews, Gouge considers the payment of tithes to Melchisedec by Abraham and explains the apostle's meaning of the phrase "... the sons of Levi ... have a commandment to take tithes of the people according to the law" (Heb.7:5). From this single phrase, Gouge demonstrates that this commandment is reflective of the Judicial,

---

[32] An excellent resource with summary information is presented on the website, "Reformed Books Online." The creator of the site has a thorough discussion on the principle of *general equity*, including interchangeable phrases, at this location: https://reformedbooksonline.com/topics/topics-by-subject/covenant-of-grace/the-mosaic-covenant/the-civil-law/, accessed May 28, 2018.

THE NECESSITY OF ABSOLUTES

Ceremonial, and Moral Laws and further explains how a Judicial Law remains binding in its Moral substance even when that Judicial application has expired with the nation-state of Israel. The commandment to take tithes of the Israelites for the maintenance of the Levites demonstrates the Judicial Law because the Levites had no tribal/geographical inheritance (property rights) with the rest of their brethren. Because the Levites served in the ceremonies of Old Testament worship, their maintenance by the tithes for that service was a reflection of the Ceremonial Law. With the expiration of the Judicial Law and the abrogation of the Ceremonial Law, there yet remains the abiding principle of the Moral Law in its universal application of the principle of *general equity*. Gouge states: "The general equity, that they who communicate unto us spiritual matters, should partake of our temporals; and that they who are set apart wholly to attend God's service, should live upon that service, is moral."[33] With the

---

[33] William Gouge, *Commentary on Hebrews* (Grand Rapids: Kregel Publications, 1980), 490. [Gouge demonstrates this principle even more fully, with several

fulfillment of ceremonial and civil precepts particular to Israel as the Old Testament Church and unique Theocracy of God (the Ceremonial Law and the *particular equity* of Judicial Law), what Moral precepts remain (the *general equity*) continue to have abiding authority and lasting application to the New Testament Church and modern nations.

The application of this *general equity* to all nations and at all times, as distinct from the *particular equity* of those Judicial Laws to ancient Israel, is best expressed by William Perkins. He states:

> ... the Judicial laws of Moses according to the substance and scope thereof must be distinguished; in which respects they are of two sorts. Some of them are laws of particular equity, some of common equity. Laws of particular equity, are such as prescribe justice according to the particular estate and condition of the Jews' commonwealth & to the circumstances thereof: time, place, persons, things, actions. ... Judicials of common equity are such as are made according to the law or instinct of nature common to all men: and these in respect of their substance, bind the consciences not only of the Jews but also of the

---

examples, when answering "objections" to the perpetuity of the tithe in his comments on Heb. 7:2, 475-76.]

THE NECESSITY OF ABSOLUTES

> Gentiles. ... Again judicial laws, so far forth as they have in them the general or common equity of the law of nature are moral: and therefore binding in conscience, as the moral law.[34]

By this definition, it becomes clear that the Westminster divines were presenting and defending a view of the Judicial Law that was already common among the Puritan divines long before their seating in Westminster Abbey. They brought with them a thorough knowledge of English jurisprudence and a long-established understanding of the principles of both general and particular equity. "So 'equity' looks beyond the letter of the law to discover the moral principles lying behind it, and the adjective 'general' limits the equity to those judicial laws which address the moral situation of all nations and not just the particular conditions of Israel."[35] Whatever parts of

---

[34] William Perkins, *A Discourse of Conscience* (Cambridge: John Legate, 1596), 17-19.

[35] Matthew Winzer, "The Westminster Assembly & the Judicial Law: A Chronological Compilation and Analysis: Part Two: Analysis," in *The Confessional Presbyterian*, vol. 5, 2009 (Dallas: Confessional Presbyterian Press, 2009), 71.

The Ceremonial Law Abrogated and Judicial Law Expired

the Judicial Law were particular to the Jews in their specific time and unique station as a Theocratic nation were no longer binding upon any other nation—either in ancient or modern times—since the dissolution of Israel in 70 AD. Those aspects of the Judicial Law, however, that were of general equity were express applications of both Tables of the Moral Law and, as such, remain binding upon every civil magistrate of every nation and in every age, simply because this was the will of God to all of mankind first revealed to Adam at his creation and engraved on the hearts of all mankind descending from him.

Specific examples of Judicial Laws of *particular equity* may be cited. These include the requirement for a man to take the widow of his deceased brother, having died childless, and raising up seed to his brother's name (Dt. 25:5-10). Another example of *particular equity* is the set of specific laws respecting the Sabbath Year and the Year of Jubilee (Lev. 25:1-17). Such laws were specific to Israel as a unique body politic under the LORD, but never pressed upon any other nation. Upon all nations, however, there remain those Judicial Laws of *general equity*. As Gouge explains:

THE NECESSITY OF ABSOLUTES

> There were other branches of the judicial law which rested upon common equity, and were means of keeping the moral law: as putting to death idolaters and such as enticed others thereunto; and witches, and willful murderers, and other notorious malefactors. So likewise laws against incest and incestuous marriages; laws of reverencing and obeying superiors and governors; and of dealing justly in borrowing, restoring, buying, selling, and all manner of contracts, Exod. xxii. 20; Deut. xiii. 9; Exod. xx. 18; Num. xxxv. 30; Lev. xx. 11, &c., xix. 32, 35.[36]

As such, when the Judicial Laws address specific judicial action against open violators of the Ten Words, because this Moral Law is binding upon all men in all ages—and by extension, to every *nation* on earth—each nation-state has an obligation before God to punish law-breakers.

If only some of the Judicial Laws are still binding because they are precepts of general equity consonant with the Moral Law, it is next to be considered whether the Old Testament civil punishments remain in force. Turretin states, "Thus in laws concerning the punishment of crimes, the substance of the punishment is of

---

[36] Gouge, 505.

natural right, but the manner and degree of punishment is of particular right and on that account mutable."³⁷ Rutherford concurs and elucidates when he states,

> But we conceive, the whole bulk of the judicial Law, as judicial, and as it concerned the Republic of the Jews only, is abolished, though the moral equity of all those be not abolished; also some punishments were merely Symbolical, to teach the detestation of such a vice ... the punishing of a sin against the Moral Law by the Magistrate, is Moral and perpetual; but the punishing of every sin against the Moral Law, *tali modo*, so and so, with death, with spitting on the face: I much doubt if these punishments in particular, and in their positive determination to the people of the Jews, be moral and perpetual.³⁸

Even when Judicial Laws remain binding upon all nations because of the rule of general equity, the specific penalties for those crimes are to be determined by the individual magistrate according

---

[37] Turretin, II:167.

[38] Samuel Rutherford, *The Divine Right of Church-Government and Excommunication* (London: John Field for Christopher Meredith, 1646), 493-94.

THE NECESSITY OF ABSOLUTES

to the needs of his nation, in consultation with the ancient civil penalties of Israel.

With the realization that the civil magistrate is responsible for the enforcement of both Tables of the Moral Law, it becomes immediately evident that any nation whose civil magistrate promotes any false religion or persecutes Christ's true Church is in gross error and open rebellion against the living God. Likewise, any nation that fails to create and enforce laws establishing the worship of the one, true and living God or that forbids the establishment of the Biblical religion is equally guilty of rebellion against God. Such is the sad case of the United States of America. In the Bill of Rights, the First Amendment states, "Congress shall make no law respecting an establishment of religion, or prohibiting the free exercise thereof."[39] When the LORD commands "thou shalt have no other gods before Me" in the First Commandment, He demonstrates the exclusive nature of His Religion. Since the establishment of the Bill of Rights, the United States has declared itself openly hostile to the

---

[39] "Bill of Rights."

Triune God by preventing the establishment of Biblical Christianity while protecting every pagan and satanic religion under the sun. A bare permission to practice the worship of the living God while simultaneously forbidding the establishment of His Religion is equivalent to open rebellion against Him and His Moral Law.

THE NECESSITY OF ABSOLUTES

4. *Theonomy* Considered in Light of Westminster

The Westminsterian view of Biblical Law, with its Biblical and historic tripartite division; emphasis upon the perpetuity and universality of the Moral Law; abrogation of the Ceremonial Law; and expiration of the Judicial Law, except for the abiding principle of *general equity*, is a viewpoint that has largely been abandoned by the professing Christian Church including many founded upon a Reformed heritage. This is unsettling, especially if the Westminster divines produced the best human summary of what the Scriptures principally teach. Most distressing is the abandonment of this presentation of Biblical Law even by those Churches that profess to be both Presbyterian and Confessional. By the second half of the twentieth century, in response to the rise of liberalism and modernism, there was a widespread movement among Reformed bodies to recover the legacy and heritage of their Puritan and historic Presbyterian roots. The republication of long out of print writings of the Reformers, Puritans, and Covenanters led to

The Ceremonial Law Abrogated and Judicial Law Expired

concerted efforts to recover the orthodox position of the orthodox divines of the First and Second Reformation periods. Much glory has been given to God with these efforts as Confessionalism, purity of worship, and Biblical apologetics all began to see a resurgence within the Reformed Churches in this nation. The nature of Biblical Law and its applicability to modern society were also raised as matters of concern, and efforts were made to restore that Law to the Church and the culture. It must be stated at the outset that the effort to reclaim a Biblical ethic for the glory of God in modern society is a Godly pursuit and many of the men who led the charge to do so demonstrated a sincere love for God, His Word, and His honor before men. Unhappily, some of these efforts—while certainly filled with zeal—were misguided and have caused deep fissures in the Body of Christ, especially within American Reformed circles. Rather than a return to the Westminsterian position of Biblical Law, the leaders of this movement introduced an old error with respect to the perpetuity of the Judicial Law. For the purpose of this discussion, the

THE NECESSITY OF ABSOLUTES

term *theonomy*[40] will be used to compare and contrast this movement with the Westminsterian position.

The modern "Christian Reconstruction" movement had its origin in the 1970s with the publication of *Institutes of Biblical Law* by Rousas John Rushdoony (1973) and *Theonomy in Christian Ethics* by Greg Bahnsen (1977). While the movement has taken on a wide variety of iterations and has crossed ecclesiastical and theological lines, it originated within the confessional Reformed camp and continues to

---

[40] *Theonomy* is a term used by the leading proponents of this view. However, this is a very inappropriate term for this particular theological movement. Meaning "the law of God," *theonomy* as presented by Rousas John Rushdoony and Greg Bahnsen is not a restoration of a Biblical view of God's Law, but a recapitulation of an old error combated by many divines throughout the centuries, notably John Calvin. In reality, the term *Theonomy*, properly applied relates to the unadulterated application of God's Law consonant with the Holy Scriptures and orthodox theology, most consistently articulated in the Westminster Standards. The proponents of the "Christian Reconstruction" school of thought have erroneously appropriated the term *theonomy* and unjustly applied it to their system. It is to be noted, however, that Rushdoony and Bahnsen differed sufficiently to distinguish between them.

have a significant presence in Reformed circles.[41] Against the prevalence of antinomianism, these men sincerely advocated a return to Biblical Law. What they presented in their writings, however, was altogether different than the Westminsterian position. Specifically, their teachings and writings emphasized

> ... the continued normativity not only of the moral law but also of the judicial law of Old Testament Israel, including its penal sanctions; and belief that the Old Testament judicial law applies not only to Israel, but also to Gentile nations, including modern America, so that it is the duty of the civil government to enforce that law and execute its penalties. Christian reconstruction hence has the appeal of claiming to apply biblical principles to contemporary

---

[41] Both Dr. Rushdoony and Dr. Bahnsen were ordained ministers in the Orthodox Presbyterian Church (OPC) and, as such, responded in the affirmative to the vow: "Do you sincerely receive and adopt the Confession of Faith and Catechisms of this Church, as containing the system of doctrine taught in the Holy Scriptures?" [OPC Book of Church Order, Ch. XXIII, par. 8, qu. 2].

society in a way that will express the dominion of Christ.[42]

While the intent is unquestionably noble, *theonomy* takes a dramatically different approach to the abiding authority of the Judicial Law than that of the Westminster divines. To explain this distinction, Sinclair Ferguson states,

> A feature of theonomistic thinking that has come to be seen as its distinctive mark is the view that the only truly consistent ... theonomy is that which regards the Judaic civil laws as binding still today and therefore necessarily applicable *mutatis mutandis* to all ages and nations. A particularly emotive implication of this view is, of course, that the death penalty is as fitting in the New Testament era as it was in the Old Testament, not only for murder ... but for other deeds ... and that the civil authorities today remain under obligation to God to punish such acts as capital crimes under the legal code of the state.[43]

---

[42] William S. Barker and W. Robert Godfrey, eds. *Theonomy: A Reformed Critique* (Grand Rapids: Zondervan House, 1990), 9-10.

[43] Sinclair B. Ferguson, "An Assembly of Theonomists? The Teaching of the Westminster Divines on the Law of God," in *Theonomy: A Reformed Critique*, 315-16.

The Ceremonial Law Abrogated and Judicial Law Expired

Ferguson's comment is a fair reflection of Bahnsen's insistence that

> because Christ confirmed every stroke of God's law in the Sermon on the Mount and that law includes direction for the civil magistrate. ... Every detail of God's law has abiding validity from the time of Christ's advent to the time of His return ... magistrates in the era of the New Testament are under obligation to those commands in the Book of the Law which apply to civil affairs and social penology. ... Because the penal sanctions of God's law are imperatives delivered with divine authority and approval, the follower of Christ should teach that the civil magistrate is yet under moral obligation to enforce the law of God in its social aspect.[44]

It is very clear that there are two contradictory systems of thought regarding the Law of God at play here. On the one hand is the Westminsterian system with its fundamental premise of the Tripartite division of the Law—Moral, Ceremonial, and Judicial—with the abiding and binding authority of the Moral Law upon all men, at all times, in all nations; the full abrogation of the

---

[44] Greg L. Bahnsen, *Theonomy in Christian Ethics*, 3rd ed. (Nacogdoches, TX: Covenant Media Press, 2002/1977), 311-12.

THE NECESSITY OF ABSOLUTES

Ceremonial Law with its fulfillment in Christ; and the expiration of the Judicial Law with the cessation of Israel as a distinct nation, *except* insofar as the *general equity* of those Judicial Laws, as reflective of the Moral Law, remains obligatory to every civil magistrate in every nation. On the other hand is the system of *theonomy* that treats the Old Testament Laws as a single unit, insisting that all of them remain binding (except, perhaps, for most of the Ceremonial Laws), down to the jot and tittle of the Mosaic penal code. This latter position dismisses the Tripartite division and reduces it to Moral and Ceremonial only and openly rejects the Reformation and Second Reformation consensus on *general equity*. Even a cursory review of the subject matter makes it impossible to conclude that *theonomy* is Westminsterian.

Bahnsen's view of Biblical Law begins with a division of the Old Testament laws into two groups (rather than three); namely, the Ceremonial Law and the Moral Law. He believed that the Ceremonial Law was subdivided into those ceremonies that specifically pointed to Christ (e.g., the

The Ceremonial Law Abrogated and Judicial Law Expired

tabernacle/temple and the sacrificial system) and those which inculcated a wall of separation from the Gentile nations (e.g., the dietary laws). He states that, while these ceremonials are not practiced the same way they were during the Old Testament period (having been fulfilled in Christ), they still have a valid place in the New Testament because

> ... they are confirmed for us. The *principle* they taught is still valid ... in the New Testament the outward form of such laws has been surpassed—the spreading of the redeemed community to the Gentiles render all meats clean (Acts 10) and the sacrifice of Christ has put the system of ordinances which separated the Jews and Gentiles out of gear (Eph. 2:11-20)—but their basic requirement of holy separation from the unclean world of unbelief is still confirmed and in force (2 Cor. 6:14-7:1).[45]

While this language does differ from that of the Westminster divines, it is not on the surface entirely discordant with their position.

---

[45] Greg L. Bahnsen, *By This Standard: The Authority of God's Law Today* (Tyler, TX: Institute for Christian Economics, 1985), 136-37; Bahnsen's emphasis.

THE NECESSITY OF ABSOLUTES

It is in his presentation of the Moral Law that Bahnsen demonstrates his radical departure from the theology and scope of the Westminster Standards. Completely rejecting the historic, orthodox, and Reformed division of Moral and Judicial Laws, Bahnsen insists that all of the remaining laws, outside of the Ceremonial, constitute the Moral Law. He explains,

> The *moral law* of God can likewise be seen in two subdivisions, the divisions having simply a literary difference: (1) general or summary precepts of morality—for instance, the unspecified requirements of sexual purity and honesty, 'thou shalt not commit adultery' and 'thou shalt not steal,' and (2) commands that specify general precepts by way of illustrative application—for instance, prohibiting incest, homosexuality, defrauding one's workers, or muzzling the ox as he treads.[46]

This section is of vital importance to the understanding of the theonomic system, especially in terms of how dramatically different it is than that of the Westminsterian system. For Bahnsen, there are no Judicial Laws, per se.

---

[46] Ibid., 137.

The Ceremonial Law Abrogated and Judicial Law Expired

Instead, every civic, political, penal institution outside of the Decalogue is a case-law application of the Decalogue and equally as binding. Even though he concedes that the Ceremonial Law is in some sense abrogated with its fulfillment in Christ, he rejects that that aspect of the Old Testament Law referred to as "Judicial" by the Westminster divines is, in any sense, expired. Instead, Bahnsen maintains that "there is abundant evidence that the New Testament authoritatively cited and applied these case-law illustrations to current situations. ... Therefore, we conclude that Jesus has forever confirmed the moral laws of God, their summary expressions as well as their case-law applications."[47] By rejecting the Westminsterian definitions of, and separations between, the Moral Law and the Judicial Law, Bahnsen was able to make it *appear* that he could garner support from historic documents written by the Reformers and Westminster divines to support his view of the abiding and binding nature of the Old Testament penal laws to every nation in modern society.

---

[47] Bahnsen, *By This Standard*, 138.

THE NECESSITY OF ABSOLUTES

Elsewhere, Bahnsen defends the Old Testament penal code, in direct contradiction to the Confessional statements. He writes:

> ... to repudiate the penal sanctions of the Mosaic law is to be impaled on the horns of a painful ethical dilemma: one either gives up all civil sanctions against crime, or one settles for civil sanctions that are not just. Both options are clearly unbiblical and produce abusive political effects in practice. ... We are driven to conclude that the Bible offers no justification for teaching that, as a category, the 'political' provisions of God's Old Testament law have been abrogated. ... The justice of God's law, even as it touches political matters like crime and punishment, is not culturally relative.[48]

Again, he states,

> ... the law for society today is the same as that in the Older Testament, and the officials of the state are responsible today, just as ancient Israel, to enforce God's law ... the civil magistrate is obligated to follow the penal sanctions of God's Law, for those sanctions are neither arbitrary nor temporary. ... Indeed,

---

[48] Greg L. Bahnsen, "The Theonomic Reformed Approach to Law and Gospel," in *Five Views on Law and Gospel*, ed. Wayne G. Strickland (Grand Rapids: Zondervan, 1999), 134, 139.

> these sanctions are as much a part of the law as the other commandments found therein. The death penalty continues in full force in this age, and it applies to more than simply murder. The magistrate is under moral obligation, then, to apply death to those who transgress God's law at places where God requires the life of the criminal.[49]

These statements are not only radically different than the Confessional statements, they are precisely the opposite of what the divines concluded. Where the divines present a Tripartite division of the Old Testament Laws—Moral, Ceremonial, and Judicial—Bahnsen replaces this with a Twofold division—Moral (including the Judicial, or Civil, Law) and Ceremonial. Where the divines speak of the expiration of the Judicial Law, Bahnsen insists they are still binding upon every magistrate today—even to the precise enforcement of the Old Testament penal code. Where the divines preserved the *general equity* of the Judicial Law insofar as those Old Testament principles enforced the Moral Law (i.e., the Decalogue), Bahnsen would have his reader believe that the divines were

---

[49] Bahnsen, *Theonomy*, 453-54.

actually equating *general equity* with the full, unwavering enforcement of the *particular equity* of every sanction in the Mosaic penal code. This writer cannot understand how such a brilliant and precise scholar as Dr. Bahnsen could have missed the plain meaning of the divines' statement in *WCF*.XIX.4. They insist that "sundry judicial laws" (obviously separate from the Moral Law) were given by God to Israel (not to the surrounding Gentile nations) under the Old Testament "as a body politic" (a distinct and unique nation), which laws "expired together with the state of that people, not obliging any other now" (even though Bahnsen insists that those very "expired" laws are now binding upon every civil magistrate of every nation), "further than the general equity thereof may require" (their view of *general equity* having been already addressed above and directly contrary to Bahnsen's insistence that every aspect of the Old Testament law code, with the (possible) exception of the Ceremonial Law, is to be applied by every nation, in every culture, at all times, and without any exception, alteration, or amendment). One can arrive at no other conclusion than that presented by Matthew Winzer: "Westminster and theonomy disagree to such an extent on the nature of the law that they must be considered two incompatible systems of thought."[50]

It is of particular interest to note that the Westminster divines defended their insistence that the Judicial Laws had expired by citing several passages of Scripture. Two will be noted here. From the Old Testament, they cite the dying prophecy of Jacob: "The sceptre shall not depart from Judah, nor a lawgiver from between his feet, until Shiloh come; and unto him *shall* the gathering of the people *be*" (Gen. 49:10). Even before the Mosaic legislation was delivered, it was clear that the specific institutions of the nation of Israel as a nation-state were temporary and not intended to be perpetual and universally binding. From the New Testament, they quote Peter: "Submit yourselves to every ordinance of man for the Lord's sake: whether it be to the king, as supreme; or unto governors, as unto them that are sent by him for the punishment of evildoers, and for the praise of them that do well" (1 Pet. 2:13-14). Together with the statement of

---

[50] Winzer, 72.

THE NECESSITY OF ABSOLUTES

Paul, "Let every soul be subject unto the higher powers. For there is no power but of God: the powers that be are ordained of God. Whosoever therefore resisteth the power, resisteth the ordinance of God: and they that resist shall receive to themselves damnation" (Romans 13:1-2), one can readily deduce, by good and necessary consequence, that the faithful Christian is to obey the laws of the civil magistrate, though the specific legislations of non-Jewish governments differ in wording and penalty from the Judicial Laws of the Mosaic economy. Both Peter and Paul were speaking to Christians under the authority of the Roman government. With the destruction of the Jewish state in 70 AD came the complete and final expiration of the Judicial Laws.

Whatever else may be said of Bahnsen's *theonomy*, this much should become immediately apparent: he departed largely from the sixteenth and seventeenth century divines by redefining the term "moral law" as including the Judicial Law. And yet a cursory reading of these same divines speaks against *theonomy* as Bahnsen presented it. He quotes, for example, with much approbation the writings of John Calvin. That same author, however, speaks directly against Bahnsen's view. A careful reading of the *Institutes* (Book IV) exposes the disparity between Calvin and Bahnsen. Calvin begins by asserting that the laws of all the nations are, indeed, bound to the principle of general equity. But Calvin's understanding of general equity aligns with that of the Westminster divines and directly contradicts Bahnsen. Rather than the insistence that every jot and tittle of the Old Testament Judicial Law is applicable to the nations today, Calvin insisted that *equity* equated to the application of the Moral Law, i.e., the Decalogue—not the Judicial Laws (unlike Bahnsen, as shown above, Calvin was a consistent adherent to the Tripartite division). It is within this context that Calvin insists:

> Whatever laws shall be framed to that rule [of equity to the Moral Law], directed to that goal, bound by that limit, there is no reason why we should disapprove of them, *howsoever they differ from the Jewish law, or among themselves.*
>
> For the statement of some, that the law of God given through Moses is dishonored when it is abrogated and new laws preferred to it, is utterly vain. For others are not preferred to it

THE NECESSITY OF ABSOLUTES

> when they are more approved, not by a simple comparison, but with regard to the condition of times, place, and nation; or when that law is abrogated which was never enacted for us. *For the Lord through the hand of Moses did not give that law to be proclaimed among all nations and to be in force everywhere;* but when he had taken the Jewish nation into his safekeeping, defense, and protection, he also willed to be a lawgiver especially to it; and—as became a wise lawgiver—he had special concern for it in making its laws.[51]

Yet there is another divine that Bahnsen appeals to as the sixteenth century champion for theonomy. He looks with great approbation at one of the Scottish Commissioners to the Westminster Assembly, none other than George Gillespie. A surface examination of one of his anonymous writings does, at first blush, *appear* to lend some support to *theonomy*. However, a closer examination will produce precisely the opposite conclusion. Gillespie was an unwavering proponent of the Tripartite division of the Law. He did, however, promote a clear examination and even implementation of some

---

[51] Calvin, *Institutes*, II:IV.20.16, 1504-5 (emphasis mine).

of the Judicial Laws. So, if one looks only at the surface of *Wholesome Severity*, one might conclude (as Dr. Bahnsen did) that Gillespie was an early theonomist. To understand Gillespie's arguments in that brilliant essay, one must understand the *context* in which it was written. Gillespie was *not* addressing all the nations in the world; instead he was addressing England specifically (being, at the time of writing, at the Westminster Assembly). England, it must be remembered, was both declaratively and practically a *Christian Magistracy*. Furthermore, the English (Long) Parliament, as lawful authority in that Kingdom, had bound itself with an oath before God to fulfill "The Solemn League and Covenant" (as, it might be added, would King Charles II do in both 1650 and 1651 — with crossed fingers behind his back). In part, this meant that they were sworn to "… endeavor … the reformation of religion in the kingdoms of England and Ireland … [and] in like manner … endeavour the extirpation of Popery, Prelacy, superstition, heresy, schism, profaneness, and whatsoever shall be found contrary to sound doctrine and the power

THE NECESSITY OF ABSOLUTES

of godliness."[52] His remarks then must be understood in that context of skillful articulation in presenting the humble advice of the Church to the Civil Magistrate which was already Christian and had sworn to seek further Reformation throughout the English Church and Kingdom.

Again, it must be remembered that, for a significant portion of this essay, Gillespie was quoting Johannes Piscator (1546-1625). But even Piscator cannot be relied upon to support Bahnsen's *theonomy* without exception. Piscator's thesis is as follows:

> ... the magistrate is obliged to those judicial laws which teach concerning matters which are immutable and universally applicable to all nations, but to those which teach concerning matters which are mutable and peculiar to the Jewish or Israelite nations for the times when those governments remained in existence.
>
> Things common to all nations (that is, which befall all) and are immutable with respect to

---

[52] "The Solemn League and Covenant," par. I and II, in *The Westminster Confession* (Edinburgh: Banner of Truth Trust, 2018), 528.

> their own nature and merits are moral offenses, that is, against the Decalogue, such as murder, adultery, theft, seduction from the true God, blasphemy, and smiting parents.
>
> Those laws which are mutable and which were peculiar to the Jews for that time are things such as the emancipation of Hebrew slaves in the seventh year, Levirate marriage, releasing of debts in the appointed year, marriage with a woman from one's own tribe, and if there were any other of the same sort. Likewise, these include ceremonial offenses such as touching a dead body, touching a woman suffering her menstrual cycle, and others of the same sort.[53]

It is with reference to this passage that Gillespie states, "to conclude therefore this point, though other judicial or forensical laws concerning punishments of sins against the moral law may, yea, must be allowed of in Christian Republics and Kingdoms; provided always, they are not contrary or contradictory to God's own judicial laws."[54] When it is remembered that Gillespie was

---

[53] Johannes Piscator, *Disputations on the Judicial Laws of Moses*, tr. Adam Johnathan Brink, ed. Joel McDurmon (Powder Springs, GA: American Vision Press, 2015), 4-5.

[54] George Gillespie, "Wholesome Severity Reconciled with Christian Liberty," in *The Anonymous Writings of George Gillespie*, ed. Chris Coldwell (Dallas: Naphtali Press, 2008), 58.

THE NECESSITY OF ABSOLUTES

defending the civil enforcement of the Moral Law by a Christian Nation that had sworn to reform further the established, national Church and the laws of that nation and basing his defense upon the Westminsterian view of Biblical Law, founded upon the Tripartite Division of that Law, it becomes clear that Gillespie cannot be relied upon as an advocate of Bahnsen's *theonomy*. Such an appeal could not— and would not—have been delivered to the Turks, the Italians, or to the United States of 150 years later! The appeal to those magistrates would have been precisely what it must be today: a call to the highest authority of the land to repent of their idolatry and blasphemy and to bow the knee before the only true King of kings and Lord of lords and to seek guidance from the Scripture in the framing of law.

Even so, every nation and its civil magistrate has the same obligation before God to enforce both tables of the Moral Law. The application of the principle of *general equity* would then mandate a careful examination and application of those Judicial Laws that clearly enforce obedience to the Decalogue. Professing this principle in order "to prevent arbitrary injustice," Piscator contends that "... the magistrate ought to be *the keeper of both tables of the law*."[55] But the professed Christian magistrate has the superadded duty of defending and protecting the true Christian religion against all who would raise up a contrary religion within his commonwealth. This is not, however, the same as Bahnsen's insistence that every minute part of the whole of the Judicial Laws remains in full effect in every nation on earth.

Without question, Dr. Bahnsen was a brilliant scholar and a sincere and zealous Christian. However, in considering his system of *theonomy* and the statements he made to defend that system, in all fairness and with all respect, Dr. Bahnsen found himself at odds with the *Westminster Confession of Faith* on this point. As Dewey Roberts observes: "Theonomy teaches that all of God's judicial laws have continuing validity in exhaustive detail. No Reformed confession has ever taken that view of the judicial laws."[56]

---

[55] Piscator, 7. [Emphasis Piscator's]

[56] Dewey Roberts, *Historic Christianity and the Federal Vision: A Theological Analysis and Practical Evaluation* (East Peoria, IL: Versa Press, Inc., 2016), 190.

THE NECESSITY OF ABSOLUTES

Westminsterian Position	*Theonomic* Position
Threefold division of the Law (Moral, Ceremonial, Judicial)	Twofold division of the Law (Moral/Judicial, Ceremonial
Moral Law forever binding; Ceremonial Laws abrogated; Judicial Laws expired, except insofar as the *general equity* thereof requires	Moral/Judicial Laws forever binding in exhaustive detail; Ceremonial Laws (largely) expired
Principle of *general equity* is the civil magistrate's responsibility to enforce against violations of the Moral Law, as evidenced by the Judicial case laws of OT Israel	Redefines *general equity* into a form of *particular equity*, in exhaustive detail, for every civil magistrate, with strict enforcement of the Moral and all Judicial Laws
Specific penalties imposed against violations of the Moral Law are mutable	Specific penalties against violations of the Moral/Judicial Laws are immutable

The Ceremonial Law Abrogated and Judicial Law Expired

*****

A consistent Confessional view of Biblical Law must include the application of the Tripartite division of the Law, with its insistence upon the perpetuity and universality of the Moral Law, the abrogation of the Ceremonial Law, and the expiration of the Judicial Law except insofar as the principle of *general equity* applies. The Westminster divines produced a Scriptural, wise, and careful document that presents Christ in all His glory and protects the Church against deviations from the clear teaching of the Word. To return the Law to its proper place in the Church and to defend against brilliant but erroneous doctrines, the Reformed pastor today must return to the clear teaching of the *Confession* on the Ceremonial and, especially, Judicial Laws. Only with this firm foundation—professed, adhered to, and taught—will the Church be an effective witness to lawless society and pagan magistrates to repent of their idolatry and to "serve the LORD with fear, and rejoice with trembling. Kiss the Son, lest He be angry, and ye perish *from* the way, when His wrath is kindled but a little" (Ps. 2:11-12).

Chapter Five

The Law for Today: Defense and Practice

> Now the God of peace, that brought again from the dead our Lord Jesus, that great shepherd of the sheep, through the blood of the everlasting covenant, make you perfect in every good work to do his will, working in you that which is well-pleasing in his sight, through Jesus Christ; to whom *be* glory for ever and ever. Amen.
> (Heb. 13:20-21)

The foregoing discussion of the Westminsterian view of Biblical Law has demonstrated that the assembled divines labored to produce a consistently Scriptural presentation of the Law of God, especially as it applies to the New Testament

THE NECESSITY OF ABSOLUTES

Church. Their efforts resulted in the most complete and judicious treatment of the Law ever produced, yet in full agreement with the orthodox divines who preceded them in the period of the First Reformation. Given the nature of the work and the skill with which the confessional statements were produced, one might conclude that there would be universal approbation of the system of thought emanating from the Assembly. Rather, as has been shown already in the case of *theonomy*, there are many who oppose the conclusions of the Assembly. Some, like the *theonomists*, are convinced that they are in agreement with the Westminster divines while maintaining contrary positions. Others are open enemies to the work of the Assembly and dismiss their labors as the efforts of "legalists." But, just as there are no new orthodox doctrines, there are also no new heresies. The Church has been plagued with those who hate God's Law throughout her history and, sadly, she is riddled with such opponents today. Reformed presbyters must renew their knowledge of and commitment to the Biblical presentation of the Law in the

The Law for Today: Defense and Practice

Westminster Standards in order to defend the honor of the Legislator and teach the sheep of Christ the right way of walking before Him regardless of what enticements are presented to them by detractors.

More than this, however, the Presbyterian and Reformed Church must instruct the saints in the Scriptural use and application of the Law. As has been shown, Christ is the end of the Law for justification but, by the indwelling of His Holy Spirit, the Lord Jesus points His people back to the Law as their Standard of obedience in order that His people may truly be conformed to His own perfect Image. Through Christ, the Moral Law is no longer a dreadful demonstration of condemnation but, for the saints, it has become the beautiful rule of obedience for those who have been justified by Christ and His righteousness as applied to them and received by faith alone. Being new creatures and filled with the awe and the deep thanksgiving of a people redeemed, the saints today look to the Moral Law as a gift from God set before them as His appointed means to show their love and thankfulness for the infinitely great gift of salvation and as that tool in the Hands of the Holy Spirit

THE NECESSITY OF ABSOLUTES

whereby they are being fitted to behold the Face of the Triune God forever in that eternal Sabbath soon to come.

The Law for Today: Defense and Practice

1. Antinomianism and New Covenant Theology

Having presented the Westminsterian position on the perpetual place of the Moral Law as the rule of obedience for the redeemed, it also must be reported that there have been many detractors and opponents to this view. The divines at Westminster did not produce anything "new," either in doctrine or practice, for Christ's Church. Rather, they advanced the Reformation in the truest sense of that term. They clarified and furthered the work of the First Reformation divines, addressing issues (such as ecclesiology and the doctrine of the Covenants) that were not fully developed during the turbulent years of the sixteenth century. More than anything else, the Assembly of Divines at Westminster should be viewed as the fullest and most mature expression of what the Scriptures principally teach, with respect to the whole Biblical Corpus, and in perfect harmony with the unwavering testimony of the orthodox Church since the days of Christ and His apostles. This is particularly true in regard to their statements concerning the nature of Biblical Law and the

THE NECESSITY OF ABSOLUTES

abiding and binding nature of the Moral Law, specifically. But, just as the early Church had to contend with Libertines, Nicolaitans, and Gnostics (even during the days of the apostles), so did the Westminster divines have to contend with various strains of antinomianism in their own day.

A brief survey of the sixteenth century conflict over the place of the Moral Law in the lives of the saints, especially at the Westminster Assembly, produces a rather confusing summary of various degrees of a particular type of antinomianism that could, perhaps, be best described as a misguided correction against Arminianism. The type of antinomianism with which the divines dealt was based upon exegetical errors in respect to the doctrine of the Covenants and that of Justification, combined with a resultant error in the understanding of the place of the Law in the lives of believers. In particular, the writings of John Eaton, Tobias Crisp, John Saltmarsh, and Robert Towne received scathing rebuttals from such notable

The Law for Today: Defense and Practice

divines as Burgess and Rutherford.[1] As Beeke and Jones observe, "A number of peculiarities separated the English Antinomians from Reformed orthodoxy, but the obvious dividing line centered on whether an individual rejected the moral law as a rule of life for believers."[2] Let there be no mistake that there were serious errors in the writings of these men, but let this fact be tempered with the realization that their intentions to defend the faith from the heresy of Arminianism led them simply too far in the opposite direction. Crisp, in particular, was so concerned to defend the Biblical principle of salvation by grace alone apart from works that he concluded: "I say, that faith, as it lays hold upon the righteousness of Christ, doth not bring this righteousness of Christ to the soul, but only declares the presence of it in the soul that was there, even before faith was."[3] Ridgeley speaks of

---

[1] See Burgess, xx; Samuel Rutherford, *A Survey of the Spirituall Antichrist* (London: Printed by J.D. & R.I. for Andrew Crooke, 1648), xx.

[2] Beeke and Jones, 324.

[3] Tobias Crisp, *Christ Alone Exalted, in the Perfection and Encouragement of the Saints, Notwithstanding Sins and Trials; Being the Complete Works of Tobias Crisp, D.D.*, vols. 1-2, ed. John Gill (London: Printed for John Bennett, 1832), 2:219.

THE NECESSITY OF ABSOLUTES

Crisp and others who held this view as men of upright moral character

> ... who nevertheless, do great disservice to the truth, and, it may be, give occasion to some to be licentious, by advancing unguarded expressions which will admit of a double construction, without condescending to explain some bold positions which they occasionally lay down. Thus, when they maintain eternal justification, without considering it as an immanent act in God, or as his secret determination not to impute sin to those who are given to Christ, but ascribe that to it which is only to be applied to justification, as it is the result of God's revealed will, in which respect it is said to be by faith; and when they encourage persons from hence to conclude that their state is safe, and maintain that it is the duty of every one to believe that he is thus justified; they certainly advance positions which have a tendency to lead some out of the way of truth and holiness, whether they design so or not.[4]

It was with this particular species of antinomianism that the Westminster divines were most closely associated and against which

---

[4] Ridgley, II:306.

The Law for Today: Defense and Practice

they formulated the precise wording of Paragraph 5 of Chapter XIX in the *Confession*.

A much more sinister, and prevalent, form of antinomianism has plagued the Church since the days of the apostles. That being the form associated with

> ... such as openly maintain that the moral law is not a rule of life in any sense; that good works are not to be insisted on as having any reference to salvation; that, therefore, if persons presume, as they, according to them, ought to do, that Christ died for them, and that they are justified before they had a being, they may live in the practice of the greatest immoralities, or give countenance to those who do so, without entertaining the least doubt of their salvation; and that it is a preposterous thing, for those who thus presumptuously conclude themselves to be justified, to confess themselves guilty of sin, since to do so would be to deny that they are in a justified state.[5]

This latter perversion of justification more closely fits the general tenor of what one most often associates with the term antinomianism. According to one definition, "Antinomianism is an approach to Christian ethics that rejects behavioral standards

---

[5] Ridgley, 305.

THE NECESSITY OF ABSOLUTES

of any sort as instances of a fixed and inflexible legalism. Antinomian practice maintains that Christians live without reference to norms as recipients of the free grace of God."[6]

For the purpose of the remainder of this discussion, however, the following definition is offered to cover the full scope of antinomianism as it has been developed and practiced as a substitute for the Biblical view of the Law. Generally speaking, antinomianism is any doctrine that presents a view of Biblical Law differing from that which is recorded in the Scriptures as rightly summarized in the Westminster Standards. More specifically, antinomianism comes in a variety of forms: (1) a system that states that the Moral Law has no binding influence on the lives of New Testament believers (such as that presented in the above definition of antinomianism); (2) a system that insists that the Moral Law—or the Moral Law *plus* the traditions of men—is the ground and basis for justification (e.g., legalism and

---

[6] Love L. Sechrest, "Antinomianism," in *Dictionary of Scripture and Ethics* (Grand Rapids: Baker Group, 2011), 72.

The Law for Today: Defense and Practice

Romanism); or (3) a system that attempts to replace the Moral Law as the rule of obedience for the saints with a new law, which neither Scripture nor sound reason produces (e.g., those insisting that the New Testament saints are under a "law of love" or "the law of Christ," specifically, proponents of New Covenant Theology). Each of these specific strains of antinomianism exemplifies a usurpation of the absolute authority of the Divine Lawgiver and Judge by replacing, adding to, or wholly rejecting God's Moral Law. Rightly understood, these particular views are dangerous and must not go unchallenged since the Moral Law of the Scriptures is a reflection of the holiness and righteousness of God Himself. To replace His Moral Law as the abiding and binding Standard for all men (to include the saints) is an affront to His authority and majesty.

The previous section addressed the errors of theonomy as an un-Biblical binding of the conscience. But, an up and coming doctrine, calling itself New Covenant Theology (hereafter NCT), needs to be considered in the light of the above definition. As will become readily apparent, unlike the antinomians during the time of the Westminster

THE NECESSITY OF ABSOLUTES

Assembly who had a jealousy for salvation by grace alone to the point of erring in the wrong direction, proponents of NCT have made a concerted and systematic effort to eliminate the Biblical standard of morality from the Church. NCT is a system that inculcates a middle way between Covenant Theology and Dispensationalism into a form of hybrid theology. As one of their apologists states,

> New Covenant Theology accommodates both continuity [Covenant Theology] *and* discontinuity [Dispensationalism]. It holds that the new covenant is connected to what went beforehand, but it is *new*. New Covenant Theology is held to by those in the 'believer's church' tradition: those churches that emphasize believer's baptism and believe that the new covenant community consists of believers. The label ... is relatively new, but it is not a new method of interpretation. Several early church fathers, the Anabaptists, as well as other significant figures in church history 'put the Bible together' in a similar way.[7]

---

[7] A. Blake White, *What is New Covenant Theology? An Introduction* (Frederick, MD: New Covenant Media, 2012), 2. [Emphasis White's]

The Law for Today: Defense and Practice

Blake White's candid admission that this movement follows in the tradition of the Anabaptists distinctly places its theological motif in the line of radical Protestantism outside of the Reformed heritage. It is therefore no surprise that there is very little agreement between NCT and the Westminsterian system.

From a Reformed Dispensational perspective, an honest assessment of the distinction between Covenant theology and NCT is described by Michael Vlach. Vlach observes: "The eight specific differences between New Covenant Theology (NCT) and Covenant Theology (CT) include NCT's denial of the Covenant of Redemption, its denial of the Covenant of Works, its denial of the Covenant of Grace, its affirmation of the unity of the Mosaic Law, its affirmation of the expiration of the Mosaic Law, its teaching that Christians are under only the Law of Christ, its rejection of infant baptism, and its affirmation that the church began at Pentecost."[8] Given this accurate description, it is a genuine wonder that the proponents of NCT claim to be

---

[8] Michael J. Vlach, "New Covenant Theology Compared with Covenantalism," in *The Master's Seminary Journal*, 18:1 (Fall 2007), 201.

THE NECESSITY OF ABSOLUTES

unifying two radically different theological systems (Covenant Theology and Dispensationalism) while denying the core tenets of Covenant Theology. Once the doctrine of the Covenants has been eliminated, there is no further agreement with Reformed Federal theology, and any further attempt to harmonize it with anything else is an exercise in futility. While each of the differences listed above requires rebuttal in defense of the Biblical teaching of the Covenants, of specific relevance is a consideration of the following three NCT differences: "affirmation of the unity of the Mosaic Law, its affirmation of the expiration of the Mosaic Law, its teaching that Christians are under only the Law of Christ." While there is nothing "new" about NCT, the antinomianism it professes is dishonoring to Christ and dangerous for Christians.

The first distinction of NCT with respect to Biblical Law is to treat the whole of the Mosaic Law as a single unit, which is now entirely abrogated for the New Testament Church. This exposes the erroneous view that there is a radical bifurcation between the two Testaments and

The Law for Today: Defense and Practice

intimates either that there are two Gods in Scripture (the vengeful, lawgiving God of the Old Testament vs. the loving, law-abolishing God of the New Testament) or that God redeems His elect by different means between the two Testaments. The fundamental problem with NCT is a Biblically inconsistent theology proper. Any system of thought that claims to be Christian but is founded upon the presupposition of a mutable God simply is not Biblical. Rather, the Triune God of Scripture has revealed Himself as immutable. "For I AM the LORD, I change not; therefore ye sons of Jacob are not consumed" (Mal. 3:6). Again, "Every good gift and every perfect gift is from above, and cometh down from the Father of lights, with Whom is no variableness, neither shadow of turning" (James 1:17). This is the first, and fundamental, error of NCT and every system that deviates from a consistent Biblical theology; namely, they hold to an un-Biblical view of God.

The idea that all the laws of the Mosaic economy must be taken as a single unit is both faulty and problematic. Just like *theonomy*, NCT arrives at faulty conclusions because of their rejection of the Tripartite Division of the Law. The Biblical view of

THE NECESSITY OF ABSOLUTES

the Tripartite Division of the Law as defended by the divines at Westminster has already been presented above.[9] Lumping all expressions of the Law of God into a single "Mosaic Law unit," as NCT does, eradicates the perpetuity of the Moral Law as delivered by the Voice of God from Mount Sinai and as written (twice) with His own Finger upon tables of stone. Tom Wells and Fred Zaspel are abundantly clear on this point and completely reject the Westminsterian Tripartite division. They state: "The popular hermeneutical attempt to divide Moses' law into so many parts and then interpret NT states of the passing of the law accordingly is simplistic ... To argue that not the moral (i.e., Decalogue) but only the civil and/or ceremonial aspects of Moses are passed ... misses Paul's point. It is Moses *en toto* that he says has gone (2 Cor. 3)."[10] But this erroneous view also denies the very application of the Moral Law as uniquely suited to the saints in the New Testament. While the two tables of

---

[9] See pp. 34ff.
[10] Tom Wells and Fred G. Zaspel, *New Covenant Theology: Description, Definition, Defense* (Frederick, MD: New Covenant Media, 2002), 150-51.

stone, upon which were written the "Ten Words," were placed in the Ark of the Covenant—lost long before the incarnation of Christ—the LORD promised that He would write the same Law on the hearts of His people when Messiah came. "But this *shall be* the covenant that I will make with the house of Israel; after those days, saith the LORD, I will put My law in their inward parts, and write it in their hearts; and will be their God, and they shall be My people" (Jer. 31:33).

John Owen, commenting on Hebrews 9:5, observes,

> This law, as unto the *substance* of it, was the only *law of creation*, the rule of the first covenant of works; for it contained the sum and substance of that obedience which is due unto God from all rational creatures made in his image, and nothing else. It was the whole of what God designed in our creation unto his own glory and our everlasting blessedness. What was in the tables of stone was nothing but a transcript of what was written in the heart of man originally; and which is returned thither

again by the grace of the new covenant, Jer. 31:33; 2 Cor. 3:3.[11]

Owen's observation bears careful consideration, especially when one seriously considers his astute realization that the giving of the Moral Law on the tables of stone was temporary *in order that*, with the fulfillment of Christ, the same Moral Law would be written by the Holy Spirit on the fleshy tables of the saints' hearts. Paul reveals the fulfillment of this prophecy when he says to the Corinthians: *"Forasmuch as ye are* manifestly declared to be the epistle of Christ ministered by us, written not with ink, but with the Spirit of the living God; **not in tables of stone, but in fleshy tables of the heart**," (2 Cor. 3:3).[12] The important point to remember is that it is the *same* Moral Law that is identified as the very Law of Christ, and it remains a perpetual and binding rule of obedience for the saints in the New Testament

---

[11] John Owen, *An Exposition of the Epistle to the Hebrews*, in *Works of John Owen*, vol. 23, ed. W. H. Goold (Edinburgh: Johnstone and Hunter, 1854), 215; Owen's emphasis.

[12] Emphasis added.

The Law for Today: Defense and Practice

Church. Herman Witsius fully concurs with Owen and reinforces this point when he states:

> The Most High God was not only pleased to publish his laws to Israel with a loud voice, in the presence of the most august assembly of the whole people, but he likewise engraved them with his own finger, on tables of stone, polished by himself for that purpose. ... This writing also **signified the purpose of God, to write the law on the hearts of his elect, according to the promise of the covenant of grace**, Jer. xxxi. 33. ... Nor is it for nothing that God himself would be the author of this writing, without making use of any man or angel. For this is the meaning of the Holy Spirit. ... To intimate, that **it is the work of God alone, to write the law on the heart**, which is what neither man himself, nor the ministers of God can do, but the Spirit of God alone. And thus believers are 'the epistle of Christ, written not with ink, but with the Spirit of the living God,' 2 Cor. iii. 3.[13]

The great distinction between the application of the Moral Law to the Church of the Old Testament and the New Testament is made abundantly

---

[13] Herman Witsius, *The Economy of the Covenants Between God and Man: Comprehending a Complete Body of Divinity*, vol. II, trans. William Crookshank (London: Printed for R. Baynes, 1822), 170-71; emphasis added.

THE NECESSITY OF ABSOLUTES

evident by the writer to the Hebrews. "For by one offering [Jesus Christ] hath perfected for ever them that are sanctified. *Whereof* the Holy Ghost also is a witness to us: for after that He had said before, 'This *is* the covenant that I will make with them after those days, saith the Lord, I will put my laws into their hearts, and in their minds will I write them; and their sins and iniquities will I remember no more'" (Heb. 10:14-17). Whereas faith was always required of the elect in every age, the clarity of saving faith is made even more evident with the completion of Christ's salvific cross work and the outpouring of the Holy Spirit upon all of the redeemed. No longer is God's perfect Moral Standard written on tables of stone and enshrined within the Ark of the Covenant behind the veil. Now, the same Divine Finger etches His perfect Standard upon the hearts and minds of His people as that template used of the Holy Spirit to conform His people to the very Image of Jesus Christ. Ross fully understands this Divine transaction upon the hearts and minds of the elect when, in reference to Jeremiah 31:33, he states,

The Law for Today: Defense and Practice

> [This promise] does not go beyond the expectations of the Mosaic Law itself (Deut. 30:14). According to the *Shema* (Deut. 6:6), God always intended that the law be internalized in the hearts of his people. Indeed, if they were to obey that command to love the LORD with all their heart and with all their soul, they needed his direct operation upon their hearts (Deut. 30:6).[14]

With the lifting of the shadows and forms of the ceremonies of the Church under age, the brightness of the reality of these very things are made evident with the saints demonstrating the principle of salt and light before a dark and lawless world to the praise, honor, and glory of His matchless Name.

Considering the relevance of the Moral Law for the Church since the coming of Christ, Fred Zaspel argues that, "… the Decalogue as such has been surpassed. It no longer stands as the believer's point of reference."[15] White, as the published advocate of NCT, has summarized the un-Biblical

---

[14] Ross, 203.

[15] Fred G. Zaspel, *The New Covenant and New Covenant Theology: Two Lectures Presented at the 2008 John Bunyan Conference, Lewisburg, PA* (Frederick, MD: New Covenant Media, 2011), 37.

THE NECESSITY OF ABSOLUTES

view of the Moral Law that is a hallmark of this erroneous position. He states,

> ... we are not under the Mosaic law, but that doesn't mean we are now lawless ... the law of Christ is something distinct from the law of Moses. ... *The law of Christ can be defined as those prescriptive principles drawn from the example and teaching of Jesus and his apostles (the central demand being love), which are meant to be worked out in specific situations by the guiding influence and empowerment of the Holy Spirit.*[16]

In light of the consistent witness of Scripture with respect to the perpetuity of the Moral Law, especially to the saints upon whose hearts the Holy Spirit engraves His good Law, such a bold profession rejecting this same Law propagates a moral relativism more suited to the fallen world than to anyone professing Christ. The proponents of this aberrant doctrine should well heed the words of the Lord Jesus Christ:

---

[16] White, 31, 33, 38; White's emphasis. The last part of this quotation is emphasized by White. White states that this last statement is a modified definition taken from Douglas J. Moo and Richard Longenecker (see note 16, p. 59).

The Law for Today: Defense and Practice

> Think not that I am come to destroy the law, or the prophets: I am not come to destroy, but to fulfil. For verily I say unto you, till heaven and earth pass, one jot or one tittle shall in no wise pass from the law, till all be fulfilled. Whosoever therefore shall break one of these least commandments, and shall teach men so, shall be called the least in the kingdom of heaven ... (Matt. 5:17-19a).

Paul, having demonstrated that justification is purely by the grace of God apart from the works of the Law (by which no man can be justified), immediately turns to a defense of the Moral Law as the abiding and binding Standard of God on the saints when he concludes, "Do we then make void the law through faith? God forbid: yea, we establish the law" (Rom. 3:31). John speaks clearly against this view when he states,

> And hereby we do know that we know Him, if we keep His commandments. He that saith, I know Him, and keepeth not His commandments, is a liar, and the truth is not in him. But whoso keepeth His Word, in him verily is the love of God perfected: hereby know we that we are in Him. He that saith he abideth in Him ought himself also so to walk, even as He walked (1 John 2:3-6).

THE NECESSITY OF ABSOLUTES

Christ produced no new Moral Law during His ministry, nor did His apostles replace the Moral Law. Since the Moral Law as given by Christ from Sinai to Israel was the reflection of His own immutable holiness, the Law itself could never change. NCT, therefore, rejects the clear and consistent teaching of Scripture and produces an abhorrent antinomianism, attempting to validate it by an undefined and nonexistent "law of Christ" that is hostile to Christ and His pure Gospel.

The Law for Today: Defense and Practice

Westminsterian Position	New Covenant Theology Position
OT Laws divided between Moral Law, Ceremonial Law, and Judicial Law	No Tripartite Division
Moral Law universally and perpetually binding; Ceremonial Law abrogated; Judicial Laws expired, except insofar as the principle of *general equity* applies	All Old Testament Laws abolished, including the Moral Law
One Church in two administrations of the Covenant of Grace	Radical Bifurcation between OT Israel and NT Church
Christians still obligated to the Moral Law as their Rule of Obedience, but never as a Covenant of Works	Decalogue abolished in Christ; instead Christians are governed by the "law of love"

2. The Biblical Practice of the Law: Good Works

The consideration of Biblical Law is no mere academic exercise. It is of the utmost importance. As has been demonstrated above, the right understanding of Biblical Law as presented by the Westminster divines avoids the errors of legalism and antinomianism. More than that, however, the Moral Law remains a vital part of the Christian life. The Holy Spirit, that "sanctifying Spirit" (1 Cor. 6:11), uses the Moral Law as a precise surgical instrument to excise the remaining corruptions from His people more and more (Phil. 1:9). Good works, therefore, are enjoined upon the redeemed as demonstrations of that work of the Holy Spirit within them. These good works, however, are not left to the determination and creativity of men to determine. They are defined by the Moral Law itself. As the divines observe, "Good works are only such as God has commanded in his holy word, and not such as, without the warrant thereof, are devised by men out of blind zeal, or

The Law for Today: Defense and Practice

upon any pretense of good intention."[17] These good works are directed by the Holy Spirit Himself, recorded in His Word, and not left to the saints merely to "feel" after. Shaw observes: "The law of God is the sole rule of man's obedience, and no action, how specious soever in appearance, can be properly called good, unless required by the supreme legislator. ... Those actions which have no warrant from the word of God, but are devised by men, out of blind zeal, cannot be reckoned good works."[18] As God is the One Who has revealed Himself in the propositions of Scripture, so has He presented and preserved every ethical necessity for the daily walk of His saints as they are being fitted, by His own Hand, for heaven. The divines continue:

> These good works, done in obedience to God's commandments, are the fruits and evidences of a true and lively faith: and by them believers manifest their thankfulness, strengthen their assurance, edify their brethren, adorn the profession of the gospel, stop the mouths of adversaries, and glorify God, whose workmanship they are, created in Christ Jesus

---

[17] *WCF*, XVI.i, 78.
[18] Shaw, 162.

THE NECESSITY OF ABSOLUTES

> thereunto; that, having their fruit unto holiness, they may have the end, eternal life. Their ability to do good works is not at all of themselves, but wholly from the Spirit of Christ.[19]

The divines understood from Scripture that a "good work" is something that is directed by God in His Word but can only be performed by those who have been redeemed. "And hereby we do know that we know Him, if we keep His commandments. He that saith, I know Him, and keepeth not His commandments, is a liar, and the truth is not in him. But whoso keepeth His word, in him verily is the love of God perfected: hereby know we that we are in Him. He that saith he abideth in Him ought himself also so to walk, even as He walked" (1 John 2:3-6). The Holy Spirit so works in the hearts of the saints that they are conformed to the Image of Christ in practice, because Christ Himself perfectly kept the whole of the Moral Law. There is no replacement, no alternative, to the Moral Law in the New Testament Scriptures. Simply put, there

---

[19] *WCF*, XVI.2 & 3, 78-80.

The Law for Today: Defense and Practice

is no possibility of knowing what is good and evil, righteous and sinful, apart from the absolute Standard of God's Moral Law. And, in this regard, particular notice should be taken of the fact that, while the actual writing surface has changed from stone tablets to the human heart, the Writer and the words themselves are exactly the same as the Ten Words delivered on Sinai.

Only a heart regenerated and indwelt by the Holy Spirit has been equipped to do those works that are pleasing to God. Even if an act outwardly conforms to the Moral Law, if the heart from which the work proceeds is at enmity against God (unregenerated), then the work itself is an abomination to the majesty and holiness of God. In order for a work to be accounted as good by God, it first must be done from a regenerated heart that has complete faith in the veracity of the Word of God as the alone Standard for faith and practice. Further, it must be accepted—not for anything naturally within the man himself, but—in the Person and work of Christ the Mediator, out of obedience to, and with full reliance upon, the Holy Spirit within the heart. As the apostle states, "Wherefore, my beloved, as ye have always

THE NECESSITY OF ABSOLUTES

obeyed, not as in my presence only, but now much more in my absence, work out your own salvation with fear and trembling. For it is God which worketh in you both to will and to do of *His* good pleasure" (Phil. 2:12-13). Furthermore, the work itself is not truly good unless the motive that generates it is for no less reason than for the glory of God. Samuel Rutherford defends this position when he observes: "We judge Repentance, and Mortification of the old man, to be a personal turning from sin, and the abating of the lusts of the old *Adam*, a deadening of the heart to the pleasures of sin, a growing in heavenly disposition, *to rise with Christ, and seek the things that are above;* flowing from the death and resurrection of Christ, apprehended by faith." [20] John Colquhoun writes:

> Nothing is gospel obedience but obedience to the law in the hand of Christ as a rule of duty. The gospel is no sooner believed than obedience is yielded, both to the law as a covenant and to the law as a rule. The righteousness of Christ in the hand of faith is

---

[20] Rutherford, *Survey*, 40-41.

The Law for Today: Defense and Practice

> obedience to it in the former view, and personal holiness of heart and life to it in the latter.[21]

Salvation in Christ relieves His people from the *curse* of the Moral Law but does not free them from their obligation to obey it. Instead, it is precisely *because* of a man's salvation by the free grace of God, and the following regenerated heart and indwelling of the Holy Spirit, that he is inclined to obedience to the Moral Law as a rule of morality and expression of gratitude. Again, Colquhoun observes:

> If the law commands believers, the grace of the gospel teaches them to love, and to practice universal holiness (Titus 2:11-12). What the law as a rule of life binds them to perform, the grace of the gospel constrains and enables them to do (Leviticus 20:8; 2 Corinthians 5:14-15). That which the precept of the law requires as a duty, the promise of the gospel affords and effects as a privilege (Ezekiel 18:31 and 36:26-27). Whatever holds the place of duty in the law occupies the place of privilege in the gospel.[22]

---

[21] John Colquhoun, *A Treatise on the Law and the Gospel*, ed. Don Kistler (Grand Rapids: Soli Deo Gloria Publications, 2009/1816), 167.

[22] Colquhoun, 167.

THE NECESSITY OF ABSOLUTES

3. The Biblical Practice of the Law: Biblical Ethics

There is a universal recognition that bad things are happening in current events. Despite the optimistic voices of secular philosophy, no solution has been found for the causes of these events from Washington, Hollywood, the educational system, or science/pseudo-science. Sadly, the American church seems utterly incapable of offering any Biblical solution. What Christian voices are heard are generally combined with the voices of the ungodly who see the cure for evil in the culture's political, social, economic, or educational systems. Popular Christian teaching, leaving her Scriptural foundation, has promoted Arminianism, the "social gospel," liberalism, modernism, and humanism (although different terms with variations in nuance, all of these nomenclatures represent natural religion as opposed to Biblical and spiritual theology). Rather than identifying *sin* as the cause of evil, the church, in general, has compromised with false ideologies, turning away from the Holy

The Law for Today: Defense and Practice

Scriptures as the alone Source of Truth. To be blunt, the American church has become ineffective for society because she has abandoned the Word of God, and its ethic.

For the true Church to be effective in her service to society, she must first return to her central purpose of glorifying God by returning to the Scripture as the *alone* Standard of faith and practice by preaching the pure Gospel of Jesus Christ and convicting the world of sin, righteousness, and judgment. Since it is impossible to hold to two opposite and contrary presuppositional systems simultaneously, the Church must abandon all worldly ideologies and cease all compromise with them. What is required is the complete return to consistent, confessional, Biblical Christianity, revealed in the propositions of Scripture and systematized by the historic, Reformed, Westminsterian system of theology, as a theological system that presents a Biblically consistent, God-glorifying, and effective world and life view.

Allen Verhey states, "Ethics may be defined as disciplined reflection concerning moral conduct

THE NECESSITY OF ABSOLUTES

and character."[23] Put another way, "The field of ethics (or moral philosophy) involves systematizing, defending, and recommending concepts of right and wrong behavior."[24] Ethics deals not only with behavior, but also considers the underlying motivations behind behavior. While there are many pagan philosophical models for ethics, there is only one Biblical model for ethics. The goal of this monograph is to identify Biblical ethics as a part of a consistent Biblical system. While a few broad generalizations will be made concerning pagan ethical ideals, it should be remembered that all such unbiblical systems are irrelevant in the light of the Scriptures. The Reformed Church today must be ready to engage those systems in order to demonstrate their ultimate futility and point the unbelieving ethicist to the only possible source of right moral behavior in the Word of God, rather than to reach some form of

---

[23] Allen Verhey, "Ethics in Scripture," in *Dictionary of Scripture and Ethics* (Grand Rapids: Baker, 2011), 5.

[24] "Ethics," in *Internet Encyclopedia of Philosophy*, xx, accessed June 15, 2018, http://www.iep.utm.edu/ethics/.

The Law for Today: Defense and Practice

compromise or "agree to disagree" mentality. Professor John Murray calls attention to this when he defines Biblical ethics as

> ... that manner of life which is consonant with, and demanded by, the biblical revelation. Our attention must be focused upon divine demand, not upon human achievement; upon the revelation of God's will for man, not upon human behaviour. In the biblical ethic we are concerned with the norms, or canons, or standards of behaviour which are enunciated in the Bible for the creation, direction, and regulation of thought, life, and behaviour consonant with the will of God.[25]

Gordon H. Clark has identified the essential characteristics that must be considered when identifying and practicing Biblical ethics. His entire system of thought was founded upon the basic axiom that "the Bible alone is the Word of God."[26] W. Gary Crampton summarizes Clark's system:

> ... Gordon H. Clark did not begin his systematic approach to theology and

---

[25] John Murray, *Principles of Conduct*, 14.
[26] John W. Robbins, "An Introduction to Gordon H. Clark," in *The Trinity Review*, July-August 1993 (Unicoi, TN: Trinity Foundation, 2003), 3.

THE NECESSITY OF ABSOLUTES

philosophy with a discussion of whether or how we know there is a god, and then seek to prove that this is the God of Scripture. His starting point was propositional revelation ... from the creator God, who is truth itself.

Every philosophical system must have its starting point, which is axiomatic, that is, it cannot be proved. It is indemonstrable (if it were provable or demonstrable, then it would not be a starting point).

According to Dr. Clark, the Christian philosophical system starts with the Word of God. This is the axiom: The Bible alone is the Word of God. The Bible has a systematic monopoly on truth. Dr. Clark himself referred to this system as dogmatism, Biblical presuppositionalism, and Christian rationalism.[27]

An individual's ethic is not created in a vacuum. Instead, it grows out of an overarching philosophy which is itself based upon one or more fundamental presuppositions. A philosophical system stands or falls based on the validity of those underlying presuppositions. A presupposition cannot be proven, per se. It is the axiom that sets

---

[27] W. Gary Crampton, *The Scripturalism of Gordon H. Clark* (Unicoi, TN: The Trinity Foundation, 1999), 26-27.

The Law for Today: Defense and Practice

the foundation of an entire system of thought. However, if a presupposition can be *disproven*, the entire system constructed upon it crumbles and the system is necessarily demonstrated to be false. Obviously, if a given philosophical system is proven false because its fundamental presupposition has been demonstrated to be faulty (most notably by the Law of Contradiction), every conclusion based upon the premise of that system collapses also. Since one's ethics is only a branch that stems from a root philosophy, once the root philosophy is disproven as irrational, all of its branches necessarily fall. Every pagan system of philosophy can be proven false because they are, without exception, based upon faulty presuppositions. All pagan ethics, therefore, stemming from root philosophies that are irrational, must necessarily be false. When Christians, therefore, attempt to amalgamate their "Christian-ness" with pagan philosophical systems, they do not add stability to the pagan system of thought, rather, they weaken or destroy the Christian foundation. One's ethics ought not to be based on a compromise with one or more pagan systems of thought.

THE NECESSITY OF ABSOLUTES

Since the Bible is the Word of God, the Church must give it heed. For the subject at hand, it behooves Christians to understand what Scripture reveals concerning ethics, both theoretically and in the details. The Bible presents the Triune God as the Creator of the entire universe and the Governor of His creation. Everything that exists was made by God and for God, and it is all under God's control.[28] But in addition to being the Creator and the Governor, God is also absolute Legislator and Judge. God alone, therefore, can determine and reveal what is good or evil, right or wrong, just or unjust. In other words, to look for the definition of morality in the creature is an absurdity since the very definition of morality can only be determined by the actual Creator, Who is also Legislator and Judge. He it is that defines what is good, upright, and holy; for He Himself is the foundation of meaning for those concepts.

Since the whole of the Bible is immediately inspired by God, has been preserved entirely by His Divine providence, and was wholly

---

[28] See Romans 11:33-36 and Acts 17:28.

committed in written propositions by Him so that man can understand His will, it is of the utmost importance that one's entire foundation of thought be derived from the Scriptures alone. The modern American Church has, in general, abandoned the Reformation principle of *Sola Scriptura* for a "The Bible *and-*" type of system. The resulting attempt to harmonize Christianity with paganism inevitably results in irrationalism. This principle is clearly articulated by Paul to the Corinthian Christians where he states, by the inspiration of the Holy Spirit,

> But the natural man receiveth not the things of the Spirit of God: for they are foolishness unto him: neither can he know *them*, because they are spiritually discerned. But he that is spiritual judgeth all things, yet he himself is judged of no man. For who hath known the mind of the Lord, that he may instruct him? But we have the mind of Christ. (1 Cor. 2:14-16).

The Church is commanded to not be "unequally yoked" with unbelievers, whether in marriage, philosophy, or ethics. Presuppositionally incompatible systems simply cannot be reconciled or harmonized together. The Scriptures teach that

THE NECESSITY OF ABSOLUTES

the world's systems of thought are diametrically opposed to the Lord God and His Word. For, "love not the world, neither the things *that are* in the world. If any man love the world, the love of the Father is not in him. For all that *is* in the world, the lust of the flesh, and the lust of the eyes, and the pride of life, is not of the Father, but is of the world. And the world passeth away, and the lust thereof: but he that doeth the will of God abideth for ever" (1 John 2:15-17).

The Scriptures, and the Scriptures alone, are the very Word of God. Since this is the case, the consistent Christian will "… bring into captivity every thought to the obedience of Christ" (2 Cor. 10:5). The Scriptures present the Triune God as Creator and Governor, and *also* as Legislator and Judge. "For the LORD *is* our judge, the LORD *is* our lawgiver, the LORD *is* our king; he will save us" (Is. 33:22). Since God is the Legislator and Judge, His Law is the only standard for behavior; and obedience to Him as the Supreme Good must be the only motivation for that obedience. Here, in a nutshell, is Biblical ethics: God is God; He has given to man His Standard in His Word, therefore all human behavior must be

The Law for Today: Defense and Practice

submissive and obedient to God's revealed will and all for the purpose of glorifying God alone as the Supreme Good in Himself. But there is a serious problem with this statement. Simply put, it requires of man that which man simply cannot do. Every non-Christian system of ethics (based upon secular philosophies established upon disproven and irrational presuppositions) looks to man—whether individually or collectively—as his own arbiter of good and evil, right and wrong, because in these systems mankind is his own judge and his lack of objectivity renders his judgments tilted toward his perpetual acquittal. In other words, unregenerate systems look to man, rather than man's Creator, for definitions of right and wrong and for the ability to act morally toward his fellow man. The absurdity of this concept is self-evident, and Paul demonstrates this when he states, "For to be carnally minded is death; but to be spiritually minded is life and peace. Because the carnal mind is enmity against God: for it is not subject to the Law of God, neither indeed can be" (Rom. 8:6-7). If autonomous man is the standard of man's conduct, then there would ultimately be 7+ billion standards of morality, and no single man or group of men

THE NECESSITY OF ABSOLUTES

could be justified in imposing their morality upon anyone else. The result is moral anarchy, universal irrationalism, and perpetual self-justification in evil. As in the antediluvian days of Noah, so it is today: "And GOD saw that the wickedness of man *was* great in the earth, and *that* every imagination of the thoughts of his heart *was* only evil continually" (Gen. 6:5). When the Church compromises with worldly systems of thought, the result is moral anarchy within the Church rather than an improvement in the world as a whole. This, too, has been seen in the Church before: "In those days *there was* no king in Israel: every man did *that which was* right in his own eyes" (Judges 21:25).

This is the very reason that non-Christian systems of ethics cannot produce lasting positive results. They reject the Bible as the holy, inspired, and infallible Word of God. Therefore, they reject the authority of the Triune God Who is the Creator, Governor, Legislator, and Judge. They place their hopes in man as his own moral governor with the false notion that man is an inherently *good* being and therefore capable of governing himself ethically. Fundamentally, all

The Law for Today: Defense and Practice

human systems of ethics fail to take into account that there already is an absolute Standard by which all men shall be judged. There can be no morality—and therefore no ethics—apart from Divine Revelation. For, "although the light of nature, and the works of creation and providence, do so far manifest the goodness, wisdom, and power of God, as to leave men inexcusable; yet they are not sufficient to give that knowledge of God, and of His will, which is necessary unto salvation."[29] But God has revealed Himself and His Standard, and He has done so in the perspicuous and rational propositions of the Holy Scriptures.

> The duty which God requireth of man, is obedience to His revealed will. ... The moral law is the declaration of the will of God to mankind, directing and binding *every one* to personal, perfect, and perpetual conformity and obedience thereunto, in the frame and disposition of the whole man, soul and body, and in performance of all those duties of holiness and righteousness which he oweth to God and man: promising life upon the fulfilling, and threatening death upon the breach of it.[30]

---

[29] WCF, I.i, 3.
[30] *WLC*, Q.91 & Q.93, 254-55.

THE NECESSITY OF ABSOLUTES

This leads directly to the final point that invalidates all unbelieving systems of ethics; namely, none of these systems recognize, address, or take into account the problem of *sin*. And, "Sin is any want of conformity unto, or transgression of, the law of God."[31]

To summarize Clark's position on Biblical ethics, the following points should be considered. Biblical ethics is founded upon Biblical morality which is dependent upon the Biblical revelation, i.e., the Bible. The Bible is absolutely authoritative because it was breathed-out by God Himself, and He has revealed Himself as the absolute Creator, Governor, Lawgiver, and Judge in the direct propositions of Scripture. Ethics requires definite information as to what constitutes right and wrong, good and evil; and any such information can only be revealed by a living, communicating God. Unbiblical ethical systems, founded upon irrational philosophies, are devised by unbelieving people who insist that

---

[31] *WSC*, Q.5, 426.

The Law for Today: Defense and Practice

the principles of ethics must be constantly changing. But, as Clark observes, "The notion of a changing morality presupposes a belief in a changing god. ... If, on the other hand, men accept the Ten Commandments as permanent obligations, they must also accept the Biblical concept of an immutable God. Biblical morality and Biblical theology are inseparable."[32] But, even more important for a consistently Biblical ethic is the Bible's teaching that the God of the Scriptures is absolutely Sovereign, which is central to the discussion of ethics. The question arises, "How does one define and identify what is good or evil?" The answer, of course, is that God has revealed what is good and right vs. what is evil and wrong. But the LORD God does not do this because He has previously identified something as good or evil; as if the Law were something external to (and therefore necessarily superior to) God. God does not will something to be good because it is independently good. On the contrary, God has revealed what is good simply because God has

---

[32] Gordon H. Clark, *Essays in Ethics and Politics*, ed. John W. Robbins (Unicoi, TN: Trinity Foundation, 1992), 91-92.

willed it to be good. Calvin, paraphrasing Augustine, states, "wrong is done to God when a higher cause of things than his will is demanded."[33] Clark similarly expounds upon his predecessor:

> The sovereignty of God is the key to the basic problem of ethics. Why is anything good, right, or obligatory? Neither utilitarianism, nor pragmatism, nor emotionalism can give a rational answer. Calvin has given the answer in very precise language: 'The will of God is the highest rule of justice: so that what He wills must be considered just, for this very reason, because He wills it.' God establishes moral norms by sovereign decree.[34]

The identification of good and evil and the obligation for man's obedience to the Moral Law then is inseparably tied to the holy nature of God Himself.

Biblical Ethics is a branch of a consistently Biblical Theology founded upon an entire Biblical System exclusively rooted in the fundamental presupposition that the Bible alone

---

[33] Calvin, *Institutes*, I:I.14.1, 161.
[34] Clark, *Essays in Ethics and Politics*, 92-93.

The Law for Today: Defense and Practice

is the written Word of God. The Bible is the *very* Word of God, presented in perspicuous and rational propositions that are understandable by man as the creature made in the *Imago Dei*. Though marred by sin, man remains a creature capable of understanding those Biblical propositions. One of the clearest summaries in Scripture that reveals God's Standard for ethics is the Ten Commandments. God has shown humanity what He decrees as good and evil, right and wrong, toward Himself and our fellow man. Human beings cannot reason uprightly apart from saving faith, and they also cannot act morally apart from Divine revelation. The Moral Law of God is that Standard and continues to be eminently useful for all men in general as the foundation of civil order, for the unregenerate as the Teacher of what is right and wrong and the demonstration of what every sin deserves, and for the regenerate as the rule of obedience exercised from a heart filled with love and thanksgiving. It is the Church's responsibility to maintain and teach God's Moral Standard by instruction and example. By setting forth the Moral Law of God as the mirror before the unregenerate, the Church presents *the* valid system of ethics to the

THE NECESSITY OF ABSOLUTES

watching world. This is how the Church glorifies God before men by demonstrating the horror of man's fallen estate along with the genuine Good News that there is salvation in Christ alone through Faith alone by Grace alone according to Scripture alone and all to the Glory of God alone.

The Law for Today: Defense and Practice

*****

Despite what detractors—both from within and without the Church—may say, God's Standard of righteousness has not changed. The Moral Law remains the binding and abiding rule of obedience for all men. To the reprobate, the Moral Law is that Standard by which they are condemned as violators of the Covenant of Works, under which they are still bound. To the saints, however, the curse of the Covenant of Works has been removed since the price of its violation was paid in full for them by Christ. But the Moral Law is not annulled by the salvation of the elect. It remains their rule of obedience, proceeding from hearts that have been made new through regeneration by the Holy Spirit. Through His indwelling, sanctifying work, the Holy Spirit conforms Christians to the Image of Christ. While justification is the act of God's free grace *apart* from works, sanctification is an essential part of salvation that necessarily *includes* good works. As James stated, "Faith, if it hath not works, is dead, being alone. Yea, a man may say, thou hast faith, and I have works: shew me thy faith without thy works, and I will shew thee my faith by my works" (James 2:17-18). It is absolutely correct to

THE NECESSITY OF ABSOLUTES

say that *justification* is by faith alone apart from works. It is wrong, however, to state that *salvation* is by faith apart from works. Clark recognized this fully when he wrote, "… we are not saved without works … a true faith produces good works … faith is the root and works are the fruit. We cannot be saved without them."[35] Works are good because God has declared them to be good by commanding them. But works are only truly good if they are according to His Moral Law and accepted by God in Christ.

---

[35] Clark, *What do Presbyterians Believe?*, 163.

Conclusion

Far too often, the modern Western Church scene resembles the pagan society around it. The emphasis in many Churches is upon entertainment and the feelings of congregants. Sadly, even many professing Reformed and Confessional Churches have been stained by this practice. The Word of God is replaced with variations of pop psychology and worldly philosophy. The more the Church resembles society, the more society devolves into even grosser idolatry. The essential ingredients required to arrest this downward spiral are revival in the hearts of God's people, the Reformation of Christ's Church, and an Awakening in society by the outpouring of the Holy Spirit. The first step toward this recovery is a return to the Reformation principle of *sola Scriptura*. It is incumbent upon

THE NECESSITY OF ABSOLUTES

faithful ministers of Christ boldly, consistently, and uncompromisingly to preach the whole counsel of God, including the Biblical teaching of the Law of God. While unpopular in most Christian circles, the Law of God is an irreplaceable part of Scripture and therefore the Christian life.

The Westminster divines did not shy away from presenting their view of Biblical Law in the Standards they produced. This treatise has presented the Westminsterian view of Biblical Law, contending that it is the best human summary of what the Scriptures teach on the subject. The divines did not produce any novel approach to the Law but presented the consensus view of the subject from the purest thought of every age of the Church. Two essential stones in the foundation of this view are the primacy and authority of the inerrant, infallible, inspired Word of God and the Biblically presented Tripartite division of the Old Testament Law. As has been demonstrated, heterodox and aberrant views of Biblical Law rest upon a faulty theology and a rejection of the Tripartite division.

Conclusion

While the Ceremonial Law has been abrogated in Christ and the Judicial Law has expired with the destruction of Israel as a distinct theocracy, the Moral Law remains the abiding and binding Standard for all human beings. To those outside of Christ, the Moral Law remains a Covenant of Works before which they stand eternally condemned. To the saints, the Moral Law no longer holds the curse of the Covenant of Works over them since Christ has fully satisfied the wrath of God on behalf of His elect. Yet, the Moral Law remains their rule of life and obedience, in gratitude to Christ Who gave Himself as the perfect Sacrifice and Satisfaction for their sins. In the hands of the Holy Spirit, this same Moral Law is now a precision surgical instrument skillfully removing the remnants of corruption from their natures and fitting them for an eternity in the presence of the thrice-holy God. For the saints, then, the Moral Law is an easy yoke and a light burden that has become the delight and rejoicing of their lives. Its application to every facet of life conforms the saints more and more to the Image of Christ Who Himself perfectly kept every jot and tittle of the Law.

THE NECESSITY OF ABSOLUTES

At its heart, Biblical Law-keeping honors God, glorifies Him before men, and presents a living testimony to the great work of salvation wrought by Him upon His elect. The faithful Christian is a walking, talking, and living reflection of God's holy Law before a world of darkness and sin. This salt and light principle is carried out by that key of Godly obedience. Christ's people must be reminded by faithful ministers that they have a job to do. If the true Biblical religion were really only about "getting saved," then every Christian would immediately die upon his conversion. Except in rare cases (e.g., the thief on the cross) this simply does not happen. There is much to be done internally by progressive sanctification and much to be done outwardly in the faithful life of a child of God before a watching world.

The modern Reformed Presbyterian Church has all the tools required to present Christ as the only Savior of sinners. The faithful preaching of the Law of God demonstrates the holiness and justice of God and the fearful estate in which sinful man stands condemned before Him as the righteous Judge. But it also demonstrates the infinite mercy of Christ in His fulfilling of that Law and suffering

Conclusion

the wrath of God owed to man for violation of that Law. The Law in the Hands of the Holy Spirit awakens the hearts of the elect to their eternal need of Christ and His salvific cross work, and it becomes a beautiful rule of life and obedience to the saints whereby they are conformed more and more to the Image of Christ. Dying to themselves more and more each day, the saints live more and more to Christ and His righteousness to the praise, honor, and glory of the matchless Name of the Triune God. This is Biblical holiness and righteousness that needs to be preached in the Church today. May the Lord be pleased to raise up faithful ministers in His Church to once again preach the sound Biblical doctrine of His Law as summarized by the Godly divines at the Westminster Assembly.

Bibliography

Primary Sources

À Brakel, Wilhelmus. *The Christian's Reasonable Service in which Divine Truths concerning the Covenant of Grace are Expounded, Defended against Opposing Parties, and their Practice Advocated as well as The Administration of this Covenant in the Old and New Testaments*. 4 vols. Edited by Joel R. Beeke. Translated by Bartel Elshout. Grand Rapids: Reformation Heritage Books, 1994.

Annotations Upon all the Books of the Old and New Testament: This Third, above the First and Second, Edition so enlarged, As they make an entire Commentary on the Sacred Scripture: The like never before published in English: Wherein The Text *is Explained,* Doubts *Resolved,* Scriptures *Parallel'd, and* Various Readings *observed; By the Labour of certain* Learned Divines *thereunto appointed, and therein employed, As is expressed in the Preface.* London: Evan Tyler, 1657.

Ball, John. *A Treatise of the Covenant of Grace wherein the Graduall Breakings out of Gospel Grace from Adam to Christ Are Clearly Discovered, the Differences betwixt the Old and New Testament Are Laid Open, Divers Errours of Arminians and Others Are Confuted, the Nature of Uprightnesse, and the Way of Christ in Bringing the Soul into Communion with Himself: Together with many other Points, both doctrinally and practically profitable, are solidly handled.* London: Simeon Ash, 1645.

Beza, Theodore. *A Clear and Simple Treatise on the Lord's Supper: In Which the Published Slanders of Joachim Westphal Are Finally Refuted.* Grand Rapids: Reformation Heritage Books, 2016.

Biblia Hebraica Stuttgartensia: With Werkgroep Informatica, Vrije Universiteit Morphology; Bible. O.T. Hebrew. Werkgroep Informatica, Vrije Universiteit. Bellingham, WA: Logos Bible Software, 2006.

Bibliography

Bolton, Samuel. *The True Bounds of Christian Freedom*. Edinburgh: The Banner of Truth Trust, 1978.

Bownd, Nicholas. *Sabbathum Veteris Et Novi Testamenti: or The True Doctrine of the Sabbath: A Critical Edition with Introduction and Analysis*. Edited by Chris Coldwell. Dallas and Grand Rapids: Naphtali Press and Reformation Heritage Books, 2015.

Bucer, Martin. *De Regno Christi*. Edited by Wilhelm Pauck. In *The Library of Christian Classics: Melanchthon and Bucer*: 155-394. General Editors: John Baillie, John T. McNeill, and Henry P. Van Dusen. Louisville, KY: Westminster John Knox Press, 1969.

Bullinger, Heinrich. *The Decades of Henry Bullinger, Minister of the Church of Zurich*. 5 vols. Edited for the Parker Society by Rev. Thomas Harding. Translated by H. I. Cambridge: Cambridge University Press, 1849.

Burgess, Anthony. *Vindiciae Legis: or, A Vindication of the Moral Law and the Covenants, From the Errours of* Papists, Arminians, Socinians, *and more especially*, Antinomians. 2nd ed., corrected and augmented. Facsimile reprint. Grand Rapids: Reformation Heritage Books, 2011.

Calvin, John. *Commentary on a Harmony of the Evangelists Matthew, Mark, and Luke.* 3 vols. Translated by Rev. William Pringle. Bellingham, WA: Logos Bible Software, 2010.

_____. *Institutes of the Christian Religion.* 2 vols. Edited by John T. McNeill. Translated and Indexed by Ford Lewis Battles. Philadelphia: Westminster Press, 1960.

_____. *Tracts and Letters of John Calvin.* 7 vols. Edited and Translated by Henry Beveridge. Edinburgh: Banner of Truth Trust, 2009.

Charnock, Stephen. *The Complete Works of Stephen Charnock*, 5 vols. Edinburgh: The Banner of Truth Trust, 1986.

Coldwell, Chris, ed. *The Anonymous Writings of George Gillespie.* Dallas: Naphtali Press, 2008.

Crisp, Tobias. *Christ Alone Exalted, in the Perfection and Encouragement of the Saints, Notwithstanding Sins and Trials; Being the Complete Works of Tobias Crisp, D.D.* 2 vols. Ed. by John Gill. London: Printed for John Bennett, 1832.

Dickson, David. *Truth's Victory Over Error: A Commentary on the Westminster Confession of*

Bibliography

Faith. Transcribed and Edited by John R. de Witt. Edinburgh: Banner of Truth Trust, 2007.

Durham, James. *A Commentary on Revelation*. Willow Street: Old Paths Publications, 2000.

_____. *A Practical Exposition of the Ten Commandments*. Edited by Christopher Coldwell. Dallas: Naphtali Press, 2002.

Gillespie, George. *Wholesome Severity Reconciled with Christian Liberty, Or, The True Resolution of a Present Controversy Concerning Liberty of Conscience*. Reprinted in vol. 4, *Anthology of Presbyterian & Reformed Literature: 178-98*. Edited by Christopher Coldwell. Dallas: Naphtali Press, 1991.

Gleanings of Heavenly Wisdom: or, The Sayings of John Dod, M.A., and Philip Henry, M.A. Compiled by John Bickerton Williams. London: T. Nelson and Sons, 1851.

Gouge, William. *Commentary on Hebrews*. Grand Rapids: Kregel Publications, 1980.

Hutcheson, George. *The Gospel of John*. Edinburgh: The Banner of Truth Trust, 1985/1657.

Lightfoote, John. *Erubhin or Miscellanies Christian and Judaicall, and others. Penned for Recreation at

THE NECESSITY OF ABSOLUTES

Vacant Houres. London: G. Miller for Robert Swayne and William Adderton, 1629.

Manton, Thomas. *The Complete Works of Thomas Manton.* Birmingham: Solid Ground Christian Books, 2008.

Melanchthon, Philip. *Loci Communes Theologici.* Edited by Wilhelm Pauck. In *The Library of Christian Classics: Melanchthon and Bucer*: 1-152. General Editors: John Baillie, John T. McNeill, and Henry P. Van Dusen. Louisville, KY: Westminster John Knox Press, 1969.

Owen, John. *The Works of John Owen.* Edited by W. H. Goold. Edinburgh: T & T Clark, 1862.

Perkins, William. *A Discourse of Conscience: Wherein is set downe the nature, properties, and differences thereof: as also the way to Get and keepe good Conscience.* Cambridge: John Legate, 1596.

_____. *The Works of William Perkins: Volume 2: Commentary on Galatians.* Edited by Paul M. Smalley. General Editors: Joel R. Beeke and Derek W. H. Thomas. Grand Rapids: Reformation Heritage Books, 2015.

Piscator, Johannes. *Disputations on the Judicial Laws of Moses.* Translated by Adam Johnathan Brink.

Bibliography

Edited by Joel McDurmon. Powder Springs, GA: American Vision Press, 2015.

Rutherford, Samuel. *The Divine Right of Church-Government and Excommunication: or A peaceable Dispute for the perfection of the holy Scripture in point of* Ceremonies *and* Church Government; *in which* The removal of the Service *book is justified.* London: John Field for Christopher Meredith, 1646.

———. *A Survey of the Spirituall Antichrist: Opening the secrets of* Familisme *and* Antinomianisme *in the Antichristian Doctrine of* John Saltmarsh, *and* Will. Del, *the present Preachers of the Army now in* England, *and of* Robert Town, Tob. Crisp, H. Denne, Eaton, *and others. Part I and Part II.* London: Printed by J.D. & R.I. for Andrew Crooke, 1648.

Scrivener, F. H. A. *The New Testament in Greek.* Cambridge: Cambridge University Press, 1881.

Turretin, Francis. *Institutes of Elenctic Theology.* 3 vols. Edited by James T. Dennison, Jr. Translated by George Musgrave Giger. Phillipsburg, NJ: P&R, 1992.

Udemans, Godefridus. *The Practice of Faith, Hope, and Love.* Edited by Joel R. Beeke. Translated by

THE NECESSITY OF ABSOLUTES

Annemie Godbehere. Grand Rapids: Reformation Heritage Books, 2012.

Westminster Confession, The: The Confession of Faith, The Larger and Shorter Catechisms, The Directory for the Public Worship of God: With Associated Historical Documents. Edinburgh: Banner of Truth Trust, 2018.

Willison, John. *A Treatise Concerning the Sanctification of the Lord's Day. Wherein the Morality of the Sabbath, or the Perpetual Obligation of the Fourth Commandment is Maintained Against Adversaries; and the Religious Observation of the Lord's Day, or First Day of the Week, as our Christian Sabbath, is Strongly Proved by Scripture Arguments.* Albany: J. Boardman, 1820.

Witsius, Herman. *The Economy of the Covenants Between God and Man: Comprehending a Complete Body of Divinity.* 2 vols. Translated and Revised by William Crookshank. London: R. Baynes, 1822/1677. (Facsimile Reprint: Kingsburg, CA: den Dulk Christian Foundation, 1990.)

Bibliography

Secondary Sources and General References

Bahnsen, Greg L. *By This Standard: The Authority of God's Law Today*. Tyler, TX: Institute for Christian Economics, 1985.

———. *Theonomy in Christian Ethics*. 3rd ed. Nacogdoches, TX: Covenant Media Press, 2002.

Barker, William S. and W. Robert Godfrey, eds. *Theonomy: A Reformed Critique*. Grand Rapids: Zondervan House, 1990.

Beeke, Joel. *Puritan Reformed Spirituality*. Darlington, England: Evangelical Press, 2006.

Beeke, Joel R. and Mark Jones. *A Puritan Theology: Doctrine for Life*. Grand Rapids: Reformation Heritage Books, 2012.

Boston, Thomas. *The Complete Works of the Late Rev. Thomas Boston, Ettrick: Including His Memoirs, Written by Himself*. 12 vols. Edited by Samuel M'Millan. Stoke-on-Trent: Tentmaker Publications, 2002.

Casselli, Stephen J. *Divine Rule Maintained: Anthony Burgess, Covenant Theology, and the Place of the Law in Reformed Scholasticism*. Grand Rapids: Reformation Heritage Books, 2016.

Clark, Gordon H. *Essays on Ethics and Politics*. Edited by John W. Robbins. Jefferson, MD: Trinity Foundation, 1992.

———. *What do Presbyterians Believe? The Westminster Confession Yesterday and Today*. Unicoi, TN: Trinity Foundation, 2001.

Coffey, John. *Politics, Religion and the British Revolutions: The Mind of Samuel Rutherford*. Cambridge: Cambridge University Press, 1997.

Coldwell, Chris and Matthew Winzer. "The Westminster Assembly & the Judicial Law: A Chronological Compilation and Analysis, Parts One and Two." Vol. 5, *The Confessional Presbyterian: A Journal for Discussion of Presbyterian Doctrine & Practice*: 3-88. Dallas: Confessional Presbyterian Press, 2009.

Colquhoun, John. *A Treatise on the Law and the Gospel*. Grand Rapids: Soli Deo Gloria Publications, 2009.

Crampton, W. Gary. *The Scripturalism of Gordon H. Clark*. Unicoi, TN: The Trinity Foundation, 1999.

Cunningham, Timothy R. *How Firm a Foundation? An Exegetical and Historical Critique of the "Ethical Perspective of [Christian] Reconstructionism"*

Bibliography

Presented in Theonomy in Christian Ethics. Eugene: Wipf & Stock, 2012.

Cyclopaedia of Biblical, Theological, and Ecclesiastical Literature. 12 vols. Prepared by John M'Clintock and James Strong. New York: Harper & Brothers, 1891-94.

Dabney, Robert L. *Syllabus and Notes of the Course of Systematic and Polemic Theology Taught in Union Theological Seminary, Virginia.* 2nd ed. Edinburgh: Banner of Truth Trust, 1985.

Fairbairn, Patrick. *The Revelation of Law in Scripture: Considered with respect both to its nature, and to its relative place in successive dispensations.* Phillipsburg, NJ: P&R, 1996.

Faith Once Delivered, The: Essays in Honor of Dr. Wayne R. Spear. Edited by Anthony T. Selvaggio. Phillipsburg, NJ: P & R Publishing, 2007.

Fesko, J. V. *The Theology of the Westminster Standards: Historical Context and Theological Insights.* Wheaton, IL: Crossway, 2014.

Green, Joel B., ed. *Dictionary of Scripture and Ethics.* Grand Rapids, MI: Baker, 2011.

Gundry, Stanley N., ed. *Five Views on Law and Gospel.* Grand Rapids: Zondervan, 1999.

THE NECESSITY OF ABSOLUTES

Hastings, James, ed. *Encyclopaedia of Religion and Ethics*. Edinburgh: T. & T. Clark, 1908-26.

Hetherington, William Maxwell. *History of the Westminster Assembly of Divines*. 5th ed. Edited by Robert Williamson. New York: Anson D. F. Randolph, 1890.

Jackson, Samuel Macauley, ed. *The New Schaff-Herzog Encyclopedia of Religious Knowledge*. 15 vols. Grand Rapids: Baker Books, 1984.

Kevan, Ernest F. *The Grace of Law: A Study in Puritan Theology*. Grand Rapids: Soli Deo Gloria Publications, 2015.

Lloyd-Jones, D. Martyn. *John Knox and the Reformation*. Edinburgh: Banner of Truth Trust, 2011.

Mahoney, David D. and James J. Mahoney. *The Torah Concordance: A Reference Guide for Biblical Law*. Hebrew Heritage Learning Center, 2012.

Manton, Thomas. *The Complete Works of Thomas Manton*. 22 vols. Birmingham: Solid Ground Christian Books, 2008.

Muller, Richard A. *Dictionary of Latin and Greek Theological Terms: Drawn Principally from Protestant Scholastic Theology*. Grand Rapids: Baker Book House, 1985.

Bibliography

Murray, A.H. et al. eds. *A New English Dictionary on Historical Principles*. 10 vols. Oxford: Clarendon Press, 1884-1923.

Murray, John. *Principles of Conduct: Aspects of Biblical Ethics*. Grand Rapids: William B. Eerdmans, 1957.

Pipa, Joseph A., Jr. *Galatians: God's Proclamation of Liberty. Focus on the Bible Commentary*. Ross-Shire: Christian Focus Publications, 2010.

Reymond, Robert L. *A New Systematic Theology of the Christian Faith: Second Edition—Revised and Updated*. Nashville: Thomas Nelson Publishers, 1998.

Ridgeley, Thomas. *A Body of Divinity: Wherein the Doctrines of the Christian Religion Are Explained and Defended. Being the Substance of Several Lectures on the Assembly's Larger Catechism*. New Edition, Revised, Corrected, and Illustrated with Notes by Rev. John M. Wilson. In Two Volumes. New York: Robert Carter & Brothers, 1855.

Robbins, John W. "An Introduction to Gordon H. Clark," *The Trinity Review* (July-August 1993): 1-10. Unicoi, TN: Trinity Foundation, 2003.

Roberts, Dewey. *Historic Christianity and the Federal Vision: A Theological Analysis and Practical Evaluation*. East Peoria, IL: Versa Press, Inc., 2016.

Ross, Philip S. *From the Finger of God: The Biblical and Theological Basis for the Threefold Division of the Law*. Ross-shire, Scotland: Christian Focus, 2010.

Rushdoony, Rousas John. *The Institutes of Biblical Law*. Vol. 1. Vallecito, CA: Chalcedon Foundation, 2012. Kindle.

Selvaggio, Anthony T., ed. The *Faith Once Delivered: Essays in Honor of Dr. Wayne R. Spear*. Phillipsburg, NJ: P&R, 2007.

Shaw, Robert. *An Exposition of the Westminster Confession of Faith*. Ross-shire, Scotland: Christian Focus Publications, 1992.

Singer, C. Gregg. *From Rationalism to Irrationality: The Decline of the Western Mind from the Renaissance to the Present*. Phillipsburg, PA: Presbyterian and Reformed, 1979.

Smith, Morton H. *Systematic Theology*. 2 vols. Greenville, SC: Greenville Seminary Press, 1994.

Stephen, Leslie and Sydney Lee, eds. *Dictionary of National Biography*. 22 vols. New York: MacMillan, 1908.

Bibliography

Van Dixhoorn, Chad. *Confessing the Faith: A Reader's Guide to the Westminster Confession of Faith.* Edinburgh: Banner of Truth Trust, 2014.

Vlach, Michael J. "New Covenant Theology Compared with Covenantalism," *The Master's Seminary Journal*, 18:1 (Fall 2007): 201-219.

Wells, Tom and Fred G. Zaspel. *New Covenant Theology: Description, Definition, Defense.* Frederick, MD: New Covenant Media, 2002.

White, A. Blake. *What is New Covenant Theology? An Introduction.* Frederick, MD: New Covenant Media, 2012.

Williamson, G. I. *The Westminster Confession of Faith for Study Classes.* 2nd ed. Phillipsburg, NJ: P&R, 2004.

Winzer, Matthew. "The Westminster Assembly & The Judicial Law: A Chronological Compilation and Analysis: Part Two: Analysis," *The Confessional Presbyterian: A Journal for Discussion of Presbyterian Doctrine & Practice*, No. 5 (2009): 56-88. Edited by Chris Coldwell. Dallas: Confessional Presbyterian Press, 2009.

Zaspel, Fred G. *The New Covenant and New Covenant Theology: Two Lectures Presented at the 2008 John*

THE NECESSITY OF ABSOLUTES

Bunyan Conference, Lewisburg, PA. Frederick, MD: New Covenant Media, 2011.

Scripture Index

Genesis
2:1-3 (202 fn)
2:16-17 (38)
3:15 (49, 254)
4:3 (202 fn)
6:5 (352)
8:21 (48)
9:6 (225)
17:7, 10 (266)
26:5 (99)
49:10 (299)

Exodus
3:14 (165)
16:23 (202 fn)
19:16, 18 (103)
20:1-2 (163)
20:1 (99)
20:5 (194, 195)
20:6 (195)
20:7 (196)
20:8 (201)
20:9 (202)
20:11 (202-03, 208)
20:12 (155, 156)
20:18 (282)
22:20 (282)
24:12-31:18 (249 fn)
25:9, 40 (252)
26:33 (262)
31:18 (99)
34:28 (99)

Leviticus
11:43-45 (234)
19:17 (159, 176)
19:18 (82, 172)
19:32, 35 (282)
20:8 (341)
20:9 (155)
20:11 (282)
24:15-16 (197)
25:1-17 (281)

Numbers
15:35 (211)
35:30 (282)

Deuteronomy
4:1 (102)
4:13-14 (205)
4:14ff (249 fn)
5:12 (202)
5:15 (203, 209)
6:4-5 (172)
6:5 (82)
6:6 (331)
7:9 (195 fn)
9:10 (172)
12:5 (187)
12:29-32 (192-93)
12:32 (190)
13:9 (282)
14:1 (169)
14:1-18:22 (249 fn)
25:5-10 (281)
28:58-59 (197)
30:6 (331)
30:14 (331)

Judges
21:25 (352)

2 Chronicles
3:14 (262)
33:17 (193)

Job
1:10 (74)
9:33 (98)

Psalms
2:10-12 (271)
2:11-12 (309)
14 (237)
16:5 (74)
50:18 (161)
51:5 (122)
95:6-7 (175)
102:25-27 (167)
119:33-40 (27)
119:96 (243)
119:126-128 (29)
147:19-20 (135)

Proverbs
30:17 (156)

Ecclesiastes
7:20 (237)

383

THE NECESSITY OF ABSOLUTES

Isaiah
5:20-21 (116)
33:22 (111, 350)
54:5 (169)
56:2 (213)
58:13-14 (212)
64:6 (149)
65:17 (252)

Jeremiah
4:22 (179)
6:14 (94)
31:33 (124, 327, 328, 329)

Ezekiel
18:31 (341)
36:26-27 (152, 341)

Daniel
9:27 (186, 259)

Hosea
4:1, 6 (179-80)

Micah
6:8 (10, 73)

Habakkuk
1:13 (235)

Malachi
1:6 (22, 198)
3:6 (165, 325)

Matthew
5:1-2 (16 fn, 103)
5:17 (80, 213)
5:17-18 (72, 87)
5:17-19a (333)
5:20 (1, 17, 87)
5:21-22 (157)
5:22 (224)
5:27-28 (158)
5:28 (226)
5:48 (149)
7:7-8 (15)
7:12 (17)
7:13-14 (19)
11:29-30 (15)
12:1-14 (210 fn)
12:8 (84)
12:22-24 (201)
12:28 (172 fn)
15:7-9 (191)
22:37 (173-74)
22:37-39 (82)
22:37-40 (173)
27:50-51 (261, 263)

Luke
11:20 (172 fn)

John
1:5 (229)
1:9 (229)
1:18 (103 fn)
1:29 (11)
3:16 (18)
4:21 (187)
4:23 (180)
8:58 (166)
13:34 (81-82)
14:6 (229)
14:15 (76)
14:15-18 (138)
16:7 (152)
17:3 (229)
20:17 (169)
20:26 (207)

Acts
2:33 (152)
7:38 (103 fn)
10 (293)
13:38-39 (136-37)
15:10 (260)
15:28-29 (260)
16:4 (260-61)
17:10-11 (180)
17:28 (348 fn)
20:6-7 (207)

Romans
1:18-19 (56, 110)
1:18-32 (133 fn)
1:20 (124)
1:21 (215)
1:32 (110, 112)
2:12 (143-44)
2:13-15 (111)
2:14 (128)
2:14-15 (32, 57, 119, 133 fn)

Scripture Index

2:15 (110)
2:16 (144)
2:23-24 (200)
3:10-12 (237)
3:20 (53, 121, 136)
3:23 (122)
3:24-26 (53)
3:31 (72, 333)
5:12 (35 fn)
5:12-19 (54 fn)
5:12-21 (47)
6:1-4 (144, 145)
6:14 (133)
7:4 (133)
7:12 (60)
7:14 (151)
8:6-7 (351)
8:7 (48)
8:29 (85)
9:4 (135)
10:4 (77-8)
11:33-36 (348 fn)
13:1-6 (116)
13:1-2 (300)
13:1, 4 (271)
13:4 (129)
13:10 (71, 74)
13:14 (22)

1 Corinthians
2:14 (32-3)
2:14-16 (349)
6:11 (336)
15:33 (161)

16:1-2 (207)

2 Corinthians
1:24 (161)
3 (326)
3:3 (329)
3:6 (26 fn)
5:14-15 (341)
5:17 (252)
5:21 (106)
6:14-7:1 (293)
6:18 (169)
10:5 (350)

Galatians
3:10-12 (133 fn)
3:10-14 (104)
3:13 (133)
3:24 (253)
3:24-25 (253-54)
4:4 (95)
5:2-4 (69, 188-89, 259)
5:16 (151)

Ephesians
1:2-6 (150)
2:11-20 (293)
2:14-16 (187-88)
4:23-24 (85)
4:25 (229)
4:28 (156)
5:23, 25 (170)
6:1-3 (222)

Philippians
1:9 (336)
2:12-13 (139, 340)
2:13 (151)
2:21 (182)
3:12 (150)

Colossians
2:13-17 (245)
2:14 (262)
2:16-17 (260)
2:17 (254)
3:2, 5 (182-83)
3:5 (153)
3:5-6 (231)
3:9-10 (229)

1 Thessalonians
5:22-23 (158)

2 Thessalonians
2:13 (139)

1 Timothy
6:10 (154)

2 Timothy
3:2 (182)
3:16 (6 fn)
4:2 (161)

Titus
2:11-12 (341)

THE NECESSITY OF ABSOLUTES

Hebrews
1:10-12 (167)
2:3 (239 fn)
3:1 (81)
3:13 (159)
5:9 (151)
7:2 (279 fn)
7:5 (277)
7:19 (137)
7:22 (95)
9:1, 8-12 (250-51)
9:5 (327)
9:10 (251, 252 fn)
9:13-14 (242)
10:1 (256)
10:14-17 (330)
10:16 (124)
10:25 (160)
12:29 (197)
13:8 (167)
13:20-21 (311)

James
1:17 (325)
2:10-12 (116)
2:17-18 (359)
3:8-9 (219)
4:2-3 (231)

1 Peter
1:13-16 (234-35)
1:16 (102)
1:22 (242)
2:9 (262)
2:13-14 (299)

1 John
1:8, 10 (237)
2:3-6 (76-7, 333, 338)
2:15-16 (182)
2:15-17 (350)
3:15 (224)
4:8 (74)
5:3 (77)
5:20 (229)

Revelation
1:8 (166)
1:10 (207)
4:2-3 (105)

Justin Benjamin Stodghill (ThD, MDiv, MAR, Whitefield Theological Seminary; MA, History, American Military University) is Adjunct Professor of Moral Philosophy and Historical Theology at Whitefield Theological Seminary, Lakeland, Florida, and Assistant Pastor of Christ Covenant Reformed Presbyterian Church (RPCGA) in Wylie, Texas.

www.ingramcontent.com/pod-product-compliance
Lightning Source LLC
Chambersburg PA
CBHW022041200426
43209CB00072B/1921/J